Framing Abuse

Framing Abuse

Media Influence and
Public Understanding of
Sexual Violence Against Children

Jenny Kitzinger

Pluto Press

LONDON • ANN ARBOR, MI

First published 2004 by Pluto Press
345 Archway Road, London N6 5AA
and 839 Greene Street, Ann Arbor, MI 48106

www.plutobooks.com

British Library Cataloguing in Publication Data
A catalogue record for this book is available from the British Library

ISBN   0 7453 2332 4 hardback
ISBN   0 7453 2331 6 paperback

Library of Congress Cataloging in Publication Data applied for

302.23
K62 f
2004

10   9   8   7   6   5   4   3   2   1

Designed and produced for Pluto Press by
Chase Publishing Services, Fortescue, Sidmouth, EX10 9QG, England
Typeset from disk by Stanford DTP Services, Northampton, England
Printed and bound in the European Union by
Antony Rowe Ltd, Chippenham and Eastbourne, England

Dedication

To Sheila and Uwe – with love

Contents

Acknowledgements

I would like to thank everyone who gave their time to my research projects and were prepared to talk to me so openly. I also wish to acknowledge financial support from the Economic and Social Research Council (award no. 000233657). The collection of most of the original data presented in this volume would not have been possible without such funds. I am grateful to former colleagues at Glasgow and my current colleagues at the Cardiff School of Journalism, Media and Cultural Studies for their intellectual engagement in developing the ideas presented here. As always thank you also to my family and friends whose forebearance and support throughout the preparation of this volume have been invaluable. Special thanks to Diana, Martha and Sarah whose love and encouragement sustained me through difficult times.

Above all, this book would not have been possible without all those who have campaigned to challenge sexual violence. I am particularly indebted to the young women in the Cambridge Incest Survivors' refuge during the 1980s. It was their courage in speaking out about their abuse, and their request for information about other survivors' experiences, that first set me on the journey which has culminated in this book so many years later.

1
Introduction

We live in a media saturated society. What does this mean for how we make sense of the world around us? How do the facts, stories, images and ideas presented in the mass media relate to our common-sense knowledge and critical judgements? What rhetorical strategies do journalists and their sources use to persuade people of their point of view? How do we respond to what we are told and come to our own conclusions? This book examines the mass media's role in defining, and sometimes transforming, social issues and influencing the way we think. It focuses on the media's role in relation to one of the major social problems of our time, child sexual abuse. The book combines analysis of media coverage with interviews with survivors of childhood sexual abuse and with journalists and their sources. In addition it presents a detailed analysis of 79 focus group discussions exploring people's assumptions and fears about sexual abuse, their opinions about controversial cases, and how they relate media representations to their own experience. This unique dataset permits an examination of the significance of media content and production processes and an examination of both the extent and the limits of media influence over time. The findings from this research engage with, but also challenge, many of the contemporary debates about audience reception processes and media power.

THE RESEARCH THAT INFORMS THIS BOOK

My work in this field stretches back over 20 years and evolved in parallel with commitments both within and outside the field of media studies. Like any research it is informed by the social, political and disciplinary context in which it was conducted. This introduction outlines the diverse research initiatives that inform this volume, provides a sense of the context in which each research project was carried out, and guides the reader through the book's structure.

I first started studying sexual abuse as a result of my involvement in the Women's Liberation Movement. One of the key aims of this movement was to challenge violence against women and children,

1

especially abuse within intimate relationships.[1] Before the rise of second wave feminism, these acts of violence were often not taken seriously. Wife battering was dismissed as a domestic dispute, rape in marriage was not a criminal offence and child sexual abuse within the family was hardly acknowledged as a problem at all. During the 1970s, for example, headline news was attracted by the occasional child abduction, rape or murder, but discussion of the broader category of sexual exploitation of children in all its forms was largely taboo. There were also very limited services available for those enduring such abuse.

In the early 1980s I was part of a feminist collective in Cambridge, England, which set up a helpline and subsequently a refuge for sexually abused girls. The young women who contacted us needed accommodation and emotional support; they also desperately wanted images that reflected the reality of their own lives and they wanted to learn about other survivors' experiences. At the time there were not many books on this subject.[2] At the request of some of the girls in the refuge I started to record interviews with adult women survivors and also with some mothers of sexually abused children. Interviewees were recruited from self-help groups, through notices in community centres and waiting rooms, and through personal contacts. These interviews addressed women's experiences of abuse, its consequences and their strategies for survival. I explored how they had sought help (or not) as children and as adults, the responses of those around them and how they integrated the experiences of trauma into their political perspectives and life narratives. I conducted 40 interviews in all. This research was conducted over a time period which proved to be one of decisive social change – 1984 to 1989 – just as the media across the English-speaking world were beginning to confront the realities of sexual abuse. In the mid 1980s the topic started to be addressed in UK news and documentaries, women's magazines, discussion shows and TV dramas. (The latter were often imported from the USA where this issue had begun to attract interest a few years earlier.) Journalists, editors, programme producers and scriptwriters started to confront the sexual exploitation of children as a widespread social problem affecting all strata of society. They also began to recognise that when children are attacked it is usually by someone they know. These radical shifts in media attention had a profound impact on the women I was interviewing. Although media representation was not the focus of this research, in retrospect it is not surprising that it emerged as a crucial issue for my research participants and that, returning to these interviews now, they offer vivid testimony to the role of the media in cultural transformation.

In 1988 I moved to join the Glasgow University Media Group. This research group was already well known for its work on media bias, e.g. *Bad News* (1976) and *More Bad News* (1980). Some of the Glasgow team were now interested in looking at audiences too and I joined the group to work on a project examining the media coverage of AIDS and its impact on public understandings of the epidemic (see Kitzinger 1990; Miller *et al.* 1998). This was my first initiation into media studies as a discipline. I began to learn about the theoretical disputes and methodological issues involved in studying audiences and to integrate this with my previous training and research. Before moving to Glasgow I had been based in the Department of Social and Political Sciences at Cambridge, examining hospital staffing structures and experiences of hospital care. In this research I had looked at people as citizens, as embodied beings and as people negotiating structured power relations (collegial and doctor–patient). Prior to that I had graduated in social anthropology through which I had been taught to approach people as bearers of culture, performers of ritual and members of kinship groups. Moving to Glasgow introduced me to a novel set of questions about audience–text relations and allowed me to combine media studies traditions with the approaches with which I was already familiar from other disciplines.

Using this cumulative experience I subsequently returned to my concerns about sexual violence. In 1992 the Economic and Social Research Council gave me a grant to study the role of media in covering child sexual abuse. This project involved three strands: first, interviews with journalists and their sources (e.g. the experts cited in the media), second, analysis of a whole year's media coverage and third, focus group discussions with ordinary people to explore their responses.[3] It is these focus groups that provide the second core data resource for this book. A total of 49 focus groups (involving 275 research participants) were conducted with networks of people contacted via their work place, church, community centre or club. (The sample is described in the appendix and the rationale underlying my research approach is presented in Chapter 2.) I invited people to discuss their views about abuse with each other. How common did they believe it to be? What form did it usually take? What did they think motivated child molesters? What should be done to prevent it? What would they do if they suspected a child was being abused?

They were also asked to reflect on why they believed what they did and to think about anything that had made them change their minds. In addition I invited research participants to comment on the media coverage of child sexual abuse in general and to discuss one news story in particular. The story selected for detailed examination was a scandal involving disputed allegations of sexual abuse (the 'Orkney case'). The groups were given a set of still photographs taken from the television coverage and invited to try to reproduce a typical news bulletin. They were then asked to reflect on this process, comparing the story they had produced with what they believed actually had happened. This task encourages people to engage actively in producing meaning and to deconstruct media reporting. Working with the photographs also helps the discussion to address the visual aspects of coverage as well as focusing on what has been said.

My interest in the representation of sexual abuse has continued in other forms since the two research projects outlined above. I have analysed the ideologies embedded in self-help books for incest survivors (Kitzinger 1992), interviewed journalists and their sources to examine the emergence of 'false memory syndrome' (Kitzinger 1998) and evaluated interventions in schools (Burton *et al.* 1998). Most relevant for the present volume is my research into grassroots demands for neighbourhood notification when convicted sex offenders are released into the community (Kitzinger 1999c). This book also presents my evaluation of the first UK public awareness campaign against sexual violence: an attempt to challenge public attitudes through a high-profile advertising initiative. This last piece of research involved a further 30 focus groups and a survey of public responses (Kitzinger 1994, 1995; Kitzinger and Hunt 1993).

The eclectic nature of this body of research offers diverse ways of approaching the question of media influence. Although each of these studies is already in the public domain in some form I hope that, by bringing them together in this book, I can better draw out some of the broader theoretical implications. The sheer quantity (and, I hope, quality) of interview and focus group material allows me to examine diversity in what people say and also to look at overlaps and patterns; the common themes which emerge in conversations in different groups and settings. My multi-disciplinary and multi-method approach (including interviews, focus groups and survey data) provides different ways of approaching key questions about audience–text relations. In addition, although focused on the news media, my research also addresses such diverse genre as documentaries, soap operas and advertising, in ways that allow for some exploration about the different ways in which these might operate.

Because I have interviews with journalists and their sources, as well as a comprehensive archive of media reporting, the analysis can also be linked back to struggles at the level of media production. Who speaks to the media and how do these sources present themselves? What rhetorical devices do they employ and do these achieve their ends? What factors influence how media practitioners present stories, how do they seek to evoke empathy or appeal to common sense, and how does all this relate to media impact?

Most important of all is the longitudinal nature of my work and how this developed alongside the evolution of child sexual abuse as a public issue. The fact that I conducted interviews before, during and after the period in which the media first (re)discovered child sexual abuse offers an almost natural experiment and provides a strong basis from which to reflect on the media's role and to track changes in real time.

Child sexual abuse is an ideal case study for an investigation of media influence because it is such a high-profile issue and the focus of attention has shifted so dramatically over the last few decades. Revelation has followed revelation as new ways of identifying the problem have been opened up and/or the media have sought ever more sensational angles. The original discovery of incestuous abuse was followed by allegations about abuse in nurseries, schools, sports clubs and children's homes. Allegations against celebrities hit the headlines alongside allegations about abuse perpetrated within (and covered up by) the Catholic Church. Fears about satanic networks were followed by concerns about predators in cyberspace stalking children via the Internet.

The whole topic is also profoundly contested. Certain claims, about ritual abuse, for example, have been systematically deconstructed and reasserted (De Young 1997; LaFontaine 1998; Scott 1998, 1999). Adults' memories of childhood sexual assault have been subject to scrutiny and challenge (*Feminism and Psychology* 1997; Loftus and Ketchum 1994; Ofshe and Watters 1994; Pendergrast 1995). Protagonists in high-profile cases have organised to protest their innocence. Police, therapists, lawyers, doctors and state social services stand accused of acts of injustice, besmirching the names of innocent men and women, destroying careers or tearing happy families apart (Bell 1988). The controversies mobilise conflicting interest groups, and sometimes produce unexpected alliances involving families' rights groups, religious organisations, neighbourhood action groups, feminist activists, abuse survivors, therapists and social workers. Few lives or professions remain untouched by a debate which bridges the public and the private, involves questions about sexuality, power and childhood, and touches on key institutions: the family, religion and the state.

There are many accounts that analyse the public controversies around this topic and theorise about the media's role in promoting new cultural awareness, myths or anxieties. (See, for example, Atmore 1999; Hechler 1988; Jenkins 1992, 1996; Myers 1994, Reavey and Warner 2003; Richardson, et al. 1991.) There is a large literature that traces moral panics around issues such as ritual abuse or day care scandals (e.g. De Young 2002, 2004). Some books chart shifts in media coverage of sexual violence in general (Cuklanz 2000; Moorti 2002; Soothill and Walby 1991). Others critically address particular case studies. Depending on their perspective, critics have blamed the media for going too far, or not going far enough, for exaggerating, or for obscuring the true extent of sexual violence, or failing to place it in context. Although journalists are sometimes praised for championing the little people (e.g. parents whose children have been taken away) they are also accused of social work bashing, pursuing trial by media and of gross misrepresentation (Campbell 1988). There is a particularly rich body of feminist literature which analyses and critiques media coverage. This highlights problems of racism, victim blaming and scaremongering and criticises the media for a disproportionate focus on certain types of crime and for feeding on incest as entertainment fodder. (See, for example, Armstrong 1994, Atmore 1996, 1998; Benedict 1992; Carter 1998; Carter and Weaver 2003, Cuklanz 1996, 2000; Hirsch 1994; Kelly 1996; Kitzinger 1988, 2004; Meyers 1997; Moorti 2002; Morrison 1992; Weaver 1998.)

My approach here is rather different from most existing work in the field. My focus is on how ordinary people interpret, recall, relate to and use media coverage in making sense of child sexual abuse. I also examine how ideas derived from the media interact with other sources of knowledge. I use detailed analysis of how people discuss child sexual abuse as a theme through which to gain a more detailed understanding of the role the media might play in reproducing the status quo, or contributing to social change.

A GUIDE TO THE BOOK'S STRUCTURE

Readers primarily interested in the substantive topic of sexual violence may wish to skip the chapter that reviews academic theories of media influence (Chapter 2). They will, however, be interested in the chapters that address:

- the history of sexual abuse as a public issue, the different social constructions of the problem and struggles to define it over the last 100 years (Chapter 3)
- the rise of the 'incest survivor' as a private and public identity and the implications of changing discursive repertoires (Chapter 3)
- the role of the media in representing disputed allegations and influencing how people recall and make judgements about such scandals (Chapters 4–6)
- the representation of child protection professionals and how this influences people's willingness to seek help and their reactions to state interventions in family life (Chapters 4–6)
- how the media report stranger-danger and perpetuate stereotypes about 'paedophiles'. This chapter also maps out how this intersects with parents' everyday experiences of worrying about their children (Chapter 7)
- the ways in which press campaigns influence demands for policy change such as public notification about convicted paedophiles in the community and how this intersects with pre-existing community concerns (Chapters 7 and 8)
- public reactions to advertisements designed to promote awareness about child sexual abuse and challenge persistent myths (Chapter 9)
- recommendations for child protection strategies and guidelines for journalists (Epilogue).

Readers concerned more broadly with debates about the media's role in contemporary society will be interested in the general methodological and theoretical lessons that can be drawn from this work as a whole. The main narrative structure of the book is as follows:

Chapter 2 summarises debates about media influence. It introduces the different theories and research approaches that have evolved since the very beginnings of mass media studies, and links these to the socio-political context in which such work developed. In particular, this chapter maps out the different European and North American traditions and summarises the current controversy about the nature of media power. It concludes by outlining how my research approach tries to bridge some of the gaps.

Chapter 3 examines the shifts in media coverage of child sexual abuse and introduces data from my own work tracking its impact. This chapter reflects on three crucial theories within media studies: theories about active consumption processes, the debate about positive representation, and agenda-setting theory. This chapter extends ideas about the media's agenda-setting powers by offering evidence of the special role the media had in this case. I show how media coverage can help (re)define individuals' experiences, influence inter-personal communication and contribute to spirals of public recognition. The media do not simply help to prioritise an issue but, I argue, they can contribute to the transformation of how that issue is understood at both a personal and political level.

Chapter 4 introduces the concept of media templates. It explores how particular crises come to be defining moments in the public profile of a social issue. Successful analogies to serve as templates, helping to make sense of new events (both for journalists and their publics). I demonstrate how these templates have a powerful impact on what people believe.

Chapter 5 introduces the concept of story branding: the shorthand label used by journalists, and by their audiences, as an aide memoir to sum up the essence of a story. It examines the ways in which pressure groups compete to brand a story in a particular way and how this intersects with journalistic practices and routines as well as audience reception processes. This chapter also shows how some brandings attract people's empathy, in ways that almost guarantee their success. Although this chapter also explores audience 'resistance', I demonstrate how, once a story is successfully branded, this label can have powerful ideological effects on how controversial cases are recalled and interpreted.

Chapter 6 introduces the concept of story placing: the use of evocative descriptions of the location of a news event. It explores how journalists routinely locate a story socially and geographically in ways which rely on, and conjure up, pre-existing ideas about 'that sort of place' or 'that sort of community'. This journalistic technique draws on, and triggers, deeply embedded assumptions about safety and danger (often intertwined with stereotypes about class and ethnicity) and can influence how people assess the validity of allegations. In this chapter I also highlight people's resistance to the predominant message in news reporting. I show how people may draw on contrasting images from diverse cultural sources (including films, postcards and tourist brochures). They may, therefore, come to very different conclusions than those implied in the news coverage. This chapter questions conventional ways of interpreting such diversity and challenges the use of concepts within media studies such as 'dominant', 'oppositional' and 'negotiated' readings.

Chapter 7 introduces the concept of social currency and explores how this helps to structure risk perceptions. Here I focus on how journalists and the general population characterise those who abuse children. While highlighting the ways in which the media perpetuate stereotypes about abusers, this chapter goes beyond media representation to look at the circulation of everyday knowledge about who poses a threat. I explore the contributory role played by the ways in which anecdotes are exchanged (or withheld) and patterns of 'gossip'. Everyday interactions, I argue, routinely reinforce the association of any threat with outsiders rather than encouraging us to look within our own families and communities.

Chapter 8 broadens the approach even further. It examines media and community campaigns against convicted sex offenders. This chapter challenges any attempt to dismiss community protests as mere copy cat riots or moral panics. Instead I examine how media attention can both crystallise and reflect people's concerns about children's safety, professional competence and how their communities are treated by the powers-that-be.

Chapter 9 shifts the focus by assessing a particular advertising initiative designed to challenge attitudes around sexual violence from a feminist perspective. It presents a close analysis of people's readings of two posters about child sexual abuse and explores the different ways in which diverse audiences engage with these posters and how they negotiate or resist the intended message.

The concluding chapter, Chapter 10, rounds off the book by summarising my findings and considering their implications. I reflect on the ways in which media influence operates both through the nature of coverage (including media templates and story branding) and through the experience of the audience (the organisation of everyday knowledge, the differential social currency of diverse anecdotes and the mobilisation of personal experience). Here I also draw together all examples of the activities through which people might claim some autonomy from the media and consider their potential and their limitations. This allows me critically to reflect on key concepts such as 'decoding', 'polysemy', 'active consumption' and 'creative appropriation and identification'. This chapter concludes by suggesting some future directions for media analysis and calling for the consolidation of a body of 'New Media Influence Research'.

2
The Debate About
Media Influence

How do the media influence us? How do we make sense of what we hear and see? What is the extent, and what are the limits, of media power? These issues are of concern well beyond the ivory towers of the academy. Declarations are made, and answers sought, by public relations experts as well as parents, by capitalists as well as Marxists and by advertisers as well as anti-globalisation campaigners. Academic researchers, however, are deeply divided on these issues. They disagree about how media influence might operate and how best to investigate it. This chapter reviews the debate and then outlines my own research approach.

In order to understand the different approaches to questions about media influence it is important to recognise the diverse socio-political contexts in which they have developed. There is no international consensus and divergent research trajectories are evident on each side of the Atlantic. A mutual ignorance, and sometimes antipathy, was evident from the very beginning and continues today. As Corner and colleagues comment:

> The separate national and historical contexts occasioned by, for instance, the propaganda campaigns of 1930s European fascism, by American preoccupations post World War II, both with public opinion and with the world's most aggressive young advertising industry, and by the longstanding concern of the British literary intelligentsia about declining cultural values, produced radically different starting points for enquiry (Corner *et al.* 1997:2).

Distinct approaches have evolved whereby, for example, American communication scholars, rooted in trying to develop a behavioural science, have traditionally privileged a mass communication model whereby messages are transported to audiences. By contrast, European work usually emphasises communication 'as a process through which a shared culture is created, modified and transformed' (Carey 1977/83: 412. See also McQuail 1990; Blumler 1978, 1980).

This chapter outlines some of the most significant approaches to studying media audiences from both sides of the Atlantic.[1] It details the fierce battle between those coming from different theoretical and disciplinary perspectives and highlights some current controversies. I conclude by outlining my own approach and highlighting how the design of my research projects sought to bridge some of the gaps.

A REVIEW OF SOME KEY APPROACHES
TO AUDIENCE RESEARCH

The history of debate about audiences can be characterised as a series of pendulum swings. In some periods theorists have emphasised the media's impact, at other times they have argued that media influence is quite weak and is highly mediated by other social factors. The following section reviews theories about the power of the mass media divided under the two headings: approaches that focus on the power of the media, and approaches that focus on the power and activity of audiences.[2]

Approaches focusing on the power of the media

The Frankfurt School and hypodermic model: The origins of contemporary media studies are often identified as being located in 1930s Germany with the work of scholars such as Adorno, Marcuse and Horkheimer. These writers propose a very powerful model of media effects known as the hypodermic model because it suggests that media messages are directly injected into the hearts and minds of the masses. The Frankfurt School coined the term 'mass culture', a concept originally suggested by the Nazi propaganda machine but then applied to the American capitalist media. Their theories were developed in response to Germany's descent in to fascism and the apparent failure of the revolutionary social change predicted by Marx. They were also informed by their observations (having fled Germany for the USA) of the manipulative popular culture of the USA. Popular culture which, they argue, infiltrates our every way of being:

> The way in which a girl accepts and keeps the obligatory date, the inflection on the telephone or in the most intimate situation, the choice of words in conversation, and the whole inner life ... bear witness to [people's] attempt to make [themselves] a proficient apparatus, similar (even in emotions) to the model served up by the cultural industry (Adorno and Horkheimer 1983:383).[3]

The behavioural effects tradition: The behavioural effects tradition refers to a much more empirically grounded approach to studying audiences, adopted by psychologists using laboratory based, experimental research techniques. This often relies on methods such as testing people before and after viewing a particular film to measure changes in attitude or behaviour. Alternatively these researchers compare a control group (not exposed to the stimulus) to a group of subjects who were exposed. This work tests whether people (particularly children) are stimulated into aggressive excitement that might be acted out in violence, or whether they are influenced by role models and may imitate what they see in the media. A famous example of such work is Bandura's experiments during the 1950s. He tested children's aggression towards Bobo dolls following viewing of a violent film. (For a discussion see Livingstone 1990/98:14–15.)[4]

Cultivation theory: A very different approach to researching media effects, called 'cultivation theory', was developed by George Gerbner at the University of Pennsylvania during the 1960s. Gerbner hypothesised that media impacts were likely to be much more long-term, subtle and cumulative than laboratory based research methods implied. The power of the media, he argues, lies in its pervasiveness and its ability to cultivate a general view of reality over time. This poses a problem for traditional experimental effects research because if 'the messages are so stable, the medium is so ubiquitous, and the accumulated total exposure is what counts, then almost everyone should be effected. It is clear, then, that the cards are stacked against finding evidence of effects' (Gerbner *et al.* cited in Livingstone 1997:311). In order to explore this Gerbner adopted a large-scale quantitative research method based on analysing patterns in mass media content and using surveys to assess people's beliefs. He then looked for any statistical correlation between their beliefs about the world and the amount of television they watched. For example, a character on TV is much more likely to be involved in violence than a real person would be. Gerbner's analysis shows that statistical analysis of audiences, divided into 'heavy' and 'light' viewers, suggests that heavy viewers are more likely to overestimate the frequency of violence in the real world.

Agenda-setting: A whole new paradigm developed in the 1970s with agenda-setting theory (McCombs and Shaw 1972). The question pursued here is not what people believe about an issue but how they rank its importance. Agenda-setting theorists argue that although we might not be able to measure the media impact on what people think, it is possible to identify their impact on what people think about. 'In one sense the media only record the past and reflect a version of the present but, in doing so, they can affect the future, hence the significance of the "agenda" analogy' (McQuail 1977/83:84). Using quantitative techniques measuring the extent of media attention to diverse social issues (such as welfare, famine and drug abuse) investigators are able to show that this correlates with the degree of salience of these issues for the public. They are also able to show that public concern and policy attention rises and falls in response to shifts in media coverage (rather than changes in the actual size of the problem in the real world). In addition some scholars designed experimental research. Iyengar and Kinder, for example, produced doctored videotapes of news broadcasts by inserting extra coverage of some particular issues. They then compared research participants who viewed these tapes with a control group. They found that respondents who viewed the videotapes containing the extra news coverage rated those issues as more important than those who had not (Iyengar and Kinder 1987). Developing out of agenda-setting theory, media scholars also introduced the notion of 'priming'. This refers to the effect of a prior context on the interpretation and retrieval of information. Priming can, for example, influence the criteria by which people assess their political leaders depending on whether or not they address the concerns that people have been 'primed' to consider of key importance.

Framing: The notion of framing developed alongside agenda-setting theory as another key way of examining media power. Framing focuses on the nature of the coverage rather than the sheer amount of media attention given to an issue. Although framing has been used mainly to analyse media texts it is increasingly being used to study audiences too. This concept, as my book title implies, is a key strand in my own work and will therefore be introduced here in a little more depth than the approaches I have outlined so far.

Terms such as 'frames', 'frameworks' and 'frame analysis' are used in a variety of overlapping ways in various disciplines (sociology, linguistics, psychology and fine arts) (Fisher 1997). One key contributor to the concept of framing is Irvine Goffman. In his book *Frame Analysis* (1974) he argues that a framework is something that 'allow[s] its user to locate, perceive, identify and label a seemingly infinite number of concrete occurrences defined in its terms' (Goffman 1974:21). Other authors have defined frames as 'cognitive windows' through which stories are 'seen' (Pan and Kosicki 1993:59) or 'maps' helping us to navigate through a forest of multiple realities (Gamson 1992:117). It is not simply a question of bias or what is said or left unsaid; frames are about how an account organises reality. In editorial terms this includes the 'angle' that journalists adopt in their approach to a story.

Ideas about how stories are framed feature in many classic studies of news coverage. Chibnall, in his analysis of crime reporting, identifies 'ideological frameworks' as 'structures through which the subjective reality of things is fashioned and meaning is imposed on the social world' (Chibnall 1977:13). Gitlin, in his study of reporting of the New Left, defines frames as 'tacit theories about what exists, what happens, and what matters' which inform the ways in which we negotiate, manage and comprehend reality (Gitlin 1980:6). A similar definition features in early work by the Glasgow University Media Group. The group explored 'inferential frameworks' in economic and industrial reporting and argued that the relation between wages and prices was presented as the key factor in explaining inflation. Wage negotiations were seen as threatening and the normal workings of the economic system 'are never treated as if they themselves generate serious problems. Rather the causes of economic problems are sought largely in the activities of trade unionists' (Glasgow University Media Group 1980:112).

This area of research continues to thrive in more recent studies. These include research projects that range from examining the framing of hate speech (Miller and Andsager 1997) and 'political correctness' (Dickerson 2001) to the framing of the US peace movement (Marullo et al. 1996) or Clinton's attempts at health care reforms (Pan and Kosicki 2001).

Most of this work (including early studies by the Glasgow group and that by Chibnall and by Gitlin) focuses on analysing media texts and/or examining the claims-making activity of various stake holders. Far less research has actually addressed people's responses. The studies that have attempted to do this usually adopt survey methods and/or a quasi-experimental approach (Shah et al. 2001; Nelson and Willey 2004; Rhee 1997). In one classic study Iyengar explored the potential consequences of the whole style of news reporting. He was interested in how news reporting that is 'episodic' (depicting concrete events) might impact on people and compared this to reporting that is 'thematic' (presenting collective or general evidence). He showed some groups episodic reporting, and others thematic reporting and then examined how each group responded.

He concludes that episodic framing (the most common form of news framing) reinforces prevailing conventional wisdom and diverts attention from societal responsibility (Iyengar 1991:137).

In spite of such important work there is a lack of in-depth understanding of how media frames might operate upon or in interaction with audiences in a broader cultural context. As Hertog and McLeod conclude:

> A great deal more effort in determining how social framing of controversies affects public understandings of those controversies is needed. This research needs to move out of the laboratory and into the realm of popular culture (Hertog and McLeod 2001:160).

In fact, this task has been (and is being) addressed by an overlapping strand of work which, although not necessarily rooted in the framing tradition, offers complementary insights into this whole area. This research breaks from the survey and experimental tradition. Instead it involves in-depth qualitative analysis of how people discuss key social issues (in interviews, focus group discussions or natural settings). This research (including more recent work by the Glasgow Media Group), examines the integration of, and interaction between, media representations and everyday ways of knowing about issues ranging from AIDS to nuclear power, from gun control to racism, from economics to human genetics. I call this scattered but substantial body of work: 'New Media Influence Research'. As this emerging strand of research actually bridges the traditional division between research that prioritises the power of the text, and work that focuses on the power of the audience, I will not discuss it in any greater depth here. As it is central to my own approach, however, I will return to a discussion of such work in my conclusion.

The approaches outlined above all, in their different ways, focus on how the nature of the media message can influence people. Throughout the same time periods, however, alternative approaches were being developed which primarily focus instead on the activities of audiences. These are outlined below.

Approaches focusing on the power and activity of audiences

Two-step model of media influence: The two-step model of media influence was developed by American researchers in the 1940s and 1950s in direct opposition to the pessimistic generalisations of the Frankfurt School and its hypodermic thesis. Much of this research was based on a much narrower focus than the broad critique of popular culture which formed the basis of the hypodermic model. The two-step model developed out of empirical research into the impact of political campaigns on people's voting intentions. This suggested that the media had a much weaker and more indirect influence than had previously been thought. It highlighted the role of social networks in mediating responses to media messages. Merton's work on mass persuasion (1946) focuses on the importance of reference groups in influencing the messages that people accepted from political campaigns. Similar findings were emphasised in work by Lazarsfeld, Berelson and Gaudet, who tracked a panel of people over six months during the 1940 US presidential campaign battle between Roosevelt and Willkie. This study revealed that most people already knew how they were going to vote before the presidential campaign began, and their intentions did not alter, although they were sometimes influenced by people whose political views they trusted (Lazarsfeld *et al.* 1944). Katz and Lazarsfeld's research on personal influence (1955) reiterates this point, posing a two-step model of media effects whereby media messages are mediated by opinion leaders who influence how ideas are taken up by members of their communities.[5]

Uses and gratifications: Uses and gratifications theory was another approach developed in opposition to those who highlighted the power of the media to shape public understandings of the world. This approach turns traditional ways of thinking about media effects on their head. It replaces the question 'what do the media do to people?' with the question 'what do people do with media?' Uses and gratifications scholars explore how people actively use and process media materials in accordance with their own needs, emphasising the ways in which individuals make a conscious selection between the various items of media content, choosing what they will watch and for what purposes. The degree and kind of media effect will therefore depend on the need of the audience member concerned and is more likely to reinforce rather than change beliefs. The uses and gratifications (U and G) approach thrived during the 1970s and 1980s. However, the earliest example of U and G theory is evident in Herzog's pioneering work with radio listeners in the 1940s USA. She examined women's consumption of radio serials (the earliest form of soap opera). Her research is based on interviews with 100 women from a variety of age and income groups and provides a fascinating portrait of women's lives at that time. She demonstrates how listeners could use and interpret the same radio serial quite differently according to their own needs and identifies the types of gratification obtained from these programmes. These gratifications included: an outlet for pent-up anxieties in giving the listener a 'chance to cry', a wishful escape from isolation and drudgery and using the radio serials to help them understand the world and provide 'recipes for adjustment' (Herzog 1941:69).[6]

Reception analysis and audience decodings: Both the two-step model and Uses and Gratifications theory highlight people's choices and social interactions as important factors in how they relate to media messages. However, the most radical and influential break in theorising about media influence came in the 1970s with a new model of understanding text–audience relations that focused on how people interpret, read or 'decode' texts. This involved a reconfiguration of the whole model of communication from one which implied transmission of a fixed object (the message) from producer to receiver to one which emphasised the social and symbolic processes involved in encoding and decoding a text. The emphasis on audience decodings led to an increasing interest in 'reception research' and 'active audience' studies which explore how people responded to the same media output in different (sub)cultures, the skills people bring to their cultural consumption and how they wrest pleasure or positive images from unexpected sources. This is the body of work which (particularly within Europe) defines the contemporary audience research agenda. It is, therefore, worth addressing this theme in some detail and outlining how it has evolved.

The foundations for studying audience reception processes are usually located in the Birmingham Centre for Contemporary Cultural Studies (BCCCS) in the UK, led by Stuart Hall and, later, David Morley. It should be acknowledged, however, that parallel and overlapping insights were developing (or were already established) across continental European. Reception theory drew on the 1920s tradition of empirical studies of literature (Rosengren 1996:23) and the German branch of literary theory that focuses on the role of the reader in the reading process; a tradition developed at the University of Konstanz (Hagen and Wasko 2000:7). The emphasis on the audience (rather than the text) also built on the insights of Roland Barthes, the French philosopher and linguist, who, in 1968, famously announced the 'death of the author'. Texts, he argued, should no longer be seen as messages dispatched by their inventors, but as sites of multiple writings. Since their socially active meanings were constructed 'not in [their] origin but in [their] destination', it was time to announce 'the demise of the producer and the birth of the reader' (Barthes 1977:148).

Whatever the correct history of how reception analysis was 'discovered' across different disciplines, it is clear that the BCCC became an innovative centre of activity developing this analysis. Stuart Hall's paper 'Encoding and decoding in the television discourse' (1973) undoubtedly served as a key intervention in the debate within media studies. This paper stresses the need to take the communicative process as a whole, with the moment of programme making at one end and the moment of audience perception at the other. Hall argues that texts are 'polysemic', being open to more than one reading, and that there is no necessary correspondence between the message encoded by the film or programme maker and that decoded by audiences.

Hall clearly sees texts as carrying a 'preferred meaning' but proposes three hypothetical positions from which decodings might be constructed in practice: the dominant, the negotiated and the oppositional (terms derived from Parkin 1971). The dominant-hegemonic position is where:

> [the audience] takes the connoted meaning from, say, a television newscast or current affairs programme full and straight, and decodes the message in terms of the reference code in which it has been encoded, we might say that the viewer is operating inside the dominant code (Hall 1973:101).

The negotiated position involves accepting the legitimacy of the dominant framework in the abstract, but negotiating the application of this framework to local conditions. For example, a worker may accept a news broadcast's hegemonic definition of the economic necessity of freezing wages in the national interest in order to avoid inflation, but still be willing to oppose such measures at the level of the shop-floor. The oppositional position, by contrast, challenges the broader hegemonic framing of the problem, questioning whether wage freezes do indeed serve the national interest or only the interest of the dominant class.

Hall's distinction between encoding and decoding highlights the possibility that meaning does not lie in the text alone. Researchers cannot accurately predict how people will relate to and interpret a particular cultural product simply by analysing headlines and photographs, camera angles, lighting, sound track and scripts. Paying attention to the process of decoding also opens questions of audience diversity and allows that 'other discourses are always in play besides those of the particular text in focus – discourses ... brought into play through "the subject's" placing in other practices – cultural, educational, institutional' (Morley 1980:163).

In other words, people are not blank slates who approach a film without any pre-existing identity, experience or resources. They come to the cinema (or TV set) with sets of prior opinions, views and ideas of themselves. In order to understand the role of the media it is therefore, Hall argues, imperative to discover how different groups respond to and interpret any particular programme, to explore the resources they bring to bear on their interpretation and the discourse to which they have access.

It was this understanding which laid the groundwork for a flowering of qualitative work with audiences during the 1980s and 1990s; quite different from the text based, survey or experimental work which had preceded it. One of the first and most influential of these studies was Morley's research into responses to the popular current affairs programme *Nationwide*. David Morley and Charlotte Brundson had already conducted a textual analysis of the programme. Morley (1980) then decided to study ordinary viewers' interpretations. His aim was to produce a typology of different responses and examine how these related to people's varying socio-economic position. To this end, he showed video recordings of an episode of *Nationwide* to 29 groups of people including managers, students, apprentices and trade unionists. The video showings were followed by group discussions.

Morley's work confirms Hall's theory that there are at least three possible readings of a text; the dominant reading (accepting the preferred reading of the text), a negotiated reading and an oppositional reading. His findings show that people differed in their critique of the style of the programme and their critique of the content/framework and that this was related to class. For example, managers objected to the style of *Nationwide* but accepted the content, whereas trade unionists did the opposite. Morley also found that many people across a range of groups were well aware of the preferred meanings embedded in the programme and that 'awareness of the construction by no means entails the rejection of what is constructed' (Morley 1980:140). He also found that class alone was inadequate to explain the diversity of audience responses. There were differences between working-class people active within the trade union movement and those who were not. There were also additional cross-cutting differences to do with age, gender and ethnicity.

Domestic consumption processes: During the 1980s and 1990s researchers also engaged with the processes of consumption itself (Moores 1993). Moving on from his study of the *Nationwide* audience Morley became increasingly interested in the context of media consumption. He was concerned about the unnatural settings in which his study of *Nationwide* audiences had been conducted. His research participants might never have chosen to watch *Nationwide* in the first place, and were unlikely to have engaged in such in-depth discussion and analysis of the programme in the normal course of events. He also hypothesised that the reading a shop steward makes in company with other shop stewards may be very different from the interpretation he might make at home, the most usual viewing situation. His next study therefore focused on how people actually watched television at home and he subsequently went on to scrutinise the impact of the media as technological hardware (e.g. the effect of having a television in the home alongside other technologies such as the computer or telephone) (Morley and Silverstone 1990).

Examining how people consume cultural products has now become a thriving area of media research. Researchers examine the television set itself as a cultural object which carries symbolic meaning. For example, one's choice of media hardware can indicate status, disposable income and taste or the lack of it (Morley 1995). They also explore how cultural consumption may be integrated into people's day-to-day lives and serve particular purposes in the social organisation of the home (Hobson 1980; Modleski 1984; Winship 1987). Throughout the 1980s (in the context of second wave feminism and challenges to traditional patriarchal ways of organising family life) there was intense interest in how men and women negotiated gender relations. This research shows how men take possession of the remote control or mock women's preferred choice of programmes as trivial (Morley 1986). It also highlights the gendered division of labour in relation to different technologies, for example, men may profess to find setting the controls on the washing machine 'too complicated' but claim supremacy over the video machine (Gray 1987). Other researchers have explored the creative way in which women engage in cultural consumption in the context of traditional family life in ways which assert their own needs. 'Addiction' to soap operas, for example, may allow women to establish times when they are not available and attentive to the needs of others (Brunsdon 1981; Hobson 1982; Seiter *et al.* 1989).

Some scholars argue that this is the cutting edge of media studies, the way forward for theorising about media audience. According to proponents such as Ang, this approach enables us to conceive of 'the ideological operations of television in a much more radical way that has hitherto been done'. It allows us to see that 'If television is an "ideological apparatus" ... this is not so much because its texts transmit "messages" as because it is a cultural form through which those constraints [on structuring social relationships, identities and desires] are negotiated and those possibilities take shape' (Ang 1989:109).

The broader field of active audience studies: Research into how people engage with media technologies was paralleled by a continued fascination with audience reception processes. In particular, researchers were interested in how people might read cultural products differently depending on their own pre-existing cultural resources and competencies.

Some researchers wanted to test out the cultural colonialism thesis. (Cultural colonialism refers to the idea that the export of American cultural products will also export American cultural values.) Comparative research often seemed to challenge a simple notion of cultural colonialism because it highlighted how the same media output could be read quite differently in diverse cultures. Katz and Liebes, for example, studied how different audiences in Israel responded to *Dallas* (an internationally successful US-made soap about a Texan oil family that was seen to celebrate conspicuous consumption). Their findings contradict the cultural colonialism thesis. They found that Russian Jews, newly arrived in Israel, read *Dallas* as capitalism criticising itself, while a Moroccan Jew learned from the series that Jewishness was the right way to be, because it was clear that non-Jews lived messy and immoral lives (Katz and Liebes 1985). This supports the argument presented by the Italian theorist Eco, for example, that audiences may engage in 'semiological guerrilla warfare' (Eco 1974) and that advertising could serve as a revolutionary message in depressed areas. This is because 'For a Milanese bank clerk a TV ad for a refrigerator represents a stimulus to buy, but for a peasant in Calabria the same image means the confirmation of a world of prosperity that doesn't belong to him' (Eco 1986:141).[7]

Other researchers were fuelled by a commitment to exploring social diversity and inequalities (e.g. by age and ethnicity). This spawned a great deal of work with minority or oppressed groups. It showed that it was possible for people to take mainstream offerings and use them to reflect constructively on their own lives. Bobo's work with black women viewers of the film *The Color Purple* was a classic study informing this strand of work.[8] She aimed to 'examine the ways in which a specific audience creates meanings from a mainstream text and uses the reconstructed meaning to empower themselves and their social group' (Bobo 2003:307). A similar approach is evident in Gillespie's richly ethnographic study of TV use by British Asians. She found that *Neighbours*, an Australian soap featuring an all-white cast, attracted young British Asians who perceived it as offering 'a complex metaphor for their own social world' (Gillespie 1995:207). *Neighbours* explores the tensions that exist between families and their neighbours in a way which resonated with those young people's experiences of their communities (1995:164). Such findings parallel research with lesbians and gay men that highlights the way in which even the most mainstream heterosexual media text can be used creatively to construct positive gay identities (Whitiker 1985; Dyer 1986; Jay and Glasgow 1992; Doty 1993; Griffen 1993; Hamer and Budge 1994; Wilton 1995). Similarly, research with children shows how they use mainstream media in ways which help them to make sense of their own structural position (Hodge and Tripp 1986). Studies of *Prisoner Cell Block H*, for example, the Australian soap set in a woman's prison, found that the programme provided school students with language and cultural categories with which to think through their experiences. Teachers were given nicknames from the cast of prison guards and the children used the programme as a way of understanding and articulating their powerlessness (Curthoys and Docker 1989; Palmer 1986).

Many scholars at this time were interested in questioning the privileged status of 'highbrow' (i.e. white, male, middle class) cultural tastes. Many feminist scholars, for example, also wanted to challenge the status accorded to watching 'serious' ('masculine') television genre and attempted to reclaim disparaged pleasures and skills (Ang 1985). Extensive work was conducted on soap fans.[9] Dorothy Hobson, for example (based at the BCCCS) went to women's homes to watch a phenomenally popular soap opera called *Crossroads* with them and to discuss their enjoyment of the programme. She found that women enjoyed hypothesising about the future actions of characters and would engage in sophisticated games with soap opera characters, including them in their 'gossip' even though fully cognisant of their fictional status. Hobson emphasises how women were actively involved in bringing meaning to the programme by drawing on experiences in their own lives. Attending to audience pleasure and acknowledging their active engagement with the text challenges traditional analysis of media content. Hobson concludes:

> To look at a programme like *Crossroads* and criticise it on the basis of a conventional literary/media analysis is obstinately to refuse to understand the relationship which it has with its audience [...] To try to say what *Crossroads* means to its audience is impossible for there is no single *Crossroads*, there are as many different *Crossroads* as there are viewers (Hobson 1982:135–6).

Such statements are less an evolution from Hall's notion of audience decodings than a challenge. Hobson's formulation breaks with the notion that there is a preferred reading built into the text at all (see Barker and Brooks 1998). At its boldest, active audience research can sometimes suggest that questions of media influence are irrelevant or, at best, impossible to research. The production of meaning is so dependent on what people bring to their engagement with the media that attempts to generalise about the impact of media coverage, or to predict how texts might influence people, are misguided, or at least doomed to failure.

THE CURRENT IMPASSE:
MEDIA INFLUENCE VERSUS ACTIVE AUDIENCES

Given the diverse approaches outlined above it is perhaps not surprising that media studies in general, and audience research in particular, is a very volatile and unsettled field (see, for example, the 1983 issue of *Journal of Communication*, entitled *Ferment in the Field*; see also Corner *et al*. 1997:2). Theorising about media influence has been condemned as a messy pot-pourri with inconsistent or inconclusive conclusions (Livingstone 1999:14). The terms 'media' and 'audience' themselves incorporate such diverse conceptualisations that some of this work is barely recognisable as addressing the same object of study at all. Some studies concentrate on the impact on one type of media (e.g. television); some examine a particular genre (e.g. soap) or an individual text (e.g. a cartoon or film). Others are concerned with an all together broader canvas (e.g. the impact of popular culture or general news reporting). Studies in this field often investigate different types of media (from radio to digital television) and consider diverse time frames (from the immediate aftermath of viewing to the long-range absorption of ideas). They are looking for very different types of effect (ranging from imitation of violent acts to the framing of general ideas about 'the ways of the world'). Sometimes they are asking entirely different questions all together (e.g. what people do with television rather than what it does to them).

Some of the divisions about study design and methodology follow geographical and cultural borders. For example, research which emphasises the power of the media is stronger in the USA while that which emphases the activity of the audiences is better established within western Europe. The former has traditionally been based on quantitative and experimental work rooted in the disciplines of social and political science or mainstream experimental psychology. The latter favours in depth qualitative research and draws more on the disciplines of arts and humanities (including cultural studies, literary theory and social anthropology).

The gap between those who theorise about media influence and those who prioritise active audience research has become a seemingly unbridgeable gulf. Sometimes each side simply ignores the other, a stance made easier by the ways in which the fault-lines in this debate coincide with national, disciplinary and methodological boundaries. At other times communication across the divide takes the form of sniping (Morley 1998). Those who study active audiences accuse those who focus on media influence of a crude approach to textual interpretation, insensitivity to people's diversity and a failure to attend to nuances of gender, ethnic and sexual identity. They attack research addressing the potential effects of media coverage for casting people as 'cultural dupes', objectifying them, being elitist and pessimistic and promoting condescending attitudes to 'vulnerable' audiences (especially children and young people) (Barker and Petley 1997/2001). Theorists concerned with media influence, for their part, often challenge their opponents for romanticising audience resistance and failing to attend to systematic asymmetries in the distribution of power and resources. (For critiques see Barry 1993; Corner 1991; Eldridge *et al.* 1997; Gitlin 1991; Jakubowicz *et al.* 1994; McGuigan 1992; McLaughlin 1993; Morris 1988; Seaman 1992; Kitzinger 1993; Philo and Miller 1997.)

Each side accuses the other of failure to address the real sites of power, for example focusing on the macro at the expense of the micro, or vice versa (Corner 1991; Gray 1999). Active audience theorists are criticised for their tendency to concentrate on fictional genres and questions of pleasure, hence sometimes being seen to sideline the 'serious' public issues of the day (Barry 1993:489; Jakubowicz *et al.* 1994:23). Media influence theorists are accused of underestimating the importance of non-news genre and failing to understand complex issues around identity and the role of fantasy. Each side in the conflict accuses the other of misreading the literature, misrepresenting history and failing to understand the social and political context within which particular polemics were published (Curran 1990, 1996; Morley 1996). Each side also accuses the other of using methodologies rooted in oppressive histories or alleges that the other is pursuing an agenda which serves the powers-that-be. On the one hand, for example, it is clear that research that highlights media influence can serve institutional interests in justifying censorship and state control or allowing the media to be used as a scapegoat for social problems more properly linked to issues such as poverty and injustice. On the other hand, it is equally clear that a focus on audience creativity can be used by multi-national media conglomerates to defend monopolies or oppose efforts to maintain 'quality'. The celebration of difference can also become the mantra of global capitalism, a goldmine, rather than a threat (McLaughlin 1993:61; McGuigan 1992:164, 183; Klien 2000:115).

Some of the accusations flung across the barricades between the two sides are true for some of the theories (or for some individual theorists) at least some of the time. The fierce polemics about the history and future of audience research have served an important role in clarifying potential dangers and highlighting differences. However, the debate becomes unproductive when the argument is reduced to simplistic binaries. There is a danger of producing highly selective accounts that oppose simple 'pro-media effects' against 'active audience' division (labels that as the above outlines show, can cover a multitude of diverse work). Emphasising competing brands of thought also tends to play up the differences rather than areas of convergence. Thus, for example, in spite of the apparently unbridgeable gulf between theorists often cited in relation to the different positions outlined above, they can each agree on some core issues. In particular commentators on both sides now often seem to concur that the constraints of how texts are produced, and how people read them, are important, and that the power of audience activity should not be exaggerated. Compare, for example, the statements below that come from John Corner who has contributed a great deal to work on media influence, David Morley (of *Nationwide* fame) and Umberto Eco, a theorist more usually associated with celebrating semiological guerrilla warfare.

'so much effort has been centred on audiences' interpretative activity that even the preliminary theorisation of influence has become *awkward*' (Corner 1991:267–9, emphasis in original).

'... the rights of the interpreters have been overstressed [as if] interpretation has no context and there is a failure to examine the limitations or constraints of readings' (Eco 1990:7).

'The power of viewers to reinterpret meanings is hardly equivalent to the discursive power of centralised media institutions to construct the texts which the viewer then interprets; to imagine otherwise is simply foolish' (Morley 1996:291).

Polemics can also have the unfortunate effect of ignoring work that is more nuanced or that has tried to address the problems highlighted in the attacks and counter-attacks. Research into the active audience, for example, is sometimes summarised by reference to the more extreme statements of its more radical proponents, while studies into the influence of the media are often reviewed simply in terms of 'the effects tradition'. The effects tradition is defined predominantly by behavioural experiments and the Frankfurt School, sometimes including cultivation theory. When proponents of an active audience review research on media effects/influence they rarely give any attention to work on agenda-setting or framing, and have not taken into account the range of work that I categorise as 'New Media Influence Research'.

MY RESEARCH APPROACH

My desire to bring together a range of my own research projects into this single volume was born out of frustration with this debate. We seem to be going round in circles. Old battles are endlessly revisited while new developments are ignored. There are plenty of detailed criticisms of old effects paradigms or attacks on active audience theory and plenty of calls for research which combines attention to both textual and audience power. It is much rarer to find reviews that actually address such research as it exists. I think it is time to move on. I hope the research presented in this volume will help us to do precisely this (and, as I have already pointed out, there is plenty of other research that can also be brought into play in this debate).

The following chapters draw together a collection of studies, involving primary research, around the role of the media in relation to child sexual abuse. (These studies were briefly outlined in Chapter 1.) Much of this research was explicitly informed by active audience theory or other perspectives dedicated to recognising people as actors, rather than merely subjects. In the following section I outline the principles informing my research approach.

My interviews with incest survivors in the 1980s, although not informed by media studies scholarship, were conducted in the context of the Women's Liberation Movement. This movement insisted that women should be viewed as survivors rather than victims and challenged traditional methodological approaches. In particular, feminist theorists objected to traditional ways of objectifying research subjects. My concern, during the course of this research, was thus in how women (re)constructed their identities and took back control from their abusers. My questions focused on the process of survival and resistance, rather than the acts of victimisation. In addition, I approached women as experts on their own lives and I tried to engage with them as 'participants' in, rather than objects of, my research. (For example, I sent interviewees transcripts of their interviews for comment and discussion.)

The two main focus group studies presented in this volume also address people as active participants in the construction of meaning. These groups were conducted after I had been initiated into the debates about active audience theory. One of the studies (involving 30 focus groups) explored people's reactions to a particular social awareness campaign. The other (involving 49 focus groups) had a broader remit, exploring the role of the mass media in general.[10] Both focus group studies were explicitly designed to attend to potential influence and also to explore how people actively engage with media texts. I wanted to explore how people use the media as a resource in their day-to-day lives and to address the multiple alternative sources people might bring to bear on their readings of a text. These concerns informed my sampling strategies, the way in which the groups were composed, the choice of location in which discussion sessions were held, the games used in the focus groups and the ways in which I facilitated them. My interest in the audience's active engagement in these issues, rather than mere 'receivers' of messages, also informs my analytical approach and the way in which I have presented my data.

- My sampling strategies: Following in the footsteps of researchers such as Morley (1980), I selected the sample in order to include people with a wide range of experiences. The aim here was to maximise potential diversity, especially in relation to the specific issue under discussion. Some groups were chosen because they might be expected to have particular knowledge of, or perspectives on, sexual abuse (e.g. social workers and incest survivors support groups). Others were chosen because, as a group, they were not necessarily expected to have any special interest in this issue (e.g. a group of people attending the same community centre or youth club). Efforts were also made to meet with groups in diverse settings (social, occupational and educational) and include participants with a range of demographic characteristics. Thus some groups were specifically targeted to ensure the sample included old people as well as young, English people as well as Scottish and black people as well as white. Community centres, clubs, youth groups and schools were also approached in different areas ranging from middle-class suburbia to areas of 'inner-city deprivation' and including some rural as well as urban locations.

- The composition of the focus groups: The groups were based on pre-existing groups of people who already knew each other through living, working or socialising together. These are, after all, the 'interpretive communities' in which people might normally discuss (or evade) the sorts of issues raised in the research session (Morgan 1988; Barbour and Kitzinger 1999). I also kept the groups small, an average of five or six participants per group, in order to allow for in-depth discussion during the sessions (which usually lasted between one and three hours).

- The design of exercises used in the focus groups: Various exercises and games were used to engage people in the debates. These included games that encouraged people to actively construct and deconstruct campaign or media messages, positioning them as expert commentators upon, not just victims of the text. (The 'news game' is briefly described in Chapter 1. For fuller discussion of this exercise, see Kitzinger 1990.)

- The way the group discussions were facilitated: Focus groups have one major advantage over interviews; they are forums within which research participants can (indeed should) address each other much more than they address the researcher. This can allow closer access to everyday forms of talk. Rather than adopting a very controlling 'group leader' role, I therefore adopted a more low-key facilitating position. For example, instead of asking questions of each person in turn, group participants were encouraged to talk to one another; ask questions, exchange anecdotes, and comment on each others' experiences and points of view. I allowed 'natural' conversation to develop and evolve in the group, and was tolerant of apparent 'digressions' in an effort to gain access to the context within which people discussed this issue with one another. (For full discussion of the focus group method see Kitzinger 1994a.)

- Transcription, coding and qualitative analysis: Focus groups are only really focus groups, rather than simply group interviews, when interaction between participants is explicitly used to generate data as part of the analytical process. Analysis of transcripts should include, for example, attention to the difference between argumentative and complementary interactions (Kitzinger 1994a), and attend to the differences between common and shared knowledge. Detailed focus group analysis also pays attention to issues such as how people talk and what counts as sensitive or unusual information (Kitzinger and Farquhar 1999). In order to allow for such analysis a full transcription is invaluable. The focus groups and interviews were fully transcribed to facilitate close examination of how talk developed in interaction over the progress of the discussion. The transcripts were also coded for themes (e.g. all references to a particular scandal) but also for types of speech or interaction (e.g. jokes, laughter, declared changes of mind). For similar reasons I often present examples of the conversational exchanges between people, rather than just statements from individuals taken out of context. I also tried to attend to different notions about the nature of talk, including thinking about talk as performance, as self-narration and as action (see Gillespie 1995:205; McKinley 1997).

- Systematic examination of patterns and deviation: Most of the focus group data is indexed on computer. This allows for rigorous comparison of themes, across thousands of pages of transcript. Such quantification is sometimes seen to be out of keeping with qualitative approaches and respect for the nuances of how people talk. However, in my experience, used in the right way, such computer-assisted analysis can complement such approaches. While always keeping the context in mind, computer coding allows for a very systematic way of locating recurring themes in a very large dataset. This gave me a basis from which to present meaningful quantification alongside in-depth qualitative analysis. (This includes detailed attention to the nuances of talk.)

Throughout the book I have thus been able to indicate where ideas were common across a variety of groups, or where they were only expressed by a few people. Even if unable to precisely enumerate the number of individuals who express a certain point of view, it is important to give an idea of the distribution of ideas across groups. As Lewis argues:

> It matters whether the discourse whose presence we identify during a focus group interview is widespread within the culture (or subculture). It is important for us to know, roughly, the number of people who construct one reading of a TV programme rather than another [...] We may not be able to enumerate it, but in describing its presence we assume that it is, in some form, quantifiable. We assume that it counts (Lewis 1997:87).

In addition, computer indexing transcripts allows one to locate and attend to deviant examples and to systematically examine all examples of types of speech and interaction (e.g. jokes, unease, declared changes of mind).

I hope the approach outlined above will provide some useful suggestions for future research and that I have provided sufficient detail to help readers to evaluate and reflect on my findings. My research demonstrates that it is possible to identify how certain aspects of media coverage can influence us, sometimes even in spite of our own 'better judgement'. It is also possible to track how specific media coverage can tap into pre-existing cultural images, experiences and expectations in ways that provoke powerful responses. The mass media are rarely our sole source of information and we actively interpret and consume the media for our own purposes and pleasures. The paradox is, as this book will show, that in spite and sometimes even because of such audience engagement, the media can have a very powerful role in defining, maintaining, and even transforming the way we see the world.

3
Transformation of Private and Public Discourse: The Media 'Discovers' Sexual Abuse[1]

How do newspaper, radio and television reports contribute to the ways in which we understand our experiences and construct our identities? Do the media merely reflect society or can they actively contribute to social change? How do audiences actively engage with the media to challenge the status quo or affirm stigmatised or taboo events from their own lives? This chapter addresses such questions through focusing on the dramatic discovery of child sexual abuse in the UK and across the English-speaking world during the last two decades of the twentieth century.

Drawing on interviews conducted throughout the 1980s and 1990s I show how the massive increase in media coverage of sexual abuse during that time raised public awareness and how it influenced, and was used by, those who had endured abuse. The media did not operate alone: the coverage was situated within a broader context of social agitation, especially the Women's Liberation Movement. However, my research highlights how a sudden rise in media attention led to sexual abuse becoming a topic for public debate and personal conversation in unprecedented ways. It also encouraged the formation and expression of identities around this previously very fragmented and silenced form of sexual exploitation.

Through focusing on the substantive topic of sexual abuse and giving detailed examples from abuse survivors' own accounts, I engage with key concepts from within media studies and debate their relevance in the broader socio-political context. This chapter concludes by critically reflecting on theories about the media's role in agenda-setting and social change, identity formation and interpersonal communication.

CONSTRUCTING A NEW SOCIAL PROBLEM: A BRIEF MODERN HISTORY

This book focuses on struggles to define and redefine mainstream understandings of child sexual abuse in the West. My particular focus is on sexual abuse within the family. In this context it is vital to acknowledge that definitions of child sexual abuse vary across cultures and over time. How we understand sexual violence against children depends, for example, on how we define childhood. This is not just a question of determining the age at which a young person becomes an adult. It also depends on how we socially construct the child and define the 'essence' of childhood (James and Prout 1990). The contemporary western concept of childhood innocence, for example, is central to how assaults against children are interpreted. Sexual abuse is a 'violation of innocence' and 'robs children of their childhood' (Kitzinger 1988, 1990). Defining what counts as 'sexual' and what counts as 'abuse' can be equally fluid and involves cross-cultural controversies (Stainton Rogers 1989). Thus contemporary debates address whether definitions of sexual exploitation or abuse should include a wide range of issues such as breastfeeding older toddlers, arranged marriages for young girls, baby beauty pageants, genital cutting of children or cosmetic surgery on young people. Quite where the focus should be is also a highly political question. Children may suffer from war and poverty, for example, but 'child abuse' is not usually discussed in ways which include these forms of violence and deprivation.

Sometimes people talk as if the 'truth of child sexual abuse' were uncovered in the West without any sense of previous attempts to address such issues or controversies surrounding its definition. However, concerns about the sexual exploitation of children have a long, if chequered, history. In the late nineteenth century, for example, early UK feminist and 'social purity' campaigners tried to highlight how working-class girls were trapped into prostitution (Jeffreys 1985). Sexual abuse was also raised as a concern by the newly founded National Society for the Prevention of Cruelty to Children as well as being highlighted by organisations such as the Salvation Army (Jackson 2000a, 2000b). In 1885 the sale of young girls for sexual services gave rise to high-profile and controversial media coverage. In a dramatic episode often cited in the history of investigative reporting, the editor of the *Pall Mall Gazette*, William Stead, printed an infamous serious of articles, 'The Maiden Tribute to Modern Babylon' (6 July 1885). This was a serialised account of his adventures in purchasing a 13-year-old virgin, with the initial support of feminist activist, Josephine Butler (Barry 1979). These reports, under sub-headings such as 'I order Five Virgins', 'Strapping Girls Down' and 'Confessionals of a Brothel-Keeper' led to outrage and to spiralling circulation figures.

The newspaper was banned by major newsagents but was sold on the streets (including by George Bernard Shaw). A quarter of a million people demonstrated in Hyde Park in central London to demand an increase in the age of consent (McIntosh 1988). The Home Secretary of the time begged the editor to suspend publication for fear of national riots. Within days the Criminal Law Amendment Act that raised the age of consent to 16 was put through its second reading. 'The Maiden Tribute to Modern Babylon' coverage is credited with forcing it into law (Pearsall 1969:302; Barry 1979). Intense debate was generated again some 20 years later leading up to the 1908 Punishment of Incest Act. This was generated partly by concern about exploitation, but also driven by disgust about immorality and in-breeding within over-crowded, illiterate, working-class families (Bailey and Blackburn 1979; Bell 1993). Concern focused on 'fallen girls', eugenic considerations and problems of rural isolation or urban overcrowding and immorality (Gammon 1999; Jackson 2000a, 2000b; Smart 1999, 2000; Gordon 1988a, 1988b). (For an account of similar historical shifts in the USA see Jenkins 1998.)

Child sexual abuse as it is understood today, however, was not 'invented' until the 1980s. For most of the twentieth century, child sexual abuse, particularly by ordinary men within ordinary (middle-class) families, was a well-kept secret and a little bit of father–daughter 'seduction' was subtly tolerated. Throughout the 1920s and 1930s women active in organisations such as the Association for Moral and Social Hygiene and the National Vigilance Association fought to have sexual abuse taken seriously, but the legal profession and the media evaded their efforts (Smart 1999). Indeed, throughout the first half of the twentieth century, although evidence of sexual abuse (e.g. childhood syphilis) was confronting the legal establishment, it seemed unable to define adult–child sexual contact as abusive or harmful (Smart 2000).

During the 1950s, 1960s and 1970s, although child abduction, rape and murder were acknowledged as a real threat, other forms of abuse often went unacknowledged or were simply seen as a non-harmful practice that did not count as assault at all. Some of the professional literature rationalised incest as a functional way to preserve the family group or a process of socialisation that led to 'better adjusted' girls (see Nelson 1982:34, 35, 350). Any harm was sometimes seen as being caused by the social taboo, rather than the act itself: 'the enlightened child would not feel abused' (Jeffreys 1990:97). By the early 1970s a strong strand of liberal opinion saw the law against paedophilia as reflecting outmoded sexual prejudice (Jenkins 1998). A liberation movement even began to emerge in the form of NAMBLA (North American Man/Boy Love Association) in the USA and the Paedophile Information Exchange in the UK. There were campaigns for change in other parts of Europe too. For some radical thinkers the real problem was seen in terms of sexual liberation rather than exploitation. The prominent French feminist, Simone de Beauvoir, as well as her partner Jean-Paul Sartre were among signatories on a petition in the 1970s calling for paedophilia to be decriminalised (Henley 2001:17). The radical theorist Michel Foucault also signed. 'Intergenerational sex' was not seen as a form of violence by these thinkers at the time, it was even seen as a child's right. This caused a scandal in France when this information surfaced in 2003. However, as Philippe Sollers, recently challenged about his stance back then, comments: 'the whole problem of violence against children was simply not a social problem at the time' (cited in Henley 2001:17).

All this changed in the 1980s as the mass media began to confront the idea that father–daughter 'seduction' was an act of violence and that children were often exploited by trusted adults within their social networks, including fathers, grandfathers and uncles. (Abuse by care-workers or priests, by brothers and by women at first had a lower profile, as did the abuse of boys.)

The USA had front-page revelations about 'the reality' of abuse, including incest, from the early 1980s onwards. As the leading US publication, *Time Magazine*, declared in 1983: 'Private violence: child abuse, wife-beating, rape [...] The unspeakable crimes are being yanked out of the shadows.' 'The wall of silence', the magazine declared, 'is breaking down' (Myers 1994b). The start of broader public recognition in the UK was signalled in October 1986 with Esther Rantzen's programme, *Childwatch*. This programme launched the children's helpline, Childline, and included detailed discussions of abuse statistics and how to support victims (what to say, what to do, who to go to for help). Childline received 50,000 calls on its opening day and calls continued at a rate of 8000 to 10,000 per day after that, a fact which generated further media attention. The *Childwatch* programme was accompanied by a remarkable expansion in attention to child abuse, particularly sexual abuse, from other TV formats as well as the print media. Reporting of sexual abuse in *The Times* newspaper, for example, increased by 300 per cent between 1985 and 1987 (Kitzinger 1996). Sexual abuse within families also became an issue for flagship UK documentary series such as *Brass*

Tacks (BBC2, 7 July 1987); *Everyman* (BBC1, 8 May 1988); *Antenna* (BBC2, 10 May 1989) and *Horizon* (BBC2, 19 June 1989). Such programmes featured abuse survivors, filmed in silhouette to protect their identities, describing the horrific damage done to them, and their struggle to survive.

The development during the 1980s of the media spectacle of tabloid news, TV discussion shows and live audience discussion programmes provided another stage for revealing personal experiences of abuse. This proved to be especially pertinent with the emergence of celebrity survivors such as Oprah Winfrey (Attmore 1999:4). A key role was also played by TV films. The American made-for-TV drama, *Something about Amelia*, starring Glen Close and Ted Dansen (broadcast in the USA in 1984 and in the UK in 1989) is often credited with doing for child sexual abuse what *Cathy Come Home* did for homelessness. By the early 1990s child sexual abuse also began to appear in drama series. It features in American and British TV dramas set in police stations, hospitals and law firms (e.g. *The Bill*, ITV, 29 January 1993; *Casualty*, BBC1, 6 February 1993 and *LA Law*, Channel 4, 16 March 1994) and became the subject of 'true crime' features (Weaver 1998). It also featured in soap opera storylines. In 1993 a particularly dramatic and long-running storyline was developed by Channel 4's popular series, *Brookside*, set in a community in Liverpool, England. This two-year-long storyline portrayed a capable young survivor, Beth Jordache, determined to protect her younger sister from her father's abuse. The story culminated in Beth's mother murdering her abusive father. Together, Beth and her mother buried him under the patio (Henderson 1996).

The decade between 1985 and 1995 was thus a time of dramatic shifts in the public profile of sexual, particularly incestuous, abuse. Previously media coverage of sexual abuse had been characterised only by flurries of outrage around attacks by strangers. The debate had revolved around serial predators, most notoriously, in the UK, the Moors Murderers Ian Brady and Myra Hindley. However, by the early 1990s the media was saturated with news reports, fictional stories, real-life accounts, documentaries, discussion shows and public participation shows, all of which addressed incest. Indeed, journalists who said they had been discouraged from following up such stories in the 1970s and early 1980s were now saying that they had reported almost every possible angle and were suffering from 'abuse fatigue' (Kitzinger 1996; Skidmore 1995, 1998).

So what effect, if any, did all this media attention have? Did it make a difference to abused children or adult survivors? Did it help to create more family and social support? How did abuse survivors contribute and respond to this shift in media coverage?

PLACING NARRATIVES IN HISTORICAL CONTEXT: RECORDING PERSONAL ACCOUNTS DURING THE 1980s AND 1990s

This chapter draws on the interviews I conducted with female incest survivors between 1984 and 1989 and also focus group discussions with men and women conducted in the mid 1990s. The research participants were aged between 14 and 79 years old. This means that the data cover a broad historical period. Many abuse survivors I spoke with had been children between the 1940s and 1970s while others, interviewed for the second project, grew up during the 1980s and early 1990s. Most of those interviewed in the first project were abused during a time when the subject was completely taboo. Some, interviewed after 1986, had lived through a dramatic transition in public discussion of sexual abuse. By the time I conducted the second project the context had changed. Some younger participants who spoke to me during the mid 1990s had grown up surrounded by a plethora of media representation of sexual abuse. Teenage focus group participants interviewed in 1995, for example, had been being abused during the late 1980s or early 1990s (after the launch of Childline and during periods of intense media controversy about sexual abuse allegations).

Re-reading both sets of transcripts I was struck by the strong sense of history that emerges. These interviews clearly demonstrate how shifts in media coverage not only transformed public knowledge but were also implicated in 'private' knowledge. Media representations were used to help make sense of intimate experiences of violence within the family, providing a framework for thinking and talking about what happened, and providing foundation stones for building a sense of identity as a survivor.[2]

FROM CULTURAL VACUUM TO MULTIPLE MEDIA MEDIATION: SURVIVORS' ACCOUNTS OF THE MEDIA'S ROLE

Prior to 1986 incestuously abused children and adult survivors had to process their experiences in an almost total cultural vacuum. Some grew up thinking that abuse was perfectly normal: 'He told me it was something that all daddies do with their little girls.' Others believed that no one else had ever 'participated' in anything so unnatural and disgusting. (Although some had sisters or brothers who were also victimised, it was never discussed between them at the time.) Even as adults, survivors often had no words to define what was happening to them, other than the explanations offered by abusers. As one woman explains: 'I had absolutely no words for it, all the words I had were the ones he gave me.'

In interviews conducted during the early 1980s women struggle to articulate the literally unspeakable. They often consciously experience the interview itself as an arena for discourse construction, a process of 'putting together the pieces of the jigsaw'. During the course of talking to me they try to unpick ideas imposed on them by their abusers ('you are my little princess', 'this isn't happening', 'you want this', 'you deserve this'). They also often make observations about the interview process such as 'I'd never seen it that way until just now' or 'I've never said this before but …'.

I always offered to send women copies of their own transcripts. I adopted this practice in response to feminist theory about ethical research processes. This practice also helped generate new data. Several responded to reading their own transcripts with remarks such as 'This is the first time I've seen anything like this in black and white.' I read one young woman's transcript to her over the telephone because it was not safe to post anything to her home. Even though it recorded her own words she commented that it was the first time she had even heard such a story. She found it very shocking and it made her look at her experiences differently.

Obviously there are structural aspects to child sexual abuse that make articulating issues around the experience difficult. Abuse may always create a sense of isolation, social dislocation and confusion. Complex feelings can be generated by abusers' manipulation of reality, their position of trust and their insistence on secrecy. Issues also arise because of the very young (even pre-verbal) age at which some children are abused and their efforts to accommodate to repeated victimisation (see Summit 1983). Many young survivors today will recognise feelings described by women talking in the 1980s. However, there are now far more positive cultural resources for confronting abuse than there were 20 years ago.

As children, teenagers and adults, prior to 1986, survivors describe struggling to make sense of what had been done to them within the inadequate conventional categories available to them at that time. One describes her confusion and distress about her stepfather's 'fondling' and contrasts this with her sense of clarity when he finally forced her to have sexual intercourse. Then, and only then, could she identify his acts as assault. In a way, this was, she explains, 'a relief'.

> Afterwards I thought, 'Jesus, I've been raped, I've been raped.' Like all the stuff before was just other things. I'd never seen it as rape because whenever you're told about it in newspapers or school it's always that, it's never anything else. So I thought: 'I've actually been raped this time. He's actually raped me now.' It felt quite real. *It felt real because I could call it something.* It really happened (Liza, my emphasis).[3]

Another young woman, however, is unable to name what happened to her as assault because she feels that she displayed insufficient resistance to her father and uncle's insistence on having sex with her. In fact, she was very surprised when I referred to what happened to her as sexual violence. She countered that she did not see it as such because 'I let it happen ... rather than thinking "Oh my God, what's he going to do to me?" and being scared, I just get on with it.' She added that she also could not call it rape because her understanding of such assault was 'walking down the street and a man coming up with a knife'. Even then, she reflected, however, she could not be raped because 'I would just lie down and take it, to get it over with.'[4]

The absence of media discussion of the range and subtlety, as well as the power dynamics, of incestuous assault made it hard for many victims to identify what happened as abusive. Some had thought of it as 'being tickled somewhere he shouldn't be touching me at all', others experienced it as being punished or disciplined or even 'educated'. Deficiencies in everyday language prior to 1986 were also part of the experience of the mothers I interviewed. One interviewee recalls searching through a dictionary for information about incest. It was the only place she could think to turn to for guidance. The dictionary definition simply talked about marriage between blood relations and was of no use to her.[5] Another interviewee, whom I call Kathy, felt unable to confront the possibility of sexual abuse until she actually walked in on her husband with her daughter.

> [I felt] totally as though I was just in a nightmare and when daylight came I would wake up and it hadn't happened. And daylight came, and

it didn't go away. [...] [Finding my husband in there] confirmed what I
knew, although I didn't know I knew it (Kathy).

Throughout her account Kathy stresses how she had to respond
'like an animal' without any cultural reference points.

It felt just as though it were a primitive kind of instinct. I had to protect
her. It was just like an animal, you know, the young have been threatened
and you just have to close round them and just protect them. And
that is what I did, in any way I knew how. But I had absolutely no
model whatever, *that was the horrible part of it*. [...] I just didn't know
anything about sexual abuse. I remember thinking: 'if only I had read
something about it'. But I had never read anything about it. [...] only
awful stories in the paper [about abduction], but no useful articles in
women's magazines that said 'I did so and so'. These things just weren't
around then (Kathy, my emphasis).

Only two of the women I interviewed describe media coverage
prior to 1986 as having been a positive resource in any way. In both
cases this was not because the newspapers or television represented
abuse, but rather the opposite. One girl, Petra, used avidly to watch
TV sitcoms and use them to make up stories about her own family
life in order to disguise the abuse and neglect she suffered. Another,
Samantha, explains that media representations of happy families led
her to realise that her experiences were abnormal.

From 1986 onwards, however, the rapid rise in media coverage
helped to cultivate general public awareness and inform both parents
and children. This was clearly acknowledged in the focus groups I
conducted during the mid 1990s: 'Nobody knew about such things
when I was young, now it's even on children's programmes' (Group
35); 'I recall my parents saying: "Now don't talk to strangers" [...],
that was about the end of it. But now everyone's looking round every
corner. [...] The whole culture's changing or it's changed' (Group 37).
A few people, mostly elderly, resisted this change. They dismissed the
media attention as 'a fad'. As one man in his seventies commented:
'It's like a lot of other things in my opinion, you get people goes on
to bandwagons. One time it was invalid people, now it's child abuse,
then it's sexual harassment. All these papers jump on the bandwagon'
(Group 27, m).

Others, however, were less sceptical and some reported that the
shifts in media coverage had altered their own views. It had 'cultivated'

a greater sense of this type of danger: 'We never talked about it in my day. I've no doubt it went on, but it just wasn't discussed. It's right to be out in the open now. I realise now it's going on' (Group 58). 'Ten years ago I found it hard to believe that fathers abused their daughters. But now I realise it's often just like that. I know that largely because of the telly, it comes back to the media' (Group 5).

This recognition of changing levels of social awareness was most acute among those with direct experience of abuse and often had profound personal significance. During the late 1980s and early 1990s many adult abuse survivors finally began to find words for what had been done to them. They started to reassess what had happened to them, finally realising that it was not normal or that they did not deserve it. Others found that media coverage forced them to confront memories that they had been trying to ignore. One woman comments that until the media started to discuss incest 'I just had these funny ideas floating around in my head – I had no way of making sense of them.' Another states that, in spite of recurring nightmares, 'It was not part of my waking day at all.' The media helped to change this. Indeed, among those I interviewed during the 1980s it was media coverage, rather than comments from friends or family, which is most often identified as a trigger for confronting childhood abuse and 'grasping' what had happened to them.[6] Amy, for example, first sought therapy in 1986 because 'It were too much, it were all coming on the telly and it were starting to really get to me.' Joanne describes how her childhood abuse had been completely muffled and unspoken until the mid 1980s because:

> It started being talked about a bit more in the media and then I heard a radio programme, that made me start thinking about it ... Whenever he abused me, he never said a word. I always found this silence around it a very loud thing. It's all been so silent.

Recognition on TV and radio, in newspapers, magazines and films became a vital part of women's process of making sense of their memories. Women refer to the importance of representation in every form; from agony columns in magazines to press reports, from soap operas to current affairs documentaries or discussion programmes. Interviewees do not usually distinguish between genres or formats for these purposes (hence this chapter does not discuss such distinctions).[7] As Joanne explains:

[Whatever it is] it legitimises your experiences. It is saying 'yes, it does happen' and you know that other people are reading it and are accepting it. Whether it's fact or fiction, whether it is research or autobiography or whatever, it's adding to this. I know when I read Sarah Nelson [a newspaper journalist who wrote some of the early press articles and a book on sexual abuse] it was wonderful seeing all the basic feelings that I had there. [...] [And] it moves people forward all the time, and it isn't just odd people saying things. [...] It is actually down on paper. [...] It's not just me having a fantasy in my head about this, many people believe this.

Media reporting also, in very practical ways, helped people both to tell, and to ask, about abuse. Melissa, for example, saved two early articles about incest from women's magazines and used these to tell her mother what was happening.

I was hysterical. I'd been smoking a lot of dope and I was feeling really, really low ... I ran into the house screaming 'Mum, come and help me, I need to talk to you' and she came out and said 'Oh, what?' And she [...] couldn't understand what I was saying and I shoved these two articles from women's magazines under her nose.

Another woman explicitly used the early Esther Rantzen TV programme to provide a script enabling her to question her daughter about abuse.

I didn't know how to approach it. But I remembered Esther Rantzen's programme which suggested asking 'Has anyone ever touched you or made you feel uncomfortable?' So I asked her, and she said 'Yes, today a boy threw a ball and it hit my head' [...] I said 'Yes, that was today, what about anyone else?' And she said 'Yes, dad' and started screaming. She wept and wept, I'd never heard a child cry like that (Shiobhan).

Media coverage also encouraged women to discuss their abuse with other family members. Sometimes they would then discover that this relative had also been victimised by the same perpetrator (e.g. their grandfather). For many there was also an interplay between media representation, public discussion and the re-evaluation and revelation of experience. Liza, for example, was in her early twenties when she attended a feminist film and post-viewing discussion held in her local arts cinema. This film, *Not a Love Story*, included footage of violent pornography. She was familiar with such images because her abuser had forced her to look at them as a child. The film and surrounding discussion made her reassess what he had done to her. It also provided a context for talking about it for the first time.

> Everyone in the audience was really shocked [by the porn] and I was thinking 'God, I have seen all this before.' What got me in a state of shock wasn't that it was new, but that I had seen it all before and nobody else seemed to have. For the first time it made me think what a real bastard he is. It really brought it home to me what he had done. […] After about three-quarters of an hour of them all talking about how upsetting it was, I told them that I had seen all that when I was eight (Liza).

Examples of engaging with and using the media were even more prevalent in the focus groups I conducted in the mid 1990s. A support group for young women, for example, emphasises the value of the portrayal of incest survivor, Beth Jordache, in the soap opera *Brookside*: 'You can watch it and say – I had those feelings like Beth. That happened to me. […] We've got some kind of communication with the telly and can talk to each other about the way Beth is' (Group 48).

Another member of this group describes how a film, *Liar, Liar*, helped her mother to understand what she had been through: 'My mum watched it with me. In the film the mother doesn't believe – my ma watched it and saw what pressure the girl went through and it made her see how I could feel' (Group 48).

A third girl, whose mother was less understanding, had videotaped and repeatedly watched an audience discussion programme (*Kilroy*) because it showed supportive family reactions: 'It was on about two years ago – families talking about how they'd reacted. I've got that on video and I kept re-watching it, wishing my mum had so much sympathy' (Group 48).

These young women had a clear message for programme makers. It is vitally important to acknowledge sexual abuse, and to offer positive images for survivors. The characterisation of Beth Jordache in *Brookside* was valued by them because it was 'realistic', helping them to talk about complex or shameful feelings. They also liked the character because she was a strong and confident role model:

> Victims on TV, they're like a big shadow, all blacked out. That makes me feel terrible, they're hiding away. […] I thought 'I'm going to grow

up and I'm going to be scared of everything.' But Beth [in *Brookside*], she's so strong, she's got a grip of everything. Before that, everything I saw seemed to say that if you were abused you'd be strange, different, keep yourself in a wee corner. Watching Beth has really helped me (Group 48).

This woman was not alone in her feelings. When news leaked that the character of Beth Jordache was to commit suicide, incest survivors' groups demonstrated outside the TV studios under banners reading 'Save Our Survivor'. Such was the level of protest that the soap opera producers agreed to rewrite the plot so that Beth would die of natural causes. Headlines at the time included *'Brookside* drama draws protest' (*Scotsman*, 7 July 1995), '... uproar halts Beth's hanging' (*Sunday Mirror*, 2 July 1995) and *'Brookside* demo forces Beth pledge: Beth Jordache won't be killed off in *Brookside*' (*Daily Mirror*, 7 July 1995).

THE PRECONDITIONS FOR MEDIA DISCOVERY

The preceding discussion has explored how media attention had profound implications for what people could imagine, what they could say and what they felt they could do. It has shown how mass media attention ricocheted through the general population and became a catalyst for change at an intimate, private, as well as public, level. However, it is vital to recognise the wider social context which laid the groundwork for media attention. The media do not conjure up social problems in isolation. They serve as a conduit for, or interact with, other social forces. The sexual revolution, a *fin de siècle* anxiety and uncertainty about the future have all been identified as producing conditions conducive to recognising sexual abuse (Hechler 1988; Best 1990). Other factors, such as the previous discovery of 'battered child syndrome' had certainly also prepared people for the notion that parents were not necessarily nurturing and protective (Parton 1985; Nelson 1984). The development of therapy, medical and legal lobbies and the rise of child protection organisations and professions were also crucial and in some countries, such as the USA, the activities of Christian rights movements were also significant (Finkelhor 1984; Nelson 1984). (For a critical assessment of the role of professional organisations as self-serving bureaucracies engaged in a 'moral panic' see Jenkins 1992. For a discussion of the role of mental health professionals see Hacking 1995.)

Most important of all, in the USA, Canada, Europe, Australia, New Zealand and many other countries, the groundwork for recognising sexual abuse lay in early activities by feminists and survivors (and involved international links within the women's movement across the world). Incest was exposed through the work of battered women's refugees and rape crisis centres (Droisen and Driver 1989; Walby 1987). Years before this issue entered the public/media domain, workers in these feminist-inspired initiatives found that they were having to address the needs of women fleeing to protect their sexually abused children. They also realised that some women they were counselling were dealing with memories of their own abuse in childhood. In the late 1970s Florence Rush addressed the New York Radical Feminist Conference with a paper on child sexual abuse, entitled 'The Last Frontier'. In 1982 the National Women's Liberation Conference had as its theme 'Male Power and the Sexual Abuse of Girls' and the London Rape Crisis Centre reported that one in four of its clients was under the age of 16 when they were attacked (McFadyean 1986). Such abuse was also being exposed in consciousness raising groups as women tentatively shared experiences and sought to analyse their shared histories. Testimonies from individual survivors were crucial (Armstrong 1994). Black women were at the forefront of confronting sexual violence against children with autobiographies and novels such as *I Know Why the Caged Bird Sings* (Angelou 1969) and *The Color Purple* (Walker 1982). This work confronted such abuse while also addressing multi-layered oppressions and acknowledging the history of lynching (whereby accusations of assault against white women/girls were used routinely as racist justification for the murder of black men and boys) (Bobo and Seiter 1996). Many of the texts produced around this time highlight the resounding silence or misrepresentation against which the authors saw themselves as writing. The titles speak for themselves: *The Conspiracy of Silence* (Butler 1978); *Kiss Daddy Goodnight* (Armstrong 1978); *The Best Kept Secret* (Rush 1980); *Incest: Fact and Myth* (Nelson 1982); *Voices in the Night* (McNaron and Morgan 1982); *I Never Told Anyone* (Bass and Thornton 1983); *Father-Daughter Rape* (Ward 1984); *Intimate Intrusions* (Stanko 1985).

Without this range of interventions the media might never have discovered the issue. Certainly, to many of those active throughout the 1970s and early 1980s, the media seemed tardy in the extreme in taking this issue on board. Journalists were sceptical of the allegations, or did not take them seriously, or considered them too shocking for a family newspaper. However, when the media did finally become involved, their impact was vital. The media's role in defining the public domain is such that, had newspapers, magazines, radio and television reporting continued to ignore incest, this would have been a serious obstacle to public recognition. In addition, the mass media had a crucial role to play in these early days because other avenues for inserting sexual abuse into public discourse were limited. The isolation and taboo around abuse meant that it was a difficult subject for individuals to raise (although, many survivors did speak out). Some survivors described not only fear of stigma but a sense of the destructive power and social inappropriateness of betraying their secret: 'it would be like dropping a bomb into the conversation'; 'it would shatter everything'; 'people just wouldn't be able to hear it'. The mass media's discovery of sexual violence against children facilitated, and may have been a prerequisite, for its transition from a shameful, individual secret to becoming a more public issue.

CRITICAL REFLECTIONS ON COVERAGE
OF 'THE INCEST SURVIVOR'

The above discussion is not intended as an uncritical celebration of media recognition. The media could be sensationalist and voyeuristic in their approach, and have certainly not always treated survivors' testimony with respect. Survivor-campaigners who have regularly dealt with journalists over the years are angry about the pressure put on them to display their scars. It was as if, only by proving that they are damaged, will the unwanted touch inflicted on them in childhood be taken seriously. The suggestion that abused children might grow up to become abusers (another way of emphasising the seriousness of abuse) is also profoundly undermining. One woman said that the media had made her terrified of changing her son's nappy in case 'I'd end up like my dad and touch his bits'. The extent of media attention can also be overwhelming and media representations, even 'positive' ones, can cause considerable discomfort and distress, especially when a viewer is taken off-guard: 'When it comes on the telly, and I'm not expecting it, I go dead cold inside and it brings back memories' (Group 48).

Far from feeling that their experiences were invisible, some survivors in the 1990s felt that their experiences had been appropriated and that their lives had become public property. One, for example, described getting upset while watching the film *Liar, Liar* with her little sister: 'My wee sister says: "What are you greeting [crying] for?

It's only a film." But then she said: "Oh, that was *you*"' (Group 48). Another member of this group agreed, adding: 'You don't know if they are watching it, or putting *you* in the film and watching you' (Group 48).

Media recognition can be a double-edged sword because silence and invisibility is not the only way in which power can operate, it also operates through representation and 'the gaze' (Foucault 1990; Haaken 1999; Bell 1993). As society has increasingly recognised incest so the incest survivor has increasingly been 'subject to discourse', scrutiny and control. Survivors are targeted as mental health clients and offered terminology ranging from the 'inner child' to 'multiple personality disorder' in ways which may constrain and discipline as much as they enable and liberate (Hacking 1995). Indeed, we now see a new identity of victimhood being pedalled by discussion shows. The complexity of the early feminist analysis of how women's narratives are shaped has been obscured (Alcoff and Gray 1993; Armstrong 1994; Scott 1998:1.6). Instead the media (along with some self-help and therapy texts) have psycho-pathologised survivors (Brown and Burman 1997). Sexual abuse has become increasingly enmeshed in expert vocabularies (Kelly 1996) and the path to survivorhood is mapped out in self-help and therapy guidelines in ways that neutralise feminist analysis (Kitzinger 1992). Sometimes sexual abuse is also now adopted as a 'master narrative' to explain away all women's ills, promoting simplistic redemption narratives (Lamb 1999; Haaken 1999; Reavey and Warner 2003).

It is important to acknowledge these issues here because I do not want to over-emphasise the media's radical potential. However, none of this undermines my central argument that the media did, at least at first, have a powerful and positive impact simply by recognising that abuse could happen, even within 'ordinary' families. Acknowledging and analysing this history is a vital part of understanding the media's role.

REVISITING THREE MEDIA STUDIES THEORIES: ACTIVE CONSUMPTION, CREATIVE IDENTIFICATION AND AGENDA-SETTING

I opened this chapter with the question: How might the media contribute to the ways in which we understand our experiences and identities, and can they contribute to social change? How do audiences actively engage with the media to challenge the status quo or affirm stigmatised or taboo events from their own lives? This section summaries my findings in relation to each of these questions and reflects on three crucial theories within media studies: research which highlights active consumption processes, the debate about positive representations, and, finally, agenda-setting theory.

Active consumption processes: not just a couch potato

My research shows people actively engaging with media texts on both a practical and a conceptual level. Not only were survivors major activists in confronting the media with this issue in the first place, but they were also active as media consumers. The group of young survivors of sexual abuse who met with me during the 1990s, for example, often used the media in helping them think through and talk about their experiences. They spoke about this as a very active interaction both with the media and with each other ('We've got some kind of communication with the telly and can talk to each other about the way Beth is'). They also adopted different viewing strategies to meet particular needs. Examples included recording and repeatedly watching a particular discussion show ('I kept re-watching it, wishing my mum had so much sympathy') or viewing a film with a family member ('my ma watched it and saw what pressure the girl went through and it made her see how I could feel'). My interviews conducted up to a decade earlier, during the 1980s, also reveal active consumption processes, although often of a very different nature. In particular the emerging media attention in the mid 1980s helped people to address concerns or disclose abuse that had previously been hidden (e.g. the girl who hoarded the first few magazine articles about the topic and gave these to her mother as a way of telling her what had happened).

The above examples illustrate the active engagement of consumers. However, there is nothing here to suggest that this means that audiences are 'independent' from the media. These actions cannot be separated from the nature of the texts. The survivors who spoke to me in the 1980s eagerly greeted the new media attention to child sexual abuse, and this enabled them to speak out about abuse in a climate where there were few other resources. The young women who spoke to me in the 1990s were engaging with 'positive' or 'useful' material which reflected their own lives (material which had been unavailable in previous years) and were able to discuss this in a support group with one another. This leads on to the second audience reception theory I want to address here, the strand which focused on creative appropriation.

Positive representations and the conditions for creative identification

A great deal of previous work has documented the creative way in which oppressed peoples may construct positive reflections of their own lives (see Chapter 2). Scholars describe the inventive way in which minority groups weave positive images out of the raw material of mainstream culture and write of 'nomadic subjects' moving between different interpretive communities (Radway, cited in Nightingale 1997:119). Talking about the need for 'positive images' is thus sometimes seen as a rather quaint, old-fashioned notion. Indeed, some scholars assert that concern about media misrepresentation or under-representation is based on dubious or non-existent evidence and is theoretically naive (Gauntlett 1995; Cumberbatch 1998). However, my research shows how the lack of representation of child sexual abuse until the mid 1980s left the power of definition in the hands (and words) of the abusers. The cultural vacuum within which they were operating also left many mothers incredulous and disoriented when they had to confront the sexual abuse of their children.

I could only find one example, among my 40 interviews from the 1980s, which might be described as creative appropriation. This was Petra, the young woman who was 'addicted' to sitcoms. She appropriated the events and interactions of happy families from these programmes and pretended they were her own experiences. She used them to be able to join in discussions about everyday family life at school and hide the abuse and neglect she suffered at home. This was certainly a creative way of using the media, but it stopped friends or teachers from being able to recognise that she needed support. Far from enabling Petra to reflect her own life, these images were adopted as a disguise and perpetuated her powerlessness (enabling her to hide and survive, but not to escape).

In this context it is important to recognise that the consequences of appropriation are not inherently something to celebrate.[8] It is also important to consider the conditions that facilitate or inhibit audience creativity or appropriation. My interviews from the 1980s highlight abused children's lack of resources and their isolation. These girls had no homeland, no common language, no sense of belonging from which to forge alternative 'readings' of media images.

Rather than being 'nomadic subjects' accessing diverse interpretive communities they were, to all intents and purposes, held in solitary confinement in relation to this aspect of their experience.

Clearly then we need a sense of the historical, social and biographical context of any creative activities. It is not possible to neatly transfer theories about the media's role in relation to childhood, national, class, gender or ethnic identity onto the identity of abuse survivor. This is true not least because most people are brought up in families or communities that include identifiable members of their own national, class, gender or ethnic identity. By contrast most survivors grew up ignored, invisible and isolated. If they had an image of their abused self at all it was often as a dreamer of bad dreams, 'tart', 'naughty girl' or 'freak' and 'monster'. (Similar observations are made by Gross 1998, reflecting on what it meant to grow up gay at a time when there were no positive cultural representations.)

Agenda-setting and the creation of new discursive repertoires

Quantitative surveys and experimental work around media reporting and public perceptions of issues show that mass media coverage can set priorities for social concern (McCombs and Shaw 1972). This sort of work is central to agenda-setting theory which asserts that the media may not tell people what to think, but it can tell them what to think about (Cohen 1963). This is sometimes characterised as a relatively weak notion of media effects. However, this chapter has used qualitative approaches to put some flesh on the bones of 'agenda-setting theory'. This shows how powerful such agenda-setting can be, especially when it breaks new ground and allows people to address previously taboo subjects. The media enabled people to think about the unthinkable and speak about the previously unspeakable. The plethora of media engagement with this topic opened up new channels of communication between people. It helped them to tell their stories and thus develop a social and inter-personal momentum that contributed towards a spiral of recognition.

This also suggests the need to go beyond agenda-setting theory to address the media's role in popularising new discursive repertoires and impacting on people's very sense of identity (Grodin and Lindloff 1996). The interaction between individual experience and culturally available narrative can spiral into further social change, mobilising professional and expert knowledges and policies, which, in their turn, impact on the objects of that knowledge. In this way a shifting agenda can also have profound personal impact, helping to shape our very sense of ourselves. As Hacking notes:

> You might think that the experiences speak for themselves, at least for the victims. Yes – and yet events, no matter how painful or terrifying, have been experienced or recalled *as child abuse* only after consciousness-raising. That requires inventing new descriptions, providing new ways to see old acts – and a great deal of social agitation (Hacking 1995:55).

Once a new idea takes root it can, in turn, transform the 'object of knowledge'. As Hacking puts it: 'There is a feedback effect. Classification of people and their actions affects the people and their actions, which in turn affects our knowledge about them and classification of them [...] The people who are the objects of our concept of child abuse become different' (Hacking 1998:55, 62). Overlapping perspectives have emerged from the radical survivor movement. As Alcoff and Gray argue:

> To become theorists of our own experience requires us to become aware of how our subjectivity will be constituted by our discourses and aware of the danger that even in our own confessionals within autonomous spaces we can construct ourselves as reified victims or as responsible for our own victimisation. This recognition that no experience is 'pretheoretical' does not entail a complete relativising of experience of the effects of sexual violence. It does mean that there are multiple (not infinite) ways to experience sexual violence: as deserved or not deserved, as humiliating to the victim or as humiliating to the perpetrator, or as an inevitable feature of women's lot or as a socially sanctioned but eradicable evil. And this more adequately reflects the experience most of us have had of 'coming to' our anger and even our hurt only after we have adopted the political and theoretical position that we did not deserve such treatment or bring it on ourselves (Alcoff and Gray 1993: 284) (see also Worrell 2003).

Press and TV reports can be part of this process. My interviews show how media representations can help to reconfigure memories and transform the ways in which experiences are interpreted ('I know now that I never deserved it'; 'It really brought it home to me what he had done'). The media, for better or for worse, are implicated in the very way in which we think about ourselves and relate to one another.

This is more than simply agenda-setting. The media get into our blood, our hearts, our minds. I am using such hyperbolic metaphors deliberately. To some media scholars it will recall the much scorned notion of hypodermic effects, the theory that media messages are directly injected into our hearts and minds (see Chapter 2). I am suggesting an equally intimate but more social process which takes into account the intersections between the public and private, the individual and collective and gives due attention to the interplay between cultural resources and self-narration.

Perhaps it is worth spelling out the contrast with hypodermic models. A crude hypodermic effects model could be used to argue that the recent 'epidemic' of adult survivors recalling sexual violence is due to the media injecting people with wrong-headed ideas and false memories in the context of a cultural obsession with victimisation and healing. Indeed, it is precisely this sort of model which appears in some of the literature from the false memory societies based in the UK and USA. Examples of adults recalling childhood abuse after viewing a television programme are presented as evidence of misleading cultural saturation and distortion. These sorts of dismissive explanations have accompanied each new wave of exposure of sexual violence. During the 1970s and early 1980s, for example, various experts were already noting that publicity generated by the Women's Liberation Movement was leading to an increase in what they called 'pseudo' or 'subjective rape' and women artificially reinterpreting past events. Such dismissal oversimplifies complex relations between cultural representation and the ways in which experiences are labelled, identified, recalled and reinterpreted. It also ignores how experiences may be suppressed, obscured and silenced (labelled a nightmare, a fantasy, or just normal).

My research suggests that we can track media effects, without falling into a simple hypodermic model. It is possible to see the media as helping to make sense of abuse or 'bring it home' without assuming that the media must simply be convincing people that they have been abused when, in fact, nothing ever happened to them at all. Here I agree with McKinley who reminds us of the benefits of poststructuralist insights and the need to scrutinise the idea that we are each independent authors of our own life narratives and speak with our own unique voice:

Poststructuralist theory [...] urges us to abandon [the notion that] it is *we* who think, not our culture and language that gives us the forum to think about anything. [...] Until we have a way to understand our innermost thoughts, desires and beliefs are woven with materials provided by language and culture we will be unable to move beyond arguments over whether television can 'make' us do anything [...]. As social construction shows, the enemy here is the fiction of the autonomous self: I am the unique source of my thoughts; culture and language play no role in the meanings I make (McKinley 1997:240).

CONCLUSION

This chapter has explored the media's role in the public and private transformations involved in identifying a new social problem. It has demonstrated the importance of media acknowledgement and located this in the context of historical, social and interpersonal dynamics. The activity of audiences (their conceptual work, practical actions and interpersonal dialogue) has been identified. I have highlighted the interaction between the media and society (especially feminist activists and survivors of abuse) which contributed to a dramatic spiral of discovery. My research questions some of the simple oppositions between 'media effects' research and 'active audience' theory which have become established within media studies. I argue that we should continue to ask questions about the impact of media representations, but do so with close attention to audiences and the context in which they are operating. Theories such as active consumption and creative appropriation should be understood in terms of their context and their consequences, not used as if they necessarily undermine media influence. Theories of agenda-setting can be usefully expanded by incorporating qualitative work and engaging with debates about discourse and poststructuralist theory.

The next chapter takes a closer look at developments in media coverage that followed from the initial discovery of sexual abuse. It discusses how the story of revelation was quickly overtaken by concern about false allegations and unnecessary interventions. I examine how news reporting influences the judgements people make about specific cases, scandals and crises. I ask: when the facts of the matter are in dispute, what information is used to decide what really happened? What impressions are people left with, and why?

4
Media Templates: Controversial Allegations and Analogies[1]

How do particular crises come to be defining moments in our understanding of social issues? What effects do these key events have on public debate? This chapter explores these questions through examining one early cause célèbre in the sexual abuse story; the Cleveland scandal. This was a high profile scandal involving highly contested allegations of abuse and counter allegations of inappropriate intervention into family life. I show how this case came to operate as a template through which to understand the problem of abuse, consider policy options and interpret subsequent abuse controversies. Media templates, I argue, are a very powerful way of helping to shape the ways in which we make sense of the world. Every major socio-political issue is associated with particular template events. These high-profile episodes outlive the conclusion of events on the ground and become inseparably associated with particular issues. Routinely used to highlight one perspective with great clarity, templates serve as rhetorical shorthand helping journalists and audiences to make sense of fresh news stories. They are instrumental in shaping narratives around particular social problems, guiding our thinking not only about the past, but about the present and future. These associations seem inevitable, but, as I will show, they are actually created and maintained by source strategies, social power relations, journalistic routines and audience reception processes.

THE MEDIA'S DISCOVERY OF CONTESTED CASES

During the last part of the twentieth century, in every country where sexual abuse had been acknowledged, something rather strange happened. Within a few years, or even months, of the media discovering 'The Reality of Abuse', the discussion quickly became refocused. Instead of reporting on sexual abuse itself, headline news was attracted by major scandals about false allegations and inappropriate interventions. As Hechler comments, in the US context, '[w]hat the media giveth, the media taketh away. And it was not long before the media were covering the backlash as enthusiastically as they had covered the epidemic' (Hechler 1988:6).

Hot on the heels of media acknowledgement came organised resistance. By 1984 a new pressure group was founded in the USA called VOCAL: Victims of Child Abuse Laws. The following year, in 1985, Southern Californian newspapers were carrying full-page advertisements paid for by The Friends of the McMartin Pre School Defendants (a group of childcare workers accused of abuse). The focus now was on witch-hunts, hysteria and state-initiated victimisation of innocent people (Myers 1994a). 'In the seventeenth century, innocent lives were lost or ruined because of the false accusation of the infamous Salem witch hunts', declared the advertisement. 'In the twentieth century, the same thing is happening again' (quoted in Hechler 1988:4). This case attracted peak media attention across the USA. It became the first in a long litany of high-profile cases of fiercely disputed allegations not only in the USA but across the world (Hechler 1988; Myers 1994). There was the Oude Pekela case in the Netherlands (Pyck 1994), Canada had Martinsville, New Zealand had the Christchurch and Spense scandals (Atmore 1996; Guy 1996) and the UK had first the Cleveland scandal, then the Rochdale case, quickly followed by the crisis in Orkney. Press and television reports recorded the bewildered protests of ordinary people who claimed they had been falsely accused. Reports focused on the anguish of those whose children had been taken into care, challenged the validity of diagnostic techniques, vilified the professionals involved and presented a disturbing picture of children being cajoled and bullied into making false 'confessions'. It is often said that we have seen a 'moral panic' about child sexual abuse. It might equally be argued that the real moral panic is about intervention. (For a critical assessment of these scandals as 'moral panics' see Chritcher 2003:81–117.)

This chapter examines how one such case, the Cleveland scandal, gained its place in collective memory and explores how it was used to frame understandings of subsequent crises around contested allegations. The chapter starts by providing a brief overview of media reporting of events in Cleveland at the time (1987). I go on to illustrate ways in which the scandal was referenced in ongoing media reporting and people's talk about sexual abuse many years later. Mainstream interpretations of Cleveland are then contrasted with a TV documentary which revisited the case ten years after the event and challenged some dominant assumptions. I use this to point out that, while stories such as Cleveland often seem to speak for themselves, they are not the only way of interpreting events or mapping out a social problem.

THE CLEVELAND SCANDAL: A BRIEF INTRODUCTION

The Cleveland scandal was the first, and remains the most famous, case in the UK involving contested allegations. It had a huge impact on public thinking about sexual abuse accusations and state intervention. It also had far reaching consequences for professional practice and child protection policy (Nelson in press). The crisis erupted in the spring of 1987. During a five-month period 121 children from 57 families had been taken into care in the county of Cleveland in England. All of them had been examined by one of two local paediatricians: Marietta Higgs and Geoff Wyatt. Using the anal reflex dilatation test, these doctors diagnosed the children as showing signs consistent with abuse. The parents claimed that their children had been misdiagnosed and the test was unreliable. Their Member of Parliament, Stuart Bell, and local police surgeon, Alistair Irvine, joined with parents in criticising social workers and the two paediatricians involved. Relations between police and social services broke down. Stuart Bell MP held a televised press conference to launch a dossier detailing cases of 19 families, which, he claimed, showed that they were being inappropriately targeted. Most of the children were eventually sent home.

Events in Cleveland were accompanied by a national outcry on the parents' behalf. Headlines included: 'Agony of Families in Sex Abuse Row', 'Midnight Test Ordeal of Sex Inquiry Tots' and 'The Families Broken by a Diagnosis' (headlines from the *Express* and *Independent* cited in Jenkins 1992:142). Although the contemporary media coverage was not uniform (Nava 1988), the broad thrust was that these were innocent families falsely accused by overzealous and incompetent professionals who were possibly motivated by man-hating or left-wing bias against the family as an institution.

Journalists denounced the doctors and social services, and asserted the rights of the parents. The suggestion was that the children taken into care were 'abused' only by the dictatorial actions of the social services who plucked them from loving families. Higgs and Wyatt were portrayed as applying tests for abuse to virtually every child with whom they came into contact, and trawling the children's wards to find subjects for investigation. Some newspapers suggested that the dilatation test had been the sole criteria for evaluation, and that any suspicious signs resulted in the immediate break-up of a family (Jenkins 1992:142).

Media analysts have extensively commented on the anti-professional/pro-parents emphasis and inaccuracies in the Cleveland reporting. They argue that the portrayal of Higgs was sexist and that, at times, she was presented as 'positively perverse' (Franklin and Parton 1991; see also Jenkins 1992; Ashendon 1994). They show how reporting of the subsequent inquiry gave most space to evidence provided by the parents' lawyers and conveyed little of the complexities included in the report (Donaldson and O'Brien 1995; Franklin 1990). Certain allegations against doctors and social workers persisted in the media, even after they had been challenged by the inquiry report (Franklin and Parton 1991:26). A book about the case, written by a dissenting feminist journalist (Campbell 1988), documents the ways in which some inaccurate statements emphasising social work/medical malpractice were given a high profile, while corrections were tucked away. Media coverage, Campbell argues, often conveyed false impressions. For example, when children were returned to their parents this was reported as if the obvious conclusion was that no abuse had occurred and no intervention had ever been justified. Indeed, a blanket embargo on media reporting of settlements in wardship cases meant that when children were returned home under conditions such as social services supervision, no such information was given to the public (Campbell 1988:148).

JOURNALISTS' RETROSPECTIVE REFERENCES TO CLEVELAND

Media references to Cleveland long outlived the conclusion of the main news events connected with the crisis. During 1991, for example, four years after the crisis broke, Cleveland was still mentioned over 200 times in the national UK press and TV news. Only a handful of these reports involved fresh developments in the Cleveland case itself (such as the parents' fight for compensation). Instead, most reports used references to Cleveland in passing to help tell the story of more recent events, in particular events in Orkney (as well as a 'similar' case in Rochdale). The Orkney crisis is a much smaller scale, but equally controversial, case in the history of sexual abuse disputes (this case is discussed in detail in Chapter 5). It involved nine children from four different families being taken into care, leading to a public outcry and intense media scrutiny. Although social services won an appeal against the decision to return the children home they decided they could not proceed with the case, partly because of the media coverage.

Media reports about Orkney frequently linked it with previous events in Cleveland. Headlines included: 'How the nightmare of Orkney ignored the lessons of Cleveland' (*Evening Standard*, 4 April 1991); 'How could this happen again – storm as sex abuse kids fly home' (*Daily Mirror*, 5 April 1991) and 'Cleveland, Rochdale, Orkney: What's wrong?' (*Sunday Telegraph*, 7 April 1991). Orkney was cited as another case in which parents were wrongly accused (*Scotsman*, 15 March 1991; *Daily Mail*, 4 March 1991) and, together, Cleveland and Orkney represented 'the might of faceless bureaucracy' against 'the basic rights of bewildered families' (*Mail on Sunday*, 7 April 1991). Journalists described Orkney as 'only the latest' in a series of 'monumental cock-ups by social workers' (*Daily Mirror*, 14 March 1991) and presented it as 'the bureaucratic rape of a community' (*Scotsman*, cited in Jenkins 1992:190). Headlines included: 'In the dock again. The care staff who go too far' (*Daily Mail*, 5 April 1991), 'Throw the book at child stealers' (*Today*, 29 March 1991) and 'Ban these Blunderers' (*Daily Mirror*, 14 March 1991). This line of 'cock-ups' stretching back to Cleveland justified descriptions of social workers as 'neo-fascist' (*Herald*, 15 March 1991) and the *Daily Mail* concluded that 'for the sake of all the broken-hearted families, we must get rid of the social workers and think again' (*Daily Mail*, 5 April 1991).

Diverse pressure groups and organisations sought to influence the public profile of the Orkney case, and the struggle to assert or deny links between Cleveland and Orkney was an explicit part of their media strategy. The Orkney parents quickly sought support from Parents Against Injustice (PAIN), a national group of aggrieved parents who came to prominence after Cleveland, and held a press conference drawing attention to similarities between the two scandals. Members of the Orkney social work department were left defensively denying any connection. Unable to renegotiate the public meaning of Cleveland, social services representatives in Orkney simply insisted that the two cases should not be associated. Guidelines produced after Cleveland were, they said, not wholly applicable to the Orkney situation (where organised abuse was suspected), and the actions of professionals in the two cases should not be lumped together. One *Guardian* article headlined the declaration by Orkney social services 'Orkney abuse case "unlike Cleveland"'

(*Guardian*, 30 August 1991). This was the only headline which contested the link. The very fact that this apparently rather bland statement was made into a headline is testimony to the significance placed on the Orkney/Cleveland analogy.

In 1987 Cleveland was a one-off scandal, by 1991 it was seen as part of a pattern of malpractice threatening ordinary families. Cleveland ceased to be a stand-alone case. Its symbolic power lay in its status as a template.

The template status of Cleveland was not only evident from analysing media content and source strategies. It was also illustrated in interviews with journalists; Cleveland was an important part of journalists' vocabulary and a key reference point for them. This is not surprising. Cross-linking between events is a routine part of journalists' practice as they attempt to draw together discrete episodes and uncover relationships between them (Whitney and Wartella 1992). Linking events is part of the journalistic endeavour to capture the zeitgeist or expose the need for fundamental policy reform. The cry 'Never Again!' is a classic headline and media logic tends to mean that one major disaster will lead to a flurry of media attention to related problems (Kepplinger and Habermeier 1995). A particular crisis can also 'sensitise the media so that the surveillance procedures and journalistic categories are sharpened to capture similar subsequent events' (Golding and Middleton 1982:60).

The meaning of the Cleveland case, and its links with events in Orkney, was self-evident to many journalists. One told me that not to have linked Orkney with Cleveland would have been a dereliction of duty. Media personnel were not only explicitly pointing out the links between the two cases in their reports, memories of Cleveland also influenced them in more subtle ways. 'Memories' (usually constructed from news cuttings or perceived public collective consciousness rather than direct knowledge of Cleveland) informed how some framed their reports about Orkney. Defending the tendency to report in ways that favoured the perspective of parents, against that of the social workers, one TV news editor comments: 'I mean at the time there had been several cock-ups by social workers all over the bloody country and so the assumption is that you are going to side with the families' (Group 3, m).

PUBLIC RECOLLECTIONS OF CLEVELAND

This news editor's assumptions about people's expectations were borne out by, and reflected in, the focus group discussions I conducted with 'the general public'. Many of these research participants did indeed see Orkney as the latest in a long line of social work blunders stretching back to Cleveland. When asked to talk about sexual abuse it was such cases that often first sprang to mind. Before opening the focus group discussion sessions, preliminary questionnaires were given to group participants. People were invited to note down typical headlines about sexual abuse. One in every three of the headlines generated in this way names Orkney or Cleveland or refered, in various ways, to 'botched interventions', 'dawn raids' and 'innocent families torn apart'. Child sexual abuse is clearly inextricably associated with stories about miscarriages of justice.[2] In the open discussion that followed, the Cleveland case is spontaneously named in over half of my 49 focus groups and, when prompted, is immediately recognised in most of the others. (Only seven groups had no memory of Cleveland. These consisted of four groups of young people who were children at the time of the crisis. The other three were composed of people who had not been resident in Britain at the time and/or whose first language was not English.)

Memories of Cleveland, and its rhetorical use, are strikingly similar both across and within the wide variety of groups who participated in my research. Indeed, within groups, people are often able to finish each other's sentences as they attempt to summarise the case. The following example is typical of the way in which Cleveland is discussed. Note the high level of consensus between the three speakers and how, although they start talking about Orkney, they quickly become diverted by their recollections of Cleveland:

f: Orkney, is that ... Oh no, I'm thinking of another one there. I'm thinking of Marietta Higgs.
f: No, that was the Cleveland child sex abuse. Yeah, I remember that stupid woman, because she had five kids.
f: They put something in the vagina or something and they said if the vagina dilated the child had been abused. Well, it was something incredible like that and it was this Marietta Higgs that was at the forefront of it all.
f: They were testing any child that had been taken in for any reason.
f: Bet they didn't test Marietta Higgs' children!
f: And there was a big outcry because then it was discovered that this method was not a good indication ... But of course at that point ...
f: The damage was done.
f: People's lives had been ruined and men were committing suicide (Group 46).[3]

Other groups come up with almost identical memories. People speak about 'innocent families falsely accused' through an 'arbitrary' test, which was 'completely discredited' (Group 23, f) and 'proved to be a load of rubbish' (Group 15, f). Marietta Higgs was, they remember: 'Examining children and saying that there'd been sexual abuse when there hadn't' (Group 12, f). 'She had a way of finding out, doing something with sphincter muscles or bums weren't it. But it went wrong and loads of people [were accused] and they hadn't even done it' (Group 14, m).

People often believe that the anal dilatation test had been carried out randomly and that it had been the only evidence of abuse: 'the children [were not] speaking out in Cleveland, it was the doctor that was sort of making judgements' (Group 11, f). Some also state that the paediatrician had been sacked or even struck off because of her malpractice: 'What she said was a valid test wasn't a test [and the local Authority was] left with no choice but to sack her' (Group 19, m). Considerable hostility is expressed toward Higgs, (attention invariably focusing on her rather than her male colleague, Wyatt). As one woman comments: '[Marietta Higgs was] warped, screwy ... but I accept that my thoughts about that come directly from the media and that is the media images of her' (Group 5, f).

In addition to expressing hostility to Higgs, several research participants recall their unease and disgust about anyone examining children's bottoms. They speak eloquently about their distaste for the reflex dilatation test that they assume involved actual anal penetration: 'Her test for child abuse was to stick her finger up a child's anus. Well if somebody did that to you, you'd jump. That's what I remember about it, it was a sort of stupid way to try and test' (Group 20, f).

Anal examination was, in itself, seen as an assault: 'A lot of these children could probably sue her for abusing them on the examination couch, frankly' (Group 23, f).[4] Empathy is also voiced for the children who had to endure such examinations:

f: Here you're taking your weans [children] to the hospital to get a stookie put on their leg, and afore you know where you are there are these strange people doing all these things ... All these kiddies all squealing and screaming and people doing things to them and there's no mammy and daddy.

f: Takes *us* all our time to go for a smear test, how do the weans feel? (Group 31).

Coverage of Cleveland conveyed the impression that children were whisked into care on the faintest suspicion. Asked for her memories of Cleveland, one woman says it is inextricably associated with 'being frightened to take your child to the doctors, in case ...' (Group 19, f). For some men, in particular, the Cleveland case still generates fears and inhibitions about how they interact with children (a fear reinforced by subsequent cases such as Orkney, see Chapter 5). One comments: 'You're afraid to do anything to your own family now' (Group 27). Another remarks: 'Everybody was frightened, nobody could relax. It put the fear of Christ up a lot of people.' He added: 'Kids do drop you in it, you though', before tailing off into silence with the words 'If it happened to me ...' (Group 43).

Both fathers and mothers identify with parents faced with losing children, but it tends to be fathers in the focus groups who identify with being accused of abuse:

m: You get your little girl [...] when they're about three or four, you get in bed and give them a cuddle. And now you're afraid they might go to school, [and say] 'My Dad was in bed cuddling me', you know next thing ..., you have got to be careful. [...]

Sometimes this is directly linked to media reports:

m: I think also we've got to be careful here because I read in the paper today a 17-year-old girl was sent to prison for lying. She reckoned that her stepdad raped her and buggered her and it's proved he didn't do nothing of the sort, OK. But just to get him out of the way, she built the story up (Group 10).

It was these fears and empathies around memories of and associations with Cleveland which informed reactions to subsequent reporting from Orkney. People not only confuse details of the two cases but explicitly use their memories of the former to help them recall and reconstruct what happened in the latter.[5] One man recalls Orkney as 'The exact same sort of thing as Cleveland and again I think that was found to be false. The thing with the Cleveland one, and the Scotland one, I think it was do-good social workers' (Group 36, m). Another remarks that his reconstruction of events in Orkney is entirely based on his memories of other cases: 'I don't remember anything about it [Orkney] [But] I do remember that there was strong allegations that social work had got it wrong, as usual, inefficient and incompetent' (Group 18, m). Some research participants state that it is obvious that the Orkney parents were innocent because social workers are known to indulge in 'mass hysteria' (Group 23, f) and are 'always picking on innocent people' or 'always poking their noses in and always getting it wrong' (Group 5, f). Seeing sexual abuse wherever you look has become a 'fashion' and a 'social work trend'; social workers are 'obsessed with sexual abuse' and 'jumping on the bandwagon' (Group 4, f).

Even some of those who declare themselves suspicious of media reporting or are open-minded about events in Cleveland seem to be influenced by the images, assumptions and fears generated by the case. Many, for example, have been left with a reluctance to call in social services and can only explain this with reference to such media reporting. One woman, who had, in fact, discovered that her child was being abused around the time of the Cleveland scandal, delayed seeking help because of what she had seen on television: 'I was so scared, the first thing I asked the social workers when I did see them was, "Are you going to take my children off me?" You hear it on the telly, they just grab the children off you'.

So far I have focused on the coherence and consistency of both the media reporting and of people's understandings. However, retrospective references to Cleveland did not simply mirror contemporary coverage during the crisis. There were some differences between contemporary reporting and public recall, in particular in relation to the relative roles of doctors and social workers. In order to refine an understanding of how media templates operate it is worth looking at this in more detail.

The role of paediatricians in Cleveland was a central theme in the original coverage. However, when I examined how Cleveland was referenced retrospectively it became clear that it is social workers rather than the medical profession who bear the lasting stigma of Cleveland. Marietta Higgs was not seen as typical of her profession. As one participant comments: 'It was hard to believe how a doctor could get it wrong' (Group 36, m). A similar statement about social workers is almost impossible to imagine. Over and above this some people describe Cleveland as a social work scandal with no (or only belated) mention of medical professionals at all. A few research participants even think that Marietta Higgs was a social worker. They speak of 'social workers examining children's bottoms' and 'social workers' fetish for anal dilatation' (Group 13, f) or make comments such as 'It was a mistake of this Marietta Higgs – a social worker – it was a big cock-up' (Group 14, m). Such mistakes, or shifts in emphasis, provide important clues to how templates operate and are operated upon. It would seem that as cases become associated with one another, blurring or osmosis occurs in both directions. It is not only that the template of Cleveland influences interpretations of Orkney, the influence also happens in the other direction. Understanding of template cases (in this example, Cleveland) is modified through the interaction between contemporaneous and retrospective reporting and by the other cases with which they are associated.

To summarise my argument so far, the accumulation of social work scandals around sexual abuse has become a defining feature of public debate, encouraging suspicion of social services, informing parental fears and focusing concern on false allegations. Just as phrases such as 'another Vietnam', 'another Chernobyl', or 'another Saddam' sum up a particular set of fears, so the phrase 'another Cleveland' (or another 'McMartin' or 'Oude Pekela') provokes a set of powerful pre-packaged associations.[6] References to Cleveland fix an image in many people's minds which places social workers firmly in the dock, drawing on and contributing to spirals of negative publicity surrounding the profession. Each new case of contested allegations is more readily received as evidence of professional incompetence because the image fits with what people already know. In combination all the sex abuse/ social work scandals gain an explanatory momentum, a powerful logical association, propelling audience reception in particular directions. (For the concept of 'fit' in relation to audience reception and racist images of Africa see Kitzinger and Miller 1992.)

However, not everyone accepted this way of referencing Cleveland. It is important to pay close attention to the minority of research participants who resist this template. A few draw attention to conflicting information available in some parts of the media back in 1987 and 1988 and make comments such as 'I just did not know what to believe.' However, most can only remember the more straightforward consistent accounts of Cleveland (and, of course, over time, it is only these secondary accounts that remain easily accessible to the general public). However, other research participants adopt a 'no smoke without fire' approach (a cliché in its own right which some people thought required no further explanation). There are others who refuse to accept a simple 'innocent families torn apart' narrative because of their own personal experience of abuse.[7] Positive contacts with social services or political perspective are also important. Several research participants linked the Cleveland case not to Orkney but to an apparently unrelated case concerning the consultant obstetrician Wendy Savage (who was suspended for adopting a different approach to managing childbirth than her male colleagues). The coverage of Marietta Higgs had, they said, been so 'blatantly biased' ('just like the attitude of male colleagues toward Wendy Savage') (Group 5, f):

> f: For me it is all tied up a bit with the Wendy Savage thing. That kind of labelling of women as kind of hysterical.
> f: I get the feeling that there was a little implication about her being obsessed [...] I got the inference that she was a bit frustrated and she had gone over the top with this thing [...]
> m: [...] It was almost like they drew things on [her face], to make her look kind of more ugly than she was.
> f: [...] I think this came just after the Wendy Savage thing, and it felt like there were real parallels around that, about the way it was handled in the media [...] it is also the anti-feminist line, as well, [...] it affects career women, or uppity women who challenge the establishment.
> f: Maybe that's why I think of the Wendy Savage case as well (Group 13).

These minority, diverse responses are reflected upon in Chapter 10. Here, I simply want to point to two ways in which the simple use of the Cleveland template are rejected. I have chosen to focus on these two because they are particularly pertinent for developing an understanding of how templates operate. The first involves people pointing to conflicting narratives around physical and sexual abuse. Physical abuse of children is associated with a list of names such as, in Britain, Maria Colwell, Jasmine Beckford and Tyra Henry, all children who met their deaths at home. The main accusation against social workers in these cases was their inaction and their failure to take children into care. How, then, some research participants ask, can we complain when social workers seem over-zealous? The parallel templates seemed to contradict each other.

The second example of template rejection seems to be a sort of boomerang effect (see Curran 1987). Far from seeing the Cleveland fiasco as confirmation that social workers in Orkney were likely to have acted improperly, a few comments suggested that the history of Cleveland might make some people more likely to accept that

Orkney social workers were justified. Take the following exchange between two neighbours:

> f: I don't think that the social workers would have acted like that [in Orkney] if there had not been ... They're not going to put their careers on the line.
> f: Especially after Cleveland (Group 8).

There are thus some challenges to the dominant Cleveland template in the way people respond to the coverage. There was also one striking example of a challenge to the template from within the media. It is instructive to take a closer look at this one TV programme, broadcast in 1997, which challenged pervasive understandings of Cleveland. This provides an opportunity to develop the theory of templates and concludes the empirical part of this chapter.

CHALLENGING TEMPLATES: AN ALTERNATIVE MEDIA ACCOUNT OF THE CLEVELAND SCANDAL

Although the commonly understood meaning of the Cleveland scandal was very stable in media representations during the late 1980s and early 1990s, this dominant paradigm was challenged in 1997 by one particular documentary, *Cleveland. Unspeakable Truths* (27 May 1997, 21.00–22.00, Channel 4). This programme presented a radically different image of Cleveland than had been portrayed in the mass media until that time.

The programme's tone was set in the first few minutes. It opened with a series of traditionally emotive images; a riderless rocking horse and low-angle shots of stairs in a family home. This was overlaid with statements about the ubiquitous nature of sexual abuse and questions such as 'Why are families better protected than the children that grow up within them?' The narrator's voice was then replaced by the voice of a woman who had been sexually abused as a child in Cleveland. Audiences were immediately invited to empathise with how an abused child might feel and start to think about this instead of concentrating their horror on the thought of an anal examination. The survivor's voice was followed by text appearing on the screen 'A judicial enquiry did not resolve what had happened to the children [in Cleveland]. The public was led to believe that innocent families were torn apart.' The screen then filled with the words 'This is the true story.'

Unspeakable Truths set itself up to challenge the 'myths' surrounding Cleveland. It directly contradicted the ways in which Cleveland had been routinely referenced (both in the media and in general public debates). It hailed viewers in ways that invited empathy with abused children rather than accused adults, and statements in this programme can be directly contrasted with some of the beliefs evident in my focus group discussions. The programme pointed out that most of the diagnoses in Cleveland were confirmed by an independent panel, that Higgs had not been sacked (although she was transferred), and that the anal reflex dilatation test was not as controversial as assumed. For example, police surgeon Alistair Irvine went on national TV news in June 1987 stating that the majority of his colleagues did not accept Marietta Higgs' interpretations of reflex anal dilation. However, his own professional body, the Police Surgeons Association advised its members that reflex anal dilatation 'should certainly give rise to strong suspicion that sexual abuse had occurred' (cited on *Unspeakable Truths*, 27 May 1997).

The programme stated that, contrary to media reporting at the time, the children were not in fact examined arbitrarily. There were usually prior suspicions and reflex anal dilatation was rarely the sole indicator (other evidence included venereal disease and statements by some children). The programme also informed viewers that some of the children were living with men who had been previously charged with sexual abuse. The 19 flagship families summarised in the MP Stuart Bell's highly publicised dossier in defence of the parents included three men already charged with sexual abuse and a further two fathers who were convicted sex offenders.

Unspeakable Truths went on to challenge routine understandings of Cleveland in other ways too. Where some of my research participants saw the children's return home as proof that they had not been abused, and none of the evidence stood up in court, the programme challenged this interpretation. It drew attention to protection packages under which some children were returned and the fact that some were re-referred to social services within two years because of suspected abuse. It informed viewers that no one knows what happened subsequently to the Cleveland children because, in 1989, the Department of Health decided that all records relating to them as a group should be destroyed and there should be no further follow-up.

Instead of focusing on social workers, *Unspeakable Truths* turned the spotlight on the police. It argued that police reactions made it difficult to process some cases correctly. The programme stated that Cleveland Constabulary adopted a policy whereby it virtually withdrew from investigating any sexual abuse cases diagnosed by Higgs or Wyatt. For example, one of the 121 cases involved in the Cleveland crisis concerned a girl whose father had previous convictions for sexually assaulting three other children. After Higgs diagnosed likely abuse, the five-year-old herself apparently confirmed this and her mother believed her. However no action was taken against the father. The police officer's record of her interview with the girl read as follows: 'She told me that she had a poorly tuppence which was caused by her father moving his fingers up and down inside. [...] She stated that this had been going on for some time. [...] In my opinion, there is no doubt he is responsible for the assault, but with the present policy I was unable to charge him'.

Unspeakable Truths argued that the real (or additional) scandal of Cleveland was not necessarily (or only) that so many children had been taken from their parents, but that some children had been returned, possibly to face ongoing abuse. The information it conveyed did not prove that most, or even any, of the accusations of sexual abuse were justified. However, the programme did convey facts that had not been widely promoted prior to that point (even though most of the information it presented had been available almost a decade earlier in evidence to the Cleveland inquiry). The programme also confronted some widely circulating assumptions. It certainly challenged many of the 'facts' that formed the building blocks of people's beliefs about the case as expressed in the focus group discussions. It also disrupted the status of the Cleveland scandal as a straightforward template of unnecessary intervention into innocent families. Some of the information in this programme might have changed public reactions to the case. For example, community reactions to convicted sex abusers being rehoused in local areas suggests that many people would not trust such a person in their street, let alone leave children in their care (see Chapter 9).

I do not have systematic data about how people reacted to the programme. However, discussion with colleagues, friends and acquaintances suggests that some who viewed *Unspeakable Truths* had to radically rethink their views. Because Cleveland was such a key case they had their opinions about subsequent cases (such as Orkney) disrupted too. I was also able to re-contact some of my original research participants. One woman who had taken part in a focus group discussion with me in 1993 comments that watching

Unspeakable Truths four years later left her 'really shaken. If those were the facts it really made me rethink everything I'd assumed.' Another, who in a focus group in 1993 had said she viewed Marietta Higgs as 'warped' and 'completely wrong', revised her opinion after viewing the programme (which I arranged for her to watch on video). She summarises her reactions as follows:

> From what I remember at the time, it was completely hidden that some parents already had convictions. Of course that makes a difference to what you'd think. Also, I thought Marietta Higgs had wrongly diagnosed, and the programme suggested that probably she was right ... I bought it [the original reporting] hook line and sinker, Marietta Higgs was damned. I hadn't realised that Marietta Higgs [...] hadn't been struck off – so they were clearly vindicated by their profession. I'm sorry if I said Marietta Higgs was a sleazeball. I take it back! (Focus group participant from 1993, interviewed in 1998, after viewing *Unspeakable Truths*).

Such comments provide pointers to how people's understandings of Cleveland might have been transformed if the media coverage had been different. However, in the absence of more systematic audience reception research, perhaps the most important point highlighted by the *Unspeakable Truths* documentary is that the presentation of episodes such as Cleveland is not predetermined. The meaning of such events is constructed in the course of competition between sources, routine media processes and audience reactions. Even when there is a powerful consensus, such as surrounded Cleveland, alternative accounts are possible.

DISCUSSION

Reflections on the media's role in 'the backlash'

The media are often seen as having betrayed abused children and sexual abuse survivors because of the vigour with which they pursued stories about false or contested allegations. However, the media did not cause the backlash (anymore than they caused the initial discovery of sexual abuse in the first place). What they did do was bring their own contribution to the dynamics. The news media's pursuit of new angles and the speed with which they developed 'abuse fatigue' were certainly factors influencing the attention they gave to contested cases. Coverage was also influenced by editorial lines (Franklin 1990), rules of professional and children's confidentiality and the difficulty of getting social services to talk to them. Journalists also did not have direct access to the child's voice. Other issues impacting on mainstream reporting included class and gender power, and the pre-existing image and status of childcare workers as well as the question of who journalists identified with (some clearly identified with the parents, see Kitzinger 1998, 1999).

The rise in high-profile contested cases however cannot be seen purely in terms of media dynamics. It also has to be seen in a broader social context. The media publicity helped to put aggrieved parents in touch with each other, but the social movement of resistance has its own independent momentum too. Analysts of the Cleveland and Orkney cases are divided between some who see such cases as evidence of a backlash and others who see them as necessary to rebalance the pendulum in response to the original moral panic about abuse. On the one hand, the backlash is seen as evidence of the passion with which people maintain the status quo and the power of patriarchal forces to defend men's power within the family. On the other hand, those who see the original identification of child sexual abuse through a 'moral panic' lens tend to emphasise instead how resistance was generated in response to 'preposterous' charges (Jenkins 1992:186). They criticise a self-serving system in which agencies with 'a full-time responsibility to investigate child abuse ... generated bureaucratic need to produce tangible results' (Jenkins 1992:138) and where feminists uncritically supported a 'believe the children' position because they were reluctant to lose 'an effective rhetorical weapon against the unsavoury and dangerous patriarchal nuclear family' (Jenkins 1992:174). Both sides however often point to the inexperience and lack of resources of those trying to combat sexual abuse, the mistakes they made, and the fundamental complexity and danger of trying to prevent crimes within the family. They account for the outcry over false allegations by highlighting the emotions such accusations generate, and people's underlying unease with admitting the possibility of abuse, as well as the shortcomings of the intervention system (Myers 1994).

The media, then, cannot be seen as causing the protests against child sexual abuse allegations. The dynamics are much more complex that that. What they did do, and did with emotive images, language and associations (as well as considerable enthusiasm), was spread the influence of such stories and increase fears of inappropriate intervention and scepticism about the potential validity of allegations.

The place of Cleveland in public discourse about sexual abuse has more general lessons to offer, beyond the immediate topic with which it is associated. The example of Cleveland can allow us to theorise more generally about how such template events operate in the media coverage of, and public response to, other social problems. In the final part of this chapter I reflect on how media templates might be identified in other news stories and the implications of templates for the ways in which we all think and act, whether as policy makers, journalists or ordinary members of the public.

Researching media templates: identifying and defining template events

The study reported here started by identifying and examining key reference points in public understandings of sexual abuse. This has demonstrated the importance of collective memories and historical analogies in audience reception, media representation and effects. The concept of media templates developed from analysis of this empirical data is, I believe, relevant to examining source/media/ audience relations over a broad range of issues. It can also be usefully positioned in relation to existing thinking about media influence, including work around framing, key events and icons.

Media templates are closely related to discussion of how the media frame social issues (see the discussion of framing in Chapter 2). The media template of Cleveland was used as an analogy in order to encourage a particular understanding of Orkney and to promote the frame 'innocent families torn apart (yet again)' through the 'persistent incompetence' of social workers. The Cleveland analogy thus lies somewhere between the metaphors and the exemplars identified as framing devices by Gamson and Modigliani (1989:3).

However, Cleveland was more than just another analogy. It was the dominant analogy for Orkney and a key reference point in thinking about the whole issue of sexual abuse which ran through every level of the circuit of communication, including journalists' thinking, media content and people's conversations. Cleveland had one particularly pervasive and dominant meaning which meant, in effect, that it carried with it an entire frame which closely circumscribed perceptions of the new cases to which it was successfully related. Whereas a frame is envisaged as a 'map' (Gamson 1992) or 'window' (Pan and Kosicki 1993) – and can be a rather vague concept – the template event refers specifically to the use of analogies and implies a more rigid and precisely outlined perspective (which both operates within, and contributes to, a specific substantive frame). Rather than seeing templates in terms of maps or windows, the more appropriate metaphor in this case would be the template document automatically summoned up each time one starts a new text file on a computer. Alternatively, the template might be envisaged as the pastry-cutting shapes used to cut out gingerbread figures, or the template allowing workers to stamp out identical metal pieces in a shipyard.

Media templates can also usefully be related to writing around key events and theories around news icons.[8] Bennet and Lawrence (1995), for example, examined 'icons' such as the videotaped beating of Rodney King by white police officers. They argue that icons are a nugget of condensed drama which can 'stand alone as an emblematic decisive moment that can be evoked with a simple phrase or visual reference'. They describe how such icons can be introduced into other types of stories and thus 'break down narrative boundaries and open the news to ... linkages between otherwise isolated events'. In this sense icons share some characteristics with templates. However, Bennet and Lawrence (1995) describe icons as opening up innovation and historical reflection, evoking 'contradictions and tensions'. I argue that templates operate in a rather different way; they are defined by their lack of innovation, their status as received wisdom and by their closure. In other words, far from opening up historical reflection they reify a kind of historical determinism which can filter out dissenting accounts, camouflage conflicting facts and promote one type of narrative. I wish to highlight several distinguishing features defining media templates:

- Media templates are key events that have an ongoing shelf life which extends beyond the conclusion of news happenings. Indeed, media templates are defined by their retrospective use in secondary reporting rather than contemporaneous coverage.
- Media templates are used to explain current events, as a point of comparison and, often, as proof of an ongoing problem. Templates are used to highlight patterns in particular issues or social problems.
- Media templates have a single primary meaning rather than being the focus for debate. When a template is referenced in discussion of subsequent discrete events its relevance may

be challenged (e.g. this case is/is not like Cleveland) but the template itself is rarely explicitly questioned.

The above definition of media templates has implications for how they operate:

• Simplification and distortion: In the process of transforming a key event into a media template, details may be blurred, dissenting accounts forgotten and facts (both from past and current events) misrepresented or disregarded.
• Minimal opportunity for alternative readings: Secondary reporting will often oversimplify or at least present the event pared down to its 'essence'. This minimises opportunities for alternative interpretations from people only exposed to secondary accounts. It may also influence recall of the events even among those who were aware of the original reporting.
• Osmosis: The meanings attached to template events are, in part, created by the interaction between such episodes and subsequent cases to which they are linked. Cleveland means what it means because of its link with the Rochdale and Orkney cases (and vice versa). The meaning of media templates may be both reinforced and altered as they are applied to events as they unfold (e.g. Cleveland has become a template of social work malpractice; the role of doctors has not been a reiterated theme).
• Challenging templates: Templates are very powerful, and often unquestioned, influences. However they are not inevitably self-perpetuating. They may be recognised and challenged through people's own personal experience or political perspective. Templates may be exposed and undermined through coming into conflict with contradictory templates or the creation of a boomerang effect. In addition, media personnel (particularly documentary makers) may take on the challenge of 'debunking the myths' in ways which provide an alternative to dominant templates.

The method for identifying template events is essentially retrospective; examining how past events are referenced and associated with (and transformed by) new, unfolding stories. None the less, educated predictions may be made about which contemporary events might become templates in the future. These predictions can be informed by close attention to the contemporary coverage, event timing, cultural resonance, the organisation of sources and likely future developments. For example, Cleveland might have been predicted to become a template from the perspective of observers in 1987 on several counts. It attracted peak, dramatic and vitriolic coverage, it occurred very early on in the discovery cycle of sexual abuse, and it was the first high profile case of its kind. It also tapped into strong feelings about children, social workers and family life. Given the structural and ideological context of social work it was also probable that similar controversies would happen in the future. It was likely that social workers would in the future feel compelled (and have the power) to take children into care in circumstances which seemed to go against common sense or violate parents' rights. Crucially, the Cleveland inquiry also put in place a report (and guidelines) against which subsequent interventions would be judged. Another legacy of Cleveland was the fact that source organisations were set up or galvanised (most notably PAIN) ready to draw attention to further cases of injustice. The structural as well as rhetorical foundations were thus laid for future cases to be picked up and linked with Cleveland.

Thinking with templates: implications for journalists, policy makers and the public

Identifying key moments from the past and using analogies from history is not inherently problematic. Such practices may well be essential if we are to learn from the past and make sense of the present. Journalistic references necessarily have to be condensed in the brief space provided by a bulletin or newspaper report. These constraints pose challenges, but to simply avoid referencing the past would result in media coverage being entirely a-historical. However, when some such associations and key moments become taken for granted as templates it is easy to ignore the constructed nature of these accounts. It is as if frameworks for understanding are invisible because of their all-encompassing nature and as if truth could be created by repetition. In order to reflect on the role of media templates it is useful to turn to debates within the disciplines of political science and history.

Social historians argue that it is important not to assume that records of historical events are innocent acts of memory, but rather to see them as attempts 'to persuade, to shape the memory of others' (Burke 1997:47). Historians and political scientists also note that historical analogies are often used in misleading ways. Richard Neustadt (Professor of Government at Harvard) and Ernest May (Professor of History at Harvard) analyse the use of such analogies by policy makers in their book *Thinking in Time: The Uses of History for Decision Makers*. This includes detailed analysis of tapes of White House discussions around, for example, the Cuban missile crisis. They argue that problems arise when analogies are used in an unthinking fashion. They highlight the problem of 'fuzzy analogies' where there is a failure to think about presumptions, 'stereotyped suppositions about persons or organisations' are inherent and little or no effort is made to see choices as part of a historical sequence (Neustadt and May 1988:33). Analogies can, they argue, predispose people to 'come to conclusions with the minimum of analysis'. They suggest that we need to use history more reflectively. Neustadt and May advise systematically separating the 'known', from the 'unclear' and 'presumed' and routinely analysing historical events for their likeness and difference from now (Neustadt and May 1988:40). Many analogies, they conclude, should be better used as warning lights to alert us to a potential problem, rather than a beacon by which we set an unswerving course (Neustadt and May 1988:56).

It is instructive to apply this advice to the use of Cleveland as a template, or arguably a fuzzy or at least limited analogy informed by 'stereotyped suppositions about persons or organisations' (such as families or social workers). There appears to be a consensus that Cleveland was badly handled and that it should never happen again. But what is the 'it' which should not be repeated? Here the consensus breaks down. For example, is it children being taken from their parents and/or is it some children being returned to potentially abusive situations? Is it social work malpractice or police non-co-operation? There also appears to be a consensus that we should learn the lessons of Cleveland. But this again begs the question: what are these lessons? Are they about social work practices or political intervention; childcare professionals or media reporting, or do they reflect intractable dilemmas for child protection? These questions are rarely asked. Both journalists and ordinary people talking about sexual abuse often make remarks such as 'look at Cleveland'. But this phrase is not a genuine invitation to examine the case. Rather it is a rhetorical full stop. 'Look at Cleveland' is a statement made in the sure assumption that everyone present will recall the events similarly and that what we see is self-evident. Such assumptions often prove to be justified, and dissenting voices are rarely heard.

Challenging templates: implications for media production

Given the analysis above I think we should value and seek to promote media reporting that develops the effective use of history combined with the accurate and innovative association of events, but which also adopts a questioning attitude toward templates. This is not an invitation to gratuitous historical revisionism, but a belief in reflective, responsible and in-depth journalistic enquiry. However, where one draws the line, and who defines this is a question for debate. The reaction of Stuart Bell MP to *Unspeakable Truths* was to describe it as 'a sensational rehash of half-truths and suppositions. It was a re-writing of history and perfectly useless exercise' (quoted in *Middlesbrough Evening Gazette*, 28 May 1997). By contrast his neighbouring MP, Frank Cook, stated that he was deeply shocked by some of the information revealed to him by the programme. This information, he said, had altered his understandings of Cleveland, and, had it been widely publicised at the time, might have made a difference to subsequent policy making, such as The Children's Act (speaking on *Unspeakable Truths*, 27 May 1997).

Whatever the judgement in this particular case, the point is that the news media are not well adapted for revisiting history. Iconoclastic reporting can and does occur. However, given what we know about the sociology of journalism, it may be a vain wish to hope that such reporting will become standard (Tuchman 1978; Schlesinger 1978). Alongside the usually identified barriers to such coverage including deadlines, established source–journalist relations and emphasis on news of the day, reporting around child sexual abuse is also influenced by gendered hierarchies within news production (Skidmore 1998; Kitzinger 1998). More generally, although the traditional documentary format can encourage iconoclastic approaches, even this traditional strength is being eroded by current changes. Challenging received wisdom has never been the path of least resistance for programme makers. It is not usually quick or cheap and programme makers attempting this task may confront political difficulties. When I interviewed the producer of *Unspeakable Truths* he described obstacles to the programme's production at every level; from the Department of Health's decision to destroy all records relating to the Cleveland children as a group through to the difficulty of obtaining interviews with relevant professionals.

Some of the key people who used to work in Cleveland were pressurised by their current employers not to appear on the programme. The main social worker from Cleveland, Sue Richardson, was working for the National Children's Home (NCH) in Scotland. She did co-operate with *Unspeakable Truths*. However, she resigned from her job because the NCH threatened that if she took part in the programme she risked sacking for gross misconduct. After the programme was in production Stuart Bell MP also wrote to protest and senior management at Yorkshire Tyne Teesside Television then vetoed the documentary. This decision was taken despite the fact that they had already won the commission from Channel 4. The producer, Tim Tate, was only able to complete the documentary by negotiating to be released from his contract and continuing the production through his own independent company. When I asked him about the difficulties producing this documentary compared to previous experiences he replied:

> I'm just thinking back. This is going to sound absurd, but the only comparable experience I've had was a film I made about the Chinese ... system for political prisoners, when people became non-people and black was white and green wasn't a colour at all. That's the closest I've come ... For the life of me I cannot think what is so important that you have to protect it with this chapter of lies and evasions (Interview with the author).

Tim Tate added that his confidence in the eventual release of the programme was supported by 'Channel 4's robust reputation for resisting political interference'. However, so-called 'dumbing down' as well as financial constraints and changes in organisational structure may undermine such opportunities in the future. The form and content of media productions are being influenced by changes in the long-term employment and nurturing of experienced journalists, including those who have expertise in investigative reporting and those who have followed events over time and have their own complex memories and source relations. This may mean that one-dimensional versions of events from news reporting will be increasingly recycled and converge as journalists, working to a tight schedule, rely on 'going through the cuttings'. Under these conditions journalists will rarely have the time or space to revisit history or produce in-depth investigations that might differ from mainstream opinion.

CONCLUSION

This chapter has reviewed the status and operation of a key moment in the debate about sexual abuse. It has highlighted how the Cleveland case operated as a media template. I have argued that media templates are a distinct form of key event which serve as a powerful framing device. Exploring how they operate is an important endeavour for anyone examining media coverage, source strategy, journalistic practice, audience reception, or, indeed, particular social issues.

Media templates are a crucial site of media power, acting to provide context for how we understand a problem and interpret new events, as well as informing policy responses. The paradigmatic examples and associations which surround any particular issue can come to seem natural and inevitable. It is the task of media theorists, practitioners, policy makers and audiences to question how such accounts are constructed and to ask how they might be different.

5
Story Branding and the Role of Empathy

How do stories become labelled in particular ways? What shorthand is used to identify a specific crisis or scandal? Why do some aspects of a story engage our imagination and make lasting impressions while others are ignored or forgotten? This chapter explores these questions by taking a closer look at the Orkney crisis. In particular it introduces the notion of 'story branding'. I borrow this term from commercial advertising where efforts are made to make consumers accept a series of simple brand significations ranging from 'Coca-Cola – it's the real thing' or 'Beans means Heinz' to 'Happiness is a cigar called Hamlet'. Branding, however, is not confined to the commercial world. It is used in broader PR and politics. In the UK, for example, the Labour Party successfully rebranded itself 'New Labour' and dissociated itself from its traditional close ties with the unions in order to attract more voters. The ousted Conservative Party then tried to change its image, from old fashioned and intolerant to more progressive and caring. Branding is also a crucial part of news management, as competing news sources try to assert different definitions of the heart of the story, its key characteristic.

This chapter examines the ways in which struggles to define the story were played out in the Orkney case. I show how it was successfully branded as the dawn raids case and examine the consequences of this labelling for public perceptions of the crisis. The chapter concludes that story branding can produce powerful and relatively straightforward media effects, and identifies the crucial role of generating audience empathy and identification in order to maximise brand recognition and acceptance.

ORKNEY IN THE NEWS – AN OUTLINE OF THE SCANDAL

The Orkney case hit the headlines in March 1991 after nine children from four different families living in the Orkneys (islands off the north coast of Scotland) were taken into care. This decision by social services was based on suspicions that the children were being sexually abused by their parents, in collusion with each other and the local minister. The abuse was also alleged to involve 'ritualistic elements'. The parents went public and vehemently protested their innocence. The case made front-page national and even international news during the five weeks that the children were in care. The events in Orkney were the focus of over a quarter of all national UK press coverage of child sexual abuse during that year, generating 445 news and feature articles, letters and editorials. Coverage was also intense in the Scottish national/regional press. During March and April alone there were 230 items (including feature articles, letters and editorials) in just four Scottish daily and two Sunday newspapers (*Glasgow Herald, Evening Times, Daily Record, Scotsman, Scotland on Sunday, Sunday Scot*).

The trajectory of the story over the two months of peak coverage involved first the children being taken into care at the end of February and then a series of legal battles (in the civil courts) between the parents and social services over their fate. In early April, Sheriff Kelbie ruled that the social services' actions had been fundamentally flawed and the children were immediately sent home. In June social services successfully appealed against Sheriff Kelbie's ruling. However, the case was not pursued. An inquiry into events was set up under Lord Clyde, but this did not publish its findings until the following year. Examples of the opening lines of news bulletins and headlines from press reports from the first two months of the crisis are shown below.

Television news bulletins
2 March 1991: Parents in the Orkney Islands have demanded the immediate return of nine children taken into care after allegations of ritual sex abuse. The call came after a public meeting to discuss mounting concern about the way the islands' social work department has handled the case (BBC1, *Nine O'Clock News*).
5 March 1991: The parents [...] were formally told today why the children had been taken into protective custody on the mainland. Place of Safety Orders were upheld and extended for a further 21 days in each case at a children's panel meeting (ITV, *News at Ten*).
7 March 1991: The parents of nine children taken into care over allegations of ritual abuse on the Orkney Islands today lost an appeal to have them returned (BBC1, *Nine O'Clock News*).
12 March 1991: The parents of the Orkney children [...] have told of the moment social workers took them away. In their first television interview they say the children weren't allowed to take any of their clothes or toys with them (ITV, *News at Ten*).

▶

12 March 1991: Plus the latest case of alleged child abuse, we report from the Orkneys on how social workers and police came by plane to take children away from their families. The families tell us of their horror at the dawn swoop, the authorities tell us they've acted correctly throughout (Channel 4, *Channel 4 News*).

3 April 1991: A court at Kirkwall in the Orkney Islands has begun hearing evidence into the alleged ritual sex abuse of nine children (ITV, *Lunchtime News*).

4 April 1991: The headlines at six o'clock – the Orkney child abuse case has been dismissed. Nine children held in care for five weeks will be back with their parents tonight. The Sheriff said the case was fundamentally flawed (BBC1, *Six O'clock News*).

5 April 1991: Parents of some of the nine Orkney children who were placed in care following allegations of ritual abuse say that their sons and daughters are confused and withdrawn and will need support to get over their ordeal. Ken Rees has visited one family who are getting used to being together again (ITV, *Early Evening News*).

19 April 1991: There's to be a full judicial inquiry into the ritual child sex abuse case in Orkney (BBC1, *One O'Clock News*).

Newspaper headlines

Date	Headline	Newspaper
1 March	Satan inquiry children held in dawn raids	*Daily Mail*
3 March	Orkney uproar after 'child sex abuse'	*Independent on Sunday*
4 March	Island families living in fear of knock on the door	*Glasgow Herald*
6 March	'It's a Salem witch-hunt' sobs kid-sex probe mum	*Sun*
7 March	Anger and concern on Orkney	*Independent*
8 March	Orkney appeal fails to lift care order	*Guardian*
8 March	How the world's press descended on Orkney	*Scotsman*
10 March	'Devil's isle' mums vow to fight on	*News of the World*
10 March	Islanders trapped in a nightmare	*Scotland on Sunday*
10 March	Rules that were ignored on Orkney	*Sunday Times*
15 March	Ruling 'in days' on Orkney child abuse charges	*Daily Telegraph*
16 March	2000 sign Orkney protest	*Sun*
21 March	End the agony!	*Daily Record*
26 March	Orkney orders extended	*Independent*
27 March	Parents trapped in limbo of hope and fear	*Guardian*
5 April	Orkney children home as abuse cases collapses	*Independent*
5 April	Home for a hug!	*Daily Record*

▶

5 April	Home from a nightmare	*Daily Mail*
5 April	They left here unharmed, they're coming home abused	*Daily Mirror*
5 April	Damning attack on handling of case	*Scotsman*
5 April	It was all a lie!	*Sun*
6 April	'They taught me how to nick cars, mum'	*Daily Star*
6 April	'Why did they keep putting words in my mouth?'	*Scotsman*
6 April	'Hip hooray, I'm going home today' sang a little boy	*Daily Telegraph*
7 April	Tears of rage as the horror is relived	*Observer*
8 April	Orkney inquiry call	*Guardian*

Throughout the coverage there was a battle between the parents and social services to control the news agenda, a battle that social services largely lost. From very early on the parents were talking to the media (with their backs to the camera to protect the identity of their children) condemning social work actions. First-person accounts appeared in the press under headlines such as: '"Our Nightmare". Sad dad tells of his family's agony' (*Daily Record*, 16 March 1991) and 'Mother's Day tears on Orkney' (*Sunday Post*, 10 March 1991). The parents were also interviewed extensively on the TV news, giving harrowing accounts of how their children were taken from their homes:

> Father: Well, we were asleep in bed, it would be just almost exactly seven o'clock when there was a knock at the door. It was six policemen and four social workers. They waved Place of Safety Orders at us and pushed their way in. Boys were woken, they weren't allowed to speak to us. We weren't allowed to speak to them, weren't allowed to hug them or anything (BBC2, *Newsnight*, 15 March 1991).

Parents described the devastating impact of the events on themselves and their children:

> Mother: When they actually came and took my children and there was not a thing I could do to protect them from what was happening. That had to be the worst moment in my life possibly (ITV, *Early Evening News*, 5 April 1991).

One woman described her daughter locking herself in the bathroom:

Mother: When I came into the house [my daughter] was still locked in the bathroom frightened [...] . I think she must have opened the door but, when [...] I went to get washed, the sink's leaking, she must have hung on to the sink while they dragged her out. That's a 13-year-old girl (ITV, *News at Ten*, 12 March 1991).

Television news reporters, unlike some of the press journalists, were usually careful to balance such accounts with comments from social work representatives (in accordance with their statutory obligations to give fair coverage). For example, the *News at Ten* bulletin intercut interviews with the parents quoted above with a statement from the Orkney Director of Social Services, Paul Lee. The juxtaposition was damning:

Director of Social Services, Paul Lee: I am satisfied that we did everything that we should have done in an appropriate way.
Reporter: But for one mother on the island, whose husband was away in England on the day she lost her children it wasn't like that at all.
Mother: Dropped off by the police outside my house on my own in the dark, and they just driving off having taken and shattered my whole world, taken my children. I actually came running into the house screaming for my own mother who's been dead for 20 years (ITV, *News at Ten*, 12 March 1991).

Parents invited journalists into their homes and spoke to the media at length; social workers, by contrast, often avoided commenting on the case and were legally constrained about what they could disclose. Parents or their representatives were twice as likely as social services to be quoted in the media and spoke at far greater length (Kitzinger and Skidmore 1995b). When social workers did comment, their remarks often seemed cold and clinical compared to the passionate distress of the parents. Although there were variations across diverse media, most coverage was highly critical of social services, sometimes vehemently so. Some journalists became closely allied with parents and particular newspapers campaigned on their behalf. This was explicitly acknowledged by one mother, in the euphoria of having her children back when they were eventually returned:

Mother: Oh brilliant, brilliant, just thanks, everybody. Thanks press, thank you community, wonderful to have the children home (ITV, *News at Ten*, 4 April 1991).

REMEMBERING ORKNEY AS 'THE DAWN RAIDS CASE'

The Orkney case, like that in Cleveland before it, proved to be a landmark in people's thinking about sexual abuse. My focus groups were conducted between April 1993 and December 1994, a minimum of two years after the Orkney crisis hit the media. However, when invited to note down a headline about child sexual abuse on their questionnaires at the start of the focus group session, almost one in five of the headlines explicitly identify Orkney by name.[1] These included headlines such as 'Orkney dawn swoop by social workers' (Group 7); 'Social workers to blame for Orkney child abuse fiasco' (Group 9); 'Orkney scandal' (Group 9); 'Judge slams social workers in Orkney' (Group 16); 'Social workers to blame for Orkney "farce"' (Group 8).

People often also state that they remember very little beyond such headlines and, when questioned, obvious gaps in their knowledge are exposed. They usually cannot say from where the allegations had originated (the accusations had come from children who were already in care and whose father had been convicted of abuse). Some do not know how many children were taken, a few do not even know whether or not the children had been returned home. Most cannot remember that the local minister was named as the alleged ringleader. Many think (incorrectly) that all the evidence had been evaluated before the children were returned to their parents.[2] Very few of the research participants know that social services won an appeal against Sheriff Kelbie's decision and virtually nothing is recalled about the findings from the subsequent Inquiry into the affair.[3]

Research participants sometimes draw their own conclusions about what this indicates about the influence of media coverage: 'I can't remember a thing, I don't think I really take it in'; 'It goes right out of your mind'; 'News just doesn't affect me, I never remember anything.' However, they are also struck by how much they recall about certain aspects of the case: 'Some of it did stick in your mind, but not everything' (Group 31, f); 'It's funny isn't it, how much you can remember about it, how upsetting it was' (Group 7, f).

Indeed, as they start to discuss the case, they are sometimes quite startled by how much they can recall: 'It's amazing how it sticks in your head' (Group 1, f); 'You know more than you think you know' (Group 10, f).

In spite of lacking knowledge about much, arguably crucial, information, research participants are able to recall particular phrases, facts, themes and explanatory structures. Their discussions reveal systematic patterns in their understandings of events in Orkney. People not only identify the strong similarities to the Cleveland case (see previous chapter) they also vividly recall the dawn raids. Indeed, for many people, Orkney is 'that dawn raids case'. Starting then from what people do remember, rather than what they had forgotten, it is possible to begin to explore how the media can influence what people know.[4]

Asked what came to mind when thinking about sexual abuse people often immediately volunteer descriptions of the Orkney dawn raids:

> There was one case where [...] it was a big headline, children being removed. [...] One of the children hadn't even been able to say cheerio to it's mother and they were taking the child out the door and it wasn't allowed to take its toys, I found that's the sort of thing that sticks most (Group 11, f).
> f: There was that Highland, up the Highlands.
> f: Up north, the Orkneys?
> f: Aye, it's horrible.
> f: The children getting taken off their parents [...]
> f: Going in in the middle of the night, taking the children away (Group 35).

When directly prompted to talk about Orkney, again it is the dawn raids that are usually the first thing people mention. They often identify the raids as the most memorable (and sometimes the only memorable) part of the crisis:

> m: I just remember what was in the papers, they were took screaming from their beds.
> m: Kids getting snatched at dawn.
> f: Aye, that's right, children getting taken out their homes [...] their parents not knowing anything about it (Group 28).
> f: All I know is that [they] were lifted in the middle of the night. [...] swooping on the island at four in the morning, uplifting all they weans out their beds (Group 31).
> f: Them getting taken away from their parents.
> f: In the middle of the night out of their beds, that's horrific.
> f: I mean it's tragic for the mums and dads, I mean it must have been dreadful for them, I think it was really awful, I really do (Group 26).

People recall the lack of information available to parents, the early hour at which the children were taken and that they were not allowed to take personal belongings.

> m: The children were just snatched away, at midnight.
> f: Dawn raids.
> f: That's it, dawn raid in Orkney.
> f: They never even had a chance to examine the children or talk to the parents or nothing, they just grabbed them away (Group 17).
> m: I remember the headline: 'Dawn raids' [...]
> f: Yes you do, yes, knocking the door down at three o'clock in the morning.
> f: Social workers coming in the night and taking children away in a very sort of aggressive and firm manner.
> f: They were taken off the island weren't they?
> f: They took them completely away, no contact allowed [...]
> f: That's right and not allowing children to take their teddy bears (Group 38).
> m: They knocked on the door, four o'clock in the morning, wallop, put in a helicopter to the mainland [...]
> m: That's it, they were literally dragged out the houses (Group 40).

The airlifting of the children away from Orkney to the mainland underlines the horror of the raids:

> What was so shocking was that they were removed from their homes by police, at crack of dawn and taken by helicopter to another piece of land, away from their parents. [...] That had quite an impact. The fact that they lived on this island and they were flown to the mainland and you had this image, that might be that child's first flight, and they were like almost being abducted. They were being abducted in fact, like a real childhood sort of horror story in a way. The idea of being removed and taken on a plane and whizzed off (Group 23, f).

Not surprisingly, when I subsequently asked research participants to try to reproduce a news bulletin about the Orkney case, dawn raids feature prominently. Extracts from some of the scripts that people wrote are reproduced below. These are juxtaposed against actual media reports which appeared at the time of the crisis, around two and a half to three and a half years earlier. The similarities are striking.

Examples from focus groups' scripts

In the early hours of this morning on the remote island of South Ronaldsay, children from four families were snatched in a series of dawn raids. The sleeping families were roused from their beds by heavy-handed social workers and police. The swiftness of the operation did not even allow the children time to collect personal belongings (Group 30, August 1994).

In this quiet Orkney town, tranquillity was shattered by the news this morning of 24 children being taken away from their parents by social workers. [...] A family friend said she heard the cars arrive at dawn, swoop on the houses. 'The children were crying and parents were screaming for the bairns to be brought back, it was terrible to see' (Group 38, October 1994).

The small island of South Ronaldsay [where] there were dawn raids on the homes of several families. We talked to a friend of one of the families who described the raids from first-hand knowledge. [...] She commented on how the police and social workers stole the children away at first light, not giving them a chance even to pick up any toys or clothing [...] and how the parents were just left, not knowing what was going on at that time (Group 19, February 1994).

... the peace was shattered in the beautiful islands of the Orkneys, when children were snatched from their beds [...] in dawn raids by social workers accompanied by police, the children were torn from their parents without even having time to gather their toys (Group 13, December 1993).

Actual press/TV reports about Orkney

Nine children have been snatched from their families [...] families on the close-knit island of South Ronaldsay were awoken without warning in a series of dawn raids. 'It was just like a witch hunt' said one tearful mother, 'The police came to the door with social workers and took our children. They just waved a piece of paper in our faces and left with the kids. We didn't even have time to kiss them good-bye' (*Today*, 1 March 1991).

[...] nine children from four families were dragged from their beds in a series of dawn raids [...] 'we were not allowed to give them breakfast. They left with only the clothes they had dressed in. [...] I asked to know where our children were being taken – we were told we were not allowed to know' (*Daily Mail*, 3 March 1991).

Father: 'They were just taken, just in the clothes they stood in. What really horrified us was they weren't allowed to take anything that had any element of security for them. I mean children need favourite things, I asked may they take a book or a teddy bear or personal stereo, anything, absolutely not. Just the clothes they stood in' (Channel 4, *Channel 4 News*, 12 March 1991).

Police and social workers had earlier swooped on four families and took nine children into care [...] Another mother, whose three children were taken away, said 'I feel so helpless. They wouldn't let me speak to my children' (*Daily Record*, 28 February 1991).

The dawn raids are, in most groups, recalled with great confidence. As one research participant declares 'children were removed from their beds at the crack of dawn and dragged screaming from their parents' homes. That's *fact'* (Group 23, f), or as another comments, we might not have the details but 'basically we know that's what happened' (Group 24, m). Nobody questions whether or not the raids ocurred, everyone knows that children were taken from their parents in traumatic circumstances. Most believe that their memories and the media reporting of the raids included the accurate and relevant facts. The accusations against the parents may, or may not, be plausible, but evidence that social workers went 'storming in like the SAS' is, for most people, incontrovertible and, for many, generated very strong feelings.

This, then, is an unproblematic demonstration of media effect. People are able to reconstruct news accounts from the time with striking accuracy and have strong shared understandings of the events in Orkney back in early spring 1991. At the time of the crisis, the media reporting generated a groundswell of public outrage against social workers. It has also clearly left many people with indelible memories of social services brutality. Perhaps this is not surprising. Maybe we take such media effects for granted. However, here I want to ask: when so much was forgotten, why was this aspect of the case recalled so vividly, and how does this inform the way people think about child sexual abuse? Under what circumstances can such effects occur? What are the implications for how media influence might operate?

WHY THE DAWN RAIDS MADE SUCH AN IMPRESSION

Close attention to the surrounding discussion within the focus groups suggests that the power of the dawn raids coverage is related to three key factors. These are:

- the quantity, prominence and trajectory of the dawn raids coverage
- repeated reiteration of the dawn raids label and using it as synonymous with the case
- drama, empathy and identification; i.e. the reporting of the raids and parents' personal accounts shocked people and generated empathy and identification.

The quantity, prominence and trajectory of the dawn raids coverage

The dawn raids attracted primary and peak attention. They were described extensively in the press and on TV news. Channel 4, ITV and BBC2's flagship news programme, *Newsnight*, for example all had main stories devoted to the way in which the children were taken into care. Relatively less attention was paid to later events, in particular the findings of the subsequent inquiry. The fact that the raids were the very first issue to hit the headlines also seems to have been significant. Several other studies have suggested that whoever can control the news agenda in the early weeks of a crisis often has the advantage in defining the terms of the debate (Miller 1994). This certainly seemed to be true in the Orkney scandal. People acknowledge that after the first fortnight to six weeks (when the children were returned home) they had taken less interest in the case. Some stopped paying attention to the media coverage after the immediate scandal had broken ('that's why I've no idea what happened in the end') and very few had noted the findings from the inquiry the following year. They make comments such as: 'There is only so much that you can take in' (Group 9, f) and 'You get to a point where you just switch off' (Group 18, m). Several say that they stopped reading articles on the case, just noticed the headlines. One woman describes how, even after just two or three weeks, she got into the habit of going off to make herself a cup of tea whenever she saw the typical 'establishing shot' on TV showing the harbour on the Orkney Islands (Group 10, f).

Repeated use of the 'dawn raids' label

The repeated use of the phrase 'dawn raids' in headlines and in the reports themselves also had an impact on how people remembered the case. The phrase quickly became synonymous with Orkney. It was used in more than 50 headlines in the national and Scottish press coverage during 1991 and appeared repeatedly in TV news bulletins. Some reports used the term as shorthand for the Orkney case, e.g. 'Unhappy letters of dawn raid children' (*Daily Mail*, 3 September 1991) or 'Dawn Raid Boss "had not read vital report"' (*Daily Mail*, 30 August 1991). This simple handle on the story is an important aide-memoire for people. The exact phrase, 'dawn raids', is used in 38 of the 49 groups (and others talk of dawn swoop or snatch). Mention of the phrase, dawn raids or swoop, is often greeted with cries of recognition and acknowledged as a trigger for memory. As one person comments after the phrase is used by another group member: 'Dawn raids? Yes, it's all coming back to me now.'

However, it is not just a question of repetition or pervasiveness; this label would not be so powerful had it not been for the dramatic impact of the coverage itself and the way in which it evoked not only empathy, but identification. It is this aspect of reporting which is discussed below.

The power of personal accounts and the role of empathy

The dawn raids (or rather, the reporting of them) touched a nerve in many people, especially if they had children of their own. There is nothing vague about their memories of the raids because they had engaged with the details on the basis of their own day-to-day knowledge of family life. Some speak, for example, about their horror at the way the children were taken, comparing this to the care they take when preparing a child for an aeroplane flight, or for staying away from home overnight for the first time. They describe their own offspring's distress about losing a favourite toy or being woken up during the night. 'Taking a kiddie out it's bed, I think that's terrible, I really do. I mean you know how you feel yourself if there's an emergency and you have to lift the kids. Kids are just bemused, they don't know what's happening to them' (Group 29, f).

People identify with the emotions the parents experienced ('you know how you feel yourself') and repeatedly invite each other to imagine themselves in that position: 'Can you imagine anybody coming up to your house and dragging your children out of bed at that time in the morning?' (Group 26, f). They also underline their own empathy with the parents: 'It's not hard to imagine how they must have felt' (Group 30, m); 'I imagine some of them were really terrified, some of them thought they would never see their weans again' (Group 10, f). Several people remember how they identified with the parents at the time, watching the reports all the while '... imagining how your own kids would sort of react and how would you have reacted to them getting hauled out the house' (Group 12, f). Research participants often spontaneously volunteer, with great vehemence, how they themselves would respond to being targeted in this way:

> If the social work department did anything like that to me I would probably commit murder (Group 7, f).
> I'd be violent if somebody turned up to take my child away in the middle of the night (Group 5, f).
> I would have stuck a knife in the social people (Group 26, f).

> See if a social worker came and tried to take a kid out of my house I think he'd be sorry. He'd be dead to be quite honest with you (Group 27, m).

Such imaginings were encouraged by the nature of the media coverage, which explicitly invited readers to identify with the parents. A report in *Today*, for example, opened with the words 'It is dawn and you are woken by the sound of hammering at the front door. Opening it, you find two social workers. They say they have come to take away your children. And they do' (*Today*, 29 March 1991).

Reporting also included fly-on-the wall filming in the Orkney parents' homes and dramatic reconstructions of the raids.[5] One news bulletin, for example, illustrated accounts of the raids with images of car wheels crunching on gravel, low angle shots of feet walking up to the house and a fist rapping on the door. It then showed a car being driven rapidly away (with the camera view from the back seat), the gates of an airport, a spinning aircraft propeller, feet walking up steps into the plane and the wheels on a plane beginning to turn. The report concluded with the image of a plane flying off into the sky (Channel 4, *Channel 4 News*, 12 March 1991). Several research participants specifically recall this sort of dramatic footage.

Reports of the case also emphasised that the fate suffered by the four Orkney families could happen to anyone. The raids took the parents completely by surprise, e.g. 'A voice at the door of his remote cottage at dawn first alerted the sleepy father of two that something was wrong' (*Sunday Times*, 3 March 1991). Social workers could strike without warning. No family was safe:

> I think every one of us is terrified to death (ITV, *News at Ten*, 5 March 1991).
> It's striking terror into the hearts of people with children (BBC1 *Nine O'Clock News*, 2 March 1991).
> Demonstrator 1: We are all frightened [...]
> Demonstrator 2: You are worried that it might be our children next (BBC1 *Nine O'Clock News*, 5 March 1991).

It is clear in the group discussions that parents are not just sympathising in the abstract. Their reactions were quite different to the compassion they might feel for a starving family in Africa. They feel that what happened to the families in Orkney could happen to them. This is not because they might be abusing their children (this was never even considered as a possibility), but because even innocent parents are at risk. There is widespread distrust of social services and many people lack faith in social workers' training and expertise. Many believe that taking children into care is routine once any suspicions are raised. In fact this is very rare. Gibbons and colleagues, for example, tracked what happened to children referred to the child protection system in eight different local authorities in England. They found that 'In only 4 per cent of referrals were children removed from home under a legal order during the investigation' (Gibbons, *et al*. 1995). Media reporting, however, gives a very different impression.

Several of my research participants volunteer that they feel particularly vulnerable to state intervention because of their class, sexuality, ethnicity or marital status: 'I'm a single parent and I think that [...] marks you out as being an "at-risk"' (Group 5, f). However, such concerns cross-cut all types of parents who participated in the research. Dawn raids are identified as a threat to anyone, not least because the parents in Orkney seemed 'just ordinary' and were white, middle-class and married.

Broader issues about the organisation of state services, and the power of social services also help shape people's responses here. Middle-class parents are reminded that they are not completely immune from state intervention into their lives. They confront the fact that although, under the UK system, they might be able to buy their way out of poor state education or under-resourced state health services, they cannot opt out of poor social services if their children come under the scrutiny of child protection services. The power of social workers to intervene (on the balance of probabilities) is terrifying and often feels unjust. Working-class research participants, already more tied in to state institutions and surveillance, feel their vulnerability all the more acutely. They comment that if even those sorts of 'posh' parents in Orkney were vulnerable then nobody was safe. Such abduction of their children is described as every parent's fear and people can identify with the feelings of utter helplessness. As one research participant observes:

> You do identify if you're a mother, that's the first thing you would do, think about how you would feel in that position. I think it's every woman's fear [...] that somebody's going to come in and take your kids away you know. It's going to get out of your control and you wouldn't

be able to do nothing about it like these people were, there was nothing they could do (Group 12, f).

The belief that the raids were arbitrary and sweeping made the memory particularly stark. As this woman goes on to say: 'I know that's what it highlighted for me, how easy it can be done and on such a mass scale how it can be done, it's quite frightening.' A point echoed in another group when one person comments: 'Some of it did stick in your mind, but not everything', to which her neighbour replies: 'Of course it sticks in your mind, because it could be the social worker up the morrow going and lifting your kiddies' (Group 31, f).

REFLECTIONS ON THE DAWN RAIDS BRANDING

Such media effects are perhaps not contentious in so far as children were indeed taken from their homes at an early hour and it was certainly a major trauma for both children and parents. The branding of Orkney as the dawn raids case may seem so inevitable (and justified) as to be meaningless and virtually unmediated. However, in the next part of the chapter, I want to argue that the dawn raids branding of Orkney encouraged people to accept a definition of the meaning of Orkney which excluded other ways of recalling the story and which included significant exaggerations and absences.[6]

First, it is important to acknowledge that there were other ways in which Orkney could have been defined other than as the dawn raids case. For example, it could have been recalled as a case about alleged ritual abuse. It could be told as a story of the triumph of parents against the state-sanctioned break-up of their families. It might be recalled as a story about social workers' misinterpretation of evidence or as another example of the backlash against children and professionals. Each of these versions of reality have featured in the way the events in Orkney have been covered in other accounts (see, for example, Bell 1988; Campbell 1988; Nelson in press). There is nothing inevitably or self-evidently more valid about the dawn raids branding.

A clear attempt to create an authoritative version of the story is represented by the findings from the official inquiry chaired by Lord Clyde. How might the Orkney case have been recalled if the inquiry had successfully defined the story? The Clyde report includes many damning criticisms of professionals in the Orkney case, but as far as the dawn raids are concerned, it comes to a perhaps surprising conclusion: 'The conduct of the workers in the removal of the children was efficient and supportive [...] . The timing of the removals was beyond serious criticism' (Clyde 1992: 349).

The conclusions of the Clyde report are not, of course, the definitive truth. The report may be viewed as merely another version of reality, composed under different conditions than the original media coverage. However, it includes specific information which was not widely available in media coverage at the time (and/or is not recalled by research participants). This allows for some comparisons to be drawn. Also the inquiry's endorsement of the way in which the children were removed from their homes clearly highlights that the dawn raids scandal definition of Orkney is contestable. The findings from the official inquiry can thus be used to reflect on the presentation of the raids in the media and how such presentations helped to shape people's recall of events. Four aspects of the dawn raids branding of Orkney are highlighted below:

- The use of emotive language and how this supported memories which exaggerated the brutality of the raids.
- The absence of particular information/voices in people's recall of events and how this confirmed irredeemably negative images of social workers.
- The apportioning of blame exclusively to social workers, and the lack of comment on the police.
- Armchair outrage from people who do not have to confront the practical dilemmas of how allegations can be investigated under difficult circumstances.

Emotive language and exaggerated memories

The use of the term 'dawn raids' was an evocative albeit vague phrase which helped people to frame and reconstruct memories of the case in particular ways. First, it encouraged people to think that the raids occurred at an inherently unreasonable hour. According to the Orkney inquiry report, police and social workers arrived at '7 a.m. and it was daylight' (Clyde 1992: 89). However, the time most frequently cited in the groups is 4 or 5 a.m. or earlier. The term 'raid' or 'swoop' also created an association between events in Orkney and dramatic scenes people had witnessed on television of police drug raids. The phrase thus not only guides people's focus and allows for inaccurate exaggerations, it also adds layers to their memories and tells them how to remember:

It was a swoop, it was a swoop. ... that's the word that always comes into my mind [...] it was like a drug bust to me (Group 12, f).

f: It was like a drugs raid. That is the image it gave me.

f: Yeah, in my mind it is exactly of a drugs raid [...] That kind of thing when you go in with a hammer and hurtling up the stairs and just sort of taking the children. That is the sort of image I have (Group 5).

These associations, combined with the inflammatory language used in some of the reporting, also encouraged people to exaggerate the violence of the raids in their recall of events. Reports in the media at the time compared social workers to the Gestapo, the SAS and the KGB (*Guardian*, 5 April 1991; *Sunday People*, 10 March 1991; *Sunday Times*, 14 April 1991). They were acting as if we lived in 'some sort of Nazi state' or 'Russia under Stalin' (*Sun*, 4 March; *Daily Mail*, 4 March 1991). In the focus groups people echo such language, referring to 'Gestapo methods' (Group 26, f) and 'SAS attacks' (Group 20, m). They remember, inaccurately, the police and social workers 'breaking into the house' (Group 26, f), 'swinging through the windows' (Group 20, m) and 'breaking down doors' (Group 38, m). Some think that the children were taken in their nightclothes (e.g. Group 13, m). One person even suggests that the police had been armed (Group 2, m).

Missing information and negative images of social workers

One might argue that such details are irrelevant given the horror of what actually did occur, and how close the authorities did come to breaking down a door in one case where a girl had locked herself in the bathroom (Clyde 1992:92). However, what the seamless version of social work malpractice avoids is any possibility that social workers considered the need for sensitivity at all, or that they had any rationale for the way in which they took the children.

People talk of social workers as 'cold', 'unfeeling' and 'heartless', lacking any understanding of family life.[7] One person declares 'they live on another planet and don't have families'; several others comment that social workers are often unmarried. Participants in three different groups state that social workers can be lesbians, who should not be trusted with children. There is also some specific speculation about the Director of Orkney Social Work Department, Paul Lee. He could not be a father himself, some suggest, or he would never be able to inflict such suffering: 'I just wonder, if he'd had children of his own, would he go in and tear children apart like that?' (Group 26, f).

The focus group discussions show that research participants have little recall of what social workers had to say for themselves during the crisis. When asked to suggest how the professionals might have justified their decisions in the Orkney case, all people can usually remember is 'social workers walking past cameras, trying to ignore the reporters' (Group 3, f) or 'Paul Lee [...] rushing about going "no comment"' (Group 20, m). Social services' sources had tried to convey the message that the children had been taken at 7 a.m., half an hour before the school bus arrived. This time was selected in an attempt to minimise harm. It was chosen so that all the families were likely to be together and to avoid taking the children from public venues such as school. However, very few people are aware of such explanations, this is not surprising as such explanations were not prominent in the media coverage. One research participant who is able to confidently argue the case on this point turned out to have a very special source of knowledge, she had read about the case in a journal, *Community Care*, and she was a member of the Children's Panel (part of the Scottish system for child protection and justice) (Group 8). Most research participants however lack the relevant facts. If they do try to defend social workers, they are therefore unable to do so with any success. They are overruled by other members of the groups:

> f: If you had Jasmine ..., Maria Colwell, you name it, a whole series of girls that you know died and everybody blamed social workers then, you'd be a very edgy social worker. What else would you do?
> m: Yeah but [...] they went in at dawn. [...] There would have been a logic for that if it was in the middle of London, [...] but in Orkney, there was absolutely no logic for it because you couldn't get off the island until the 11 o'clock plane or the 12 o'clock boat you know.
> f: Yeah, right, OK, yeah. Yes. OK. Scrap that (Group 32).

Apportioning blame

Blaming the social workers also fits neatly with the gaps in people's knowledge of the raids in another way; their lack of awareness or thought about the role of the police. The fact that the police were present at the dawn raids was extensively reported at the time, but they were not subject to the same level of media scrutiny as their social worker colleagues. The police are seen as mere appendages following social workers' demands and, if blamed at all, they are blamed for not challenging social workers:

> f: I actually don't really remember much about police involvement [...]
> f: Did the police not have to work with the social workers?
> f: Oh aye.
> f: Could they not have said something about, 'Do you not think it's a wee bit too early in the morning'? (Group 29).

In fact the removal was a joint operation by police and the social work department (Clyde 1992:214). Decisions about the co-ordination and timing of action were taken on police advice. However, this is not known by most people. Instead, responsibility is laid solely at the door of social workers, a profession peculiarly vulnerable to public anger. (As I have argued earlier if mud is going to stick, it will stick to social workers, rather than other professionals such as doctors or police officers, see Chapter 4).[8]

This tendency to trust the police in this context more than social workers is also reflected in the broader pattern of public debate (at least in the UK) in relation to sexual abuse. In their questionnaires I asked research participants to write two headlines about child sexual abuse, one including a reference to social workers, the other including the word 'police'. Of the headlines they produced about social workers, 72 per cent positioned this profession in a negative light (only 2 per cent were positive). By contrast 33 per cent of the headlines about the police gave them a positive role, e.g. 'Police smash paedophile ring' and 'police rescue abused boy'. This was neatly paralleled by an examination of actual headlines in all the national UK press reporting of sexual abuse in 1991. There were 70 headlines about social workers, 44 of which were explicitly negative, e.g. 'Obsession of social workers made them ignore experts' (*Daily Telegraph*, 8 March 1991) and 'Beware the social work abusers' (*Daily Telegraph*, 7 March 1991). By contrast of the 31 headlines about the police only four were critical.

Side-stepping dilemmas

This brings me to my final point, the way in which branding Orkney as the dawn raids case evaded consideration of dilemmas central to child protection. As people discuss the horror of the dawn raids they either implicitly assume that the abuse allegations are false, or suspend judgement. Their ability to empathise with the parents is based on an (at least temporarily) presumed innocence. (None of them would dream of empathising with an abuser, see Chapter 7.) Few try to imagine what it must be like to be an abused child in that situation or, indeed, how it might feel to be a social worker. The question of how children can be given space to speak out, and be protected, if the allegations were true is ignored. Few people displayed any knowledge of the disturbing comments from some of the Orkney children while they were in foster care (see Nelson in press). (Although some details about this are recorded in the Clyde inquiry report such information attracted very little media attention and did not feature in public consciousness.) The focus on the dawn raids allows armchair outrage without a genuine engagement with the dilemmas faced daily by those trying to protect children. The focus on the tragedy of the parents whose children had been taken away stopped people thinking beyond this.[9]

SOURCES OF ALTERNATIVE PERSPECTIVES

Before concluding, it is important to draw attention to those minority research participants who deviated from the common consensus and/or how they felt they resisted media influence. Not everyone was equally convinced by the coverage. Some people had personal experience of abuse that made them keep in mind the question 'but what if the children *were* being abused?' Some said they thought the coverage was 'just too pro the parents'. The reporting had seemed 'orchestrated'; 'the media [were] very slanted against the social work department. It was all staged [...] It wasn't impartial at all' (Group 1, f). One woman thought the PR system in support of the parents seemed too 'slick': 'The whole thing just seemed like cover-up', she says, 'all these jolly, respectable looking ministers and friends of parents and local sort of professionals' (Group 6). Sometimes people felt manipulated by the sheer emotiveness of the coverage. Reactions were also informed by what they perceived as long-standing patterns in media coverage such as anti-social work biases 'The media always project the social workers as the bandits. I don't think they could ever have done the right thing' (Group 18, f). People commonly expressed a scepticism about the reporting. They made comments such as 'The paper'll blow everything out of proportion anyway. You're never going to know what really happened' (Group 11, f) and 'You just know whenever you are watching the news that you are not actually getting the facts' (Group 13, m). Several research participants said they has 'switched off' from the coverage. One woman comments: 'I really don't know [what happened in Orkney], I don't read these things. No, no, head in the sand' (Group 9).

In addition to such distancing techniques a few research participants had personal knowledge which informed their response. One research participant, although accepting the 'dawn raids' label for Orkney, rejected the general negative media image of social workers because of what she had learned from her parents. They had fostered a child with gynaecological problems resulting from rape by her father:

> The authorities [...] did that very well. They were able to remove the children very delicately from the home. We're not talking about you know, dawn raids, and so on. And the man was removed from the home. There were a lot of really important things had been done to this family to keep them together, get the mother back, get her head together and this sort of thing. That was an example that doesn't appear in the media, because they did it well, so no one's ever going to know about that (Group 23, f).

A few people had had conversations with social workers or police acquaintances that led them to step back from a focus on the dawn raids. One man, for example, was strongly influenced by a statement made by a police acquaintance. While 'drowning' among a 'sea' of reporting about the dawn raids, he used this information as a way of avoiding being enveloped by the emotive accounts:

> Well, one policeman commented to me that they had to be very sure what they were doing before they went anywhere near the families. I kind of hung on to that in the middle of all the media bias, which is one of the reasons I kind of stepped back from watching that (Group 19, m).

Those with direct professional experience also emphasised the need to put the interventions in Orkney in perspective:

> f: Children still love their parents despite the fact their parents are abusing them, [...] they still want to hold hands and run down the road with the parents. [...] I've done access with children who absolutely cannot wait to see their dad, who has been abusing them for years (Group 15).

In addition, one of the few research participants to reflect on this dilemma drew on her own experience to challenge the way in which the Orkney case was being talked about. She interrupted the group's discussion of dawn raids to suggest there were other important questions to address:

> I was taken away when I was eleven, it was a terrible experience. I left my brothers and sisters there and you felt you were wrong for being lifted. I was wanting to go back home even though [the abuse] had happened. [...] [The taking of the children from Orkney] sounded a horrific experience and I noticed how we were saying how awful it was for the children, which indeed it was, but if the children were being abused, isn't it better? (Group 16).

While people may have different answers to this question, the important point here is that it was not even considered in many people's reflections on the case. The fact that the story branding of Orkney allowed this question to be evaded is perhaps the most powerful effect of all.

The ways in which personal knowledge could offer a different perspective on media representations was also vividly illustrated by the reaction of one research participant in a focus group with survivors of abuse. When I produced the photographs showing scenes from news bulletins about Orkney she became distressed. One image in particular upset her and made her feel physically sick. It was the photograph showing the children reunited with their parents. This image of apparently happy children holding hands with their parents on their way home was profoundly disturbing to her because of her own experiences of being returned to her abusive father by police.

However, the limits of peoples' ability to resist the dominant branding of Orkney were illustrated by the fact that even those who had specialist knowledge, or expressly criticised the coverage, still often talked in ways which were informed by it. People who say they do not pay any attention to a particular story have often still picked up general impressions. The research participant who declared 'I don't read these things', went on to describe Orkney as 'that dawn raid case'. The woman who only paid attention to the first few weeks of media coverage (and then routinely went to make a cup of tea whenever the Orkney case appeared on the news) had a powerful sense of the injustice done to the families, but little other contextual information. Far from being immunised against media influence, the inattentive or occasional viewer may be more vulnerable to dominant themes.

It was also clear that people who expressed distance from, or cynicism about, the media were still using information, impressions and frames from the coverage to inform their talk. In fact they sometimes held beliefs that were, on reflection, not in accord with their own preferred position on a topic. The process of discussion, and in particular the process of having to produce and critique their own news bulletin, sometimes helped them to reflect on this.

> It was when we were thinking about how to put it [the news bulletin] over, it occurred to me that it [the Orkney case] comes across in my mind as [...] they went in at dawn and that was it. [...] That's what I remember of it. Just thinking about it, these are the wrong bits, I remember them more than anything else (Group 19, m).
> What I did was, social workers I condemned and criticised and police I simply reported that they'd gone in. I was immediately aware [while doing the news game] of an attitude there in me (Group 16, f).

CONCLUSION

This chapter has illustrated the impact of press and TV news reporting about the Orkney crisis. Although some people are able to resist the message, the media can, and do, convey some impressions very powerfully and consistently, to a broad cross-section of the population. People may avoid or forget a great deal of detail but they may still find they are absorbing information and frames from the media in spite of their 'better judgement'. These impressions may be strongly adhered to, and long lasting, even after media attention has subsided.

Some theorists highlight the amount of information that people seem to lack and they present this as evidence of weak media influence (Nordenstreng 1972, cited in Morley 1992:79). The evidence presented in the preceding chapters, however, suggests this is not a useful way of looking at the phenomenon. Many details may be forgotten but news events can still have a powerful impact. Simply testing recall of predefined pertinent information presupposes what counts as important in a story. Testing people's memories after viewing particular news items also ignores the cumulative effect of reiterated media accounts (Curran 1990:152). People may recall little about one individual bulletin, but themes running consistently through a variety of coverage may make a deep impression. Such common themes can infiltrate public assumptions without being attributable to any individual TV programme or press report. This can then help to resource and maintain attitudes towards a high profile case, a country, a city, a disease, or a professional group (see Husband 1975; Van der Gaag and Nash 1987; Kitzinger and Miller 1992; Miller 1994; Cottle 1993).

This chapter has highlighted how a particularly powerful effect can be achieved when the media (or their sources) are able to successfully establish a specific thumbnail sketch of the 'essence' of a story under a particular label. I call this 'story branding'. The brand label acts as an effective aide memoir which (like template-analogies discussed in the previous chapter) taps into, and helps to maintain, a whole series of associations, highlighting some aspects of the story and sidelining others. In the Orkney case the phrase 'dawn raids' encouraged an exaggerated focus on the brutality of the intervention, a failure to engage with possible rationales for it, focused blame on social workers and evaded dilemmas about how complex allegations about organised incestuous abuse can be investigated.

The success of this branding might be attributed in part to the intensity of media interest, the timing of the story, patterns of audience attention and, of course, the poignant interviews with parents and the way in which people were drawn into the story (through camera angle and text). However, these features might not have been sufficient were it not that many people were already primed to be sceptical about social workers and that they were very ready to identify with the parents. (This 'priming' of course was partly achieved by the 'media template' that associated Orkney with Cleveland, see previous chapter.) This was not just an abstract empathy, as they read the newspapers and watched the TV reports, many people could believe that such a thing might happen to them. It was this identification, empathy and fear which underpinned the indelible impression made by the dawn raids.

6
Story Placing: Representing Localities, Landscapes and Communities in the News

This chapter introduces the notion of 'story placing'. It shows how journalists employ descriptions of place (geography, landscape and community) to frame their news reports. Selective and often highly emotive descriptions are used not only to 'give colour' to news reports, but also to give credibility to one way of understanding events rather than another.

This chapter also explores how we, as audiences, read these accounts. It highlights the ways in which our mental maps about the types of place where crime occurs help to shape reactions to news stories. Focusing on the contested allegations of sexual abuse in the Orkneys (a collection of small, isolated, rural islands off the north coast of Scotland) I draw out the diversity of people's responses to this theme of reporting. I also argue that the range of people's reactions to the Orkney landscape and community, although superficially in opposition, often share a fundamental acceptance of conventional notions about what constitutes a place of safety and a place of danger. This chapter concludes by reflecting on this data in order to question conventional theories about polysemy. I challenge the ways in which evidence of diverse decodings are sometimes used to imply that the media have little influence and that power lies with the audience rather than the texts that we consume.

THE SIGNIFICANCE OF PLACE IN NEWS REPORTING

News reports routinely include the geographical and social placing of stories: the use of descriptions and visuals which conjure up ideas about the location (and associated landscapes, peoples and cultures) where the events have occurred. One of the first lessons any trainee journalist learns is how to set the scene, and a sense of place is built into the routines of reporting practice. The conventions of TV news filming combine wide-angle establishing shots and scene-setting background images with more detailed close ups to allow viewers to imagine the location. They also often include footage from an on-location reporter (think of the time-lagged satellite footage from Iraq for example). Newspaper journalists have to be content with still photographs and opening word-pictures but, for them too, conveying a sense of place is an essential part of the journalist's trade. Viewers and readers are invited to visualise the desert landscape littered with burned out tanks after the battle, the inner-city slum which was the site of the riot or the wasteland where the child's body was found.

Descriptions and images are used to provide context and to serve as shorthand. A photograph or few seconds of film footage can, for example, be used to symbolise a whole continent such as Africa or a concept such as urban decay. Images of place introduce atmosphere and local colour (in the case of TV, images are also necessary to justify and exploit the visual nature of the medium). They also lend authority to reports; I was there, and you, the audience, can see as if with your own eyes. Over and above this, representations of place are often imbued with more than simple geography. They carry values and ideas about the social context of events and convey ideas about 'the natives' (Goffman 1990:11).

Many critics have highlighted the colonialism and racism evident in foreign reporting (Said 1978; Sreberny 2002; Bell 1995). Others have examined the 'politics of place' in crime journalism. Critics note that journalists often rely on stereotypes about where crime happens and who commits it. Constructions of 'inner city riots', 'dangerous youth', 'mugging' and 'terrorism' promote ideas about class, age, gender and ethnicity and rely on specific ideas about national identity and place (see, for example, Cottle 1993, 1994; Ericson et al. 1987, 1991; Hall et al. 1978; Golding and Middleton 1982; Miller 1994, Cohen and Young 1973; Burgess and Gold 1985). Our notions about where violence is likely to occur bear little relation to the nature of most assaults, especially when it comes to thinking about violence against women and children (Cream 1993; Valentine 1989). Such violence most commonly takes place in private inside the home, however it is public space (the street, the playground, the dark alley-way) that is often most feared. As many feminists have pointed out, the hidden dangers in our private lives are thus all but obscured by the overwhelming focus on public safety (Stanko 1990; Weaver 1998). When a women is raped or murdered (by someone other than her male partner), or a child abducted, news reporters flock to the scene. Descriptions of the place from where the victim was taken, or where the body was found, play upon and play out ideas about how safety and danger can be mapped against the world around us. Journalists evoke ideas about the wild/tame, savage/civilised, rural/urban, inner-city/countryside, familiar/strange to conjure up a sense of security and threat. Such images also run through the blossoming genre of true crime television involving endless dramatic reconstructions: the estate agent abducted from the empty property, the young woman who disappears while hitchhiking, the jogger attacked in the park by a 'pack' of 'foreigners' or the hapless tourist who wandered into a 'rough' neighbourhood (see Benedict 1992; Cuklanz 1996, 2000; Moorti 2002; Morrison 1992; Weaver 1998). There is even a flourishing tourism of sites of sexual violence; you can do a Jack the Ripper walk in London and come away with a T-shirt.[1]

What do journalists do then when sexual abuse is alleged to have occurred within the supposedly safe walls of the family home in a 'normal' community? How is story placing used in cases where the allegations are contested? The next section examines the way in which reports about Orkney evoked 'symbolic geographies' (Cream 1993) to imply that the allegations were implausible.

LOCATING THE STORY IN LANDSCAPE AND COMMUNITY: MEDIA ACCOUNTS OF ORKNEY

I forget who said 'Everywhere is a view from somewhere', but this is certainly true of media reporting. In the case of much of the reporting about Orkney, it was a view from London as London-based journalists were billeted away from the metropolis up to this outcrop of the British Isles. One had the sense that many of them needed to consult a map to locate the islands and could not quite believe that anywhere could be so far away from the capital or that anywhere so small could be the site of such a momentous story. (Reporting was, in this sense, reminiscent of reporting from the Falklands during the conflict with Argentina.) Press and TV reports showed pictures of aeroplanes or ferries, and maps emphasising the geographical isolation of Orkney. One outside news broadcast opened with the windswept reporter at the ferry terminal detailing the lengthy journey that must be taken to reach Orkney:

> The ferry at Scrabster, near John o'Groats, in the very north of Scotland. [...] serious fog has delayed all flights to Orkney for more than two days. Getting to Orkney was always difficult, but these weather conditions

only emphasise the isolation of the islands (Channel 4, *Seven O'Clock News*, 12 March 1991).

Reports from Orkney almost took the form of foreign reporting and journalists repeatedly emphasised the features that distinguished the islands from the bustling mainland, particularly mainland urban England. They portrayed Orkney as a sleepy, quiet string of islands where nothing much ever happened and their remoteness was used to underline their idyllic nature. Shots of the harbour on South Ronaldsay (the specific Orkney island which was the focus of concern), the farms or the surrounding hills were accompanied by captions and voice-overs which emphasised the traditional way of life, strong community and family values. South Ronaldsay was, we were told, 'a haven of peace' (BBC2, *Newsnight*, 15 March 1991). The accused parents were strongly associated with these values and the fact that they were all English incomers to the island was used to underline this. If the native Orcadians represented 'good working people', the incomers were identified as solidly middle-class (with a touch of 'the good life' about them). They had moved to Orkney to 'escape the rat race of contemporary urban society' (*Scotland on Sunday*, 10 March 1991) in pursuit of 'the simple' life' (Channel 4, *Seven O'Clock News*, 12 March 1991) or 'a quieter, more fulfilling' existence (*Sunday Times*, 1 September 1991). Indeed, they had chosen Orkney because 'It was regarded as a "place of safety" to bring up their children' (*Scotland on Sunday*, 10 March 1991). The latter phrase was used with deliberate irony, a 'place of safety' order is the name of the ruling used to take children away from their parents.

A picture was conjured up of an untouched place of innocent beauty (rather than, for example, a place of primitive and backward practices, which would be the other standard cultural association). Journalists used the conventions of tourist brochures to paint lyrical word pictures of the beautiful countryside, indeed some reports read rather like postcards home (of the wish-you-were-here variety). Journalists wrote, for example, of 'brilliant sunshine etching the hills and fields in spring gold' and explicitly linked this to the island's status as a secure playground for youngsters: 'It looked like the perfect safe haven for children to play ...' (*Express*, 6 April 1991). One newspaper published a picture showing the quarry where the abuse was supposed have occurred. The caption contradicted any potentially sinister readings of the image, describing the site in language reminiscent of a Laurie Lee novel: 'The farm quarry: "In that long, now lost summer, the place where the water warmed up and brought youngsters from miles around"' (*Scotland on Sunday*, 24 March 1991).

It was the social workers who were identified as the source of any discord or suspicion on the island. One of the few negative descriptions of the Orkney landscape was closely tied to negative representation of social workers and their obsessive desire to discover abuse. Where journalists often used pallets of green and gold to paint the landscape, on this occasion, the scene was conjured up entirely in greys:

> It is a story that can only be thought of in monochrome. There are houses of grey granite and a swirling Orcadian mist. At 7.00 am, as daylight breaks over the island of South Ronaldsay, social workers call on four families without warning. In their eyes is the cold hard light of those who believe they are about to strike at ultimate evil (*Daily Telegraph*, 5 April 1991).

Indeed, in some descriptions it was as if the social workers had introduced the notion of evil into some kind of contemporary Eden. One newspaper picture showed the parents looking over the Orkney landscape with the caption 'Paradise Lost'.

The corruption of childhood innocence was a recurring theme in reports of the children's experiences away from home. A much publicised interview with one of the Orkney children after his return, for example, was introduced in terms which contrasted nostalgic evocations of growing up in the countryside with the evils of urban living: 'And as he played with his dog in his South Ronaldsay farm yesterday, he spoke of learning to steal cars, roll a cannabis joint and glue sniffing' (*Daily Record*, 6 April 1991).

Light and dark, warmth and cold, sunshine and mist were also used to evoke different images of the nature of Orkney and to contrast parents and social workers. The seasons and the weather were often used rhetorically to indicate emotional states. A picture of a reunited family was accompanied by the caption 'Sunshine after the storm' (*Scotsman*, 6 April 1991), another article was headlined 'Back together. From magic summer to winter nightmare' (*Scotland on Sunday*, 7 April 1991). Indeed news reporting seemed to suggest that the weather was controlled by a benign being totally in support of the parents: 'After days of rain, the island was bathed in sunshine today, a fitting welcome back for the children' (ITV, *Early Evening News*, 17.40, 5 April 1991).

Intertwined with ideas about Orkney/South Ronaldsay as an island (its landscape, geographical location and its weather conditions) were ideas about the type of people who lived on Orkney, the nature of community relations and the islanders' collective reaction to the allegations. The community was repeatedly described as 'close-knit', and, as one native Orcadian declared: 'There are no secrets here ... If these people were guilty, we would all have known ... I would suspect myself before I suspected these people' (*Mail on Sunday*, 3 March 1991). The 'normally peaceful community' was, we were told, 'stunned and angered' by the removal of the children from their families (*News at Ten*, 5 March 1991; BBC1, *Nine O'Clock News*, 5 March 1991). It was emphasised that, even though the accused parents were incomers, 'their fellow islanders have rallied behind them' (Channel 4, *Seven O'Clock News*, 12 March 1991). As well as vox-pops with islanders, expressing their disbelief at the allegations, the media covered petitions and demonstrations in their support. Headlines included 'Islanders threaten to picket hearing into child abuse' (*Observer*, 3 March 1991); 'Islanders support families' (*Glasgow Herald*, 5 March 1991), or simply 'OUTRAGE: They all came together in the small hall to demand: give us back our children' (*Mail on Sunday*, 3 March 1991). Although a few press reports suggested some people in the community had turned against the incomers, in most reports the parents were closely identified with 'the community'. Viewers were informed that the whole community had been 'scarred' by the allegations (BBC1, *Six O'Clock News*, 4 April 1991) and the actual island was sometimes personified as sharing a single reaction. One headline read 'Fears of outraged island' (*Mail on Sunday*, 3 March 1991), another referred to 'Island anger' (*Evening News*, 4 March 1991), a third spoke of 'Village fury' (*Daily Mail*, 2 March 1991) while a fourth declared simply 'Orkney Reels' (*Scotland on Sunday*, 24 March 1991). This linguistic collapsing together of categories refuses any possible conflicts. Terms such as 'parents', 'families', 'islanders', 'village' and 'the island' were used interchangeably in a way which excluded the possibility of divergent interests between, for example, children and parents within a family and reinforced the idea that the entire community was of one mind.

There was one particularly striking exception to the pattern of reporting outlined above. This was an article in the *Evening News* (a Scottish newspaper). It challenged or inverted every feature of the reporting summarised above. The quarry (described in one example above as ' the place where the water warmed up and brought youngsters from miles around') featured in this report as 'remote', 'shrouded in mist' and 'partially filled with muddy water'. The island as a whole was described as 'a place so wild it appears to have been abandoned totally by both God and man'. The whole tone of the article was unusually negative about the accused parents and was explicitly sceptical about some of their assertions. It questioned whether the quarry the parents displayed to the journalists was, in any case, the 'right' quarry (i.e. the one that social workers considered might be a site of abuse). Far from echoing other reports of a united island, it described a tense and divided community (*Evening News*, 28 March 1991).

This exceptional report vividly illustrates the fact that the landscape and community of Orkney could be interpreted in other ways than those that predominated in most of the coverage. Its inversion of the themes also underlines the motivated and value-laden way in which a sense of place could be used to convey messages about the rights and wrongs of the case.

An analysis based on looking at the coverage alone could end here. The conclusion could be that the media overwhelmingly promoted a positive image of Orkney as a place and a community, and did so in a way which supported the parents' claims that they were victims of injustice. However, to say that the media 'promotes' a particular way of looking at an issue presupposes their effect on their audiences. If we look at how people actually responded to such imagery a rather more complex picture appears.

PEOPLE'S MEMORIES OF HOW
THE MEDIA REPRESENTED ORKNEY

As one might expect given the type of coverage indicated above, people do remember that the media had represented Orkney as an idyllic place and the site of a united community. Indeed, it is striking how, up to three and a half years after the event, people are able to echo the positive descriptions of the island and the community almost word for word. This aspect of the coverage has, for many people, made a very deep impression and the common readings of this aspect of reporting across a wide range of groups suggests this theme was a more monosemic than polysemic aspect of the coverage. Although often unable to reproduce many of the facts of

Figure 6.1 and 6.2 Orkney island harbour and an unusually sinister representation of the quarry – alleged to be the site of abuse. Two images from the television news coverage of the Orkney scandal.

the case beyond recalling the dawn raids and the link with Cleveland, people readily reconstruct news reports that described Orkney (South Ronaldsay) as a rural idyll with a tight-knit community. They often add explicit comments such as that it was 'the sort of place you wouldn't expect abuse to happen'. The following interaction while this group were attempting to reconstruct a news report about Orkney is typical:

> f1: How about we start [our news report] with [...] something like 'The sleepy something or other of, where did it take place? Was it Ronaldsay? [...]
> f2: OK, sleepy community of South Ronaldsay
> f1: Was rocked, shocked or what ...
> f3: Rocked by allegations of sexual abuse [...]
> f1: A friend of the parents, [...] reflected the community when she ...
> f1 and f2 [simultaneously]: Expressed anger and shock [laughter]
> f1: At such a decision
> f3: It's amazing how it sticks in your head
> f1: It's scary, isn't it, when you come out with the same thing (Group 1).

My research participants' reconstructions of news reports about Orkney usually open with references to 'a sleepy fishing village' (Group 23); a 'quiet wee place' (Group 11); 'a little seaside town with a population of 75' (Group 14) and a 'quiet community' in a 'small secluded village' with a 'quaint shore front' (Group 22). Social work interventions are presented as having disrupted the calm of 'the once peaceful village' (Group 21) or 'normally idyllic setting' (Group 18) and having 'shattered' the 'tranquillity' of this quiet community' (Group 46). The impact on the whole community is a recurring feature of the reconstructed reports produced by my research participants. One report opens with the words 'This [...] is a tranquil close-knit community which has been savagely shaken by the taking away of two children from one of the village's most well respected families' (Group 14). Support for, and outrage on behalf of, the parents is a central part of people's recall of the events. 'They just put the full island through misery, the full place they put through misery', comments one woman (Group 31, f). 'What I remember about Orkney', observes another, 'was that it just rocked the whole community' (Group 18, f).

The scripts that the groups produced echo many of the rhetorical devices identified in my analysis of the actual news reports. For example, the community is presented as synonymous with the families and, like the actual news reports from the time, statements often personify the place itself. One script opens with the words 'This remote and peaceful Scottish island of Orkney has been devastated' (Group 8). Others refer to South Ronaldsay 'reeling in shock' or declare that 'A sleepy Orkney hamlet today was devastated' (Group 15). 'A serene Orkney town has been ripped apart' (Group 23); 'the town was shaken' (Group 14) and 'a cloud hangs over the island' (Group 1). One script produced by my research participants concludes with the words 'The remote community in Orkney await the return of their children' (news reconstruction, Group 8).

If their scripts conclude with a happy ending with the children sent home, a return to normality is often stressed: 'homes ... were once again scenes of ... normal family life' (Group 32) and people talked about 'the town united again' (Group 4) and 'the village tries to rebuild itself' (Group 14). One script concluded: '[after] the happy reunion of the Orkney children with their parents [...] the people of Orkney will attempt to put this trauma behind them and rebuild their lives' (Group 2). Another even mentions the way the sunshine had come out and smiled on the island as the children flew back home (a point echoing almost word for word an actual report at the time, see above) (ITV, *Early Evening News*, 5 April 1991).

Clearly, the predominant media representation of Orkney has been understood and recalled.[2] But understanding and recalling a message is not necessarily the same as actually accepting it. Although aspects of reports were reproduced without criticism, others were produced in a reflective and self-conscious way, and even involved an element of parody. Occasionally research participants also deconstructed their accounts of the case, even as they reconstructed them, laughing about their own hyperbole or the clichéd way in which the media described Orkney.

The next important question is: how did the predominant media image of Orkney (as a place and as a community) relate to what people actually believed? How do they personally construct 'the geography' of safety and danger in relation to Orkney? How did media images of Orkney relate to their own ideas about the sort of place where abuse would occur or their personal knowledge, if any, of Scottish islands and rural communities? The next section examines these questions.

PEOPLE'S IMPRESSIONS AND BELIEFS

Analysis of how people relate to the news bulletins they wrote and how they discuss Orkney as a place identifies three common positions in relation to the media representation: acceptance, inversion and modification. These categories roughly parallel Stuart Hall's notion of dominant, negotiated and resistant readings (for a discussion of Hall's model see Chapter 2). However, I have chosen to use slightly different terminology to avoid some of the confusion often associated with the use of Hall's terms that conflates interpretation and reaction. My research makes it clear that people had a common 'reading' of the dominant message from the media even as they chose to respond to it in different ways. Also it is important to note none of these three responses to the coverage could be said to be truly radical, or to step outside the overarching framing of media reporting which associates sexual violence with only certain types of places/people. Only a very few group discussions were able to move beyond such common cultural notions and truly reject stereotypical associations, and this was facilitated not by media coverage, but by alternative personal and political insights.

Accepting the dominant message: 'it is just not that sort of place'

Many research participants simply accept that Orkney was just not the sort of place where abuse would happen. They speak positively of Orkney and have absorbed the image of a supportive tight-knit community and a place characterised by strong family values. Social workers, they conclude, were guilty of gross incompetence. This position closely accords with Hall's notion of a dominant reading. People taking this position do not necessarily notice the ideological content of representing Orkney as a rural idyll (although they sometimes do), and some can not imagine any alternative construction of Orkney. The research participants who adopt this perspective talk at length about the nature of life on Orkney and are sometimes able to expand on this with specific details about how children had been taken from this rural idyll and exposed to corrupting influences in care. As one comments: 'was there not something about a guy that got taught how to open cars or something like that, [...] . He'd been taken away and here's the real abuse going on' (Group 20, m).

Usually these people are totally dependent on media reports for their image of this part of the country. However a few back this up with descriptions of visiting Orkney (or 'similar' islands). A group of schoolgirls from Inverness for example, had personal knowledge of the islands. They say it was hard to believe that abuse could take place in Orkney because:

> f: [Orkney is] just small, wee crofters.
> f: Close-knit community.
> f: You wouldn't think it [abuse] would happen on a tiny little island in the north of Scotland, you'd think it would be more central, like Glasgow or Edinburgh or something.
> f: Yeah, like when you go to Orkney it's all like people fishing and taking lobsters in and selling them in the markets and that (Group 21).

Belief in the wholehearted support of native Orcadians for the accused parents informs their judgements that the parents had been unfairly victimised. Some research participants underline this perspective with their own knowledge of small community life:

> m: I really thought that it [the accusation] was a load of rubbish [...] If there was a certain proportion of the community at it the whole community would know about it. [...] I'm from a small community and they knew that the fighters were off to Libya before the national press even knew. Because it is a small community everybody knows everything. [...] But the entire community said 'we are absolutely bewildered' (Group 4, f).

The testimony of the community is crucial evidence in favour of the parents, particularly given that the parents were incomers. As one research participant who grew up in Orkney comments:

> Despite the fact they were incomers, they got the support of the locals, which was quite unusual. [...] There's usually quite a lot of antagonism. I would have expected the community not to rally round and the fact that they did suggested that it was more likely they were innocent (Group 32, m).

Inverting the dominant message: 'strange things go on in small isolated places'

A second position adopted by many research participants is in direct opposition to the perspective outlined above. This could be seen to accord with Hall's notion of oppositional reading (although quite whether this would count as a truly oppositional reading could also be disputed). These people recall that the news reporting had generally promoted a positive image of Orkney but vehemently reject this message. Those asserting this position are consciously opposed to what they identify as the dominant media presentation of Orkney. They have alternative images of the island as a sinister place, and the site of bizarre religious practices, precisely the sort of location where abuse would occur:

> Weird and strange things go on in small isolated places (Group 10, f).
> f: The Orkneys are an island aren't they? It's away from mainland society and an ideal place for witchcraft.
> m: All backwards, you think of it, don't you … ritual abuse usually happens on islands and the like (Group 14).
> It's so isolated and desolate. [...] When you think about it it's so likely that it could happen in one of these places (Group 22, f).

Sometimes they speak at length about the culture, habits, collusion, secrecy and insularity of island life:

> m: They tend to inter-marry don't they and, I mean, you don't know what's going to happen then do you?
> m: They could keep it sort of hushed up if everyone's involved [...] you could hush it up much more on a Scottish island than you could on the mainland (Group 43).
> You'd expect people to have really strong beliefs in something or other, whether it was in themselves or in God and they wouldn't expect themselves to be wrong because they don't have anyone to ask questions, you know. It's not like they wander around and get the opportunity to talk about a lot of things (Group 22, f).

From this perspective the notion that the community was close-knit is seen as a basis to suspect collusion rather than as evidence of the parents' innocence. Thus when one research participant refers to the support of 'the close-knit community' on Orkney, his co-participant replies: 'Aye, *too* close-knit' (Group 35, f).

Such ideas are not usually drawn from the media reporting of the Orkney case itself (which, as outlined above, usually eschewed such association). If people mobilise information from the media in defending this point of view it tends to involve reinterpretation of the media coverage (e.g. the 'too close-knit' comment). It also draws on broader cultural images of island life, including fictional representations. Two people, for example, say their understanding of island life had been influenced by seeing the film *The Wicker Man* (a film about devil worship in the Western Isles),[3] another comments '[Island life is] like *Lord of the Flies*, you develop your own rules' (Group 15). Others refer to the general genre of horror film in which murderers loom out of the mist to explain their negative associations with foggy, isolated islands. Several associate island living and paganism:

> Oh there was definitely some sort of cult ... all those islanders and what they're up to. I'd imagine that there'd be something weird like that going on. You hear about these magic circles [...], the sort of thing you see on the television, the drama series, I think it was *Inspector Morse*, like druids and that (Group 21, f).

On a few occasions research participants reinterpret images from the media coverage of Orkney in ways that ran directly counter to the accompanying voice-overs. For example, in a rare but striking example of the polysemy that may be invoked by images 'contradicting' words two research participants (in separate groups) recall watching television news reports from Orkney and being struck by the 'strange' appearance of the accused parents. They comment that whatever the reporter might have said, the camera actually showed parents dressed in rubber boots and woolly jumpers looking, as one put it, 'like new age hippie types'. This was an appearance which, according to these research participants, suggests they might well be 'into paganism and that kind of thing' (Group 1; Group 4).[4]

Such observations are sometimes underlined by reference to personal experience:

> I know quite a few people that have come from the islands and I know they're very, very, very secretive and they do not like outside interference. And they're definitely into cult things, and I don't think they're all innocent. I really don't think (Group 29, f).

One woman even draws, for her images of Orkney, on her late husband's experiences there over half a century ago:

> My husband was there during the First World War and he used to say there was nothing in Shetland and Orkney, it was just barren land. They

used to say 'bonny Scotland', that was a joke, it was nothing but sheep
and cattle where the soldiers were billeted. He hated it, he only done six
month there [...] He wanted back home, it was too quiet ... I'll tell you
something, there was a lot of funny things went on then (Group 35).

Others exchange anecdotes about the experiences of friends of
friends:

My friend went to Stornoway [in the Western Isles] and he was asked
to come and see the big bonfire. It was the Minister running down the
fiddlers, the Devil's music. He said there was a big pile of fiddles and he
looked at one, costs thousands of pounds, and he nearly cried when he
seen the whole lot went up in flames (Group 26, m).

These stories circulate as an alternative form of cultural repertoire
from which people can challenge the more positive images of Orkney,
and justify their suspicions that the social workers there did have
cause for concern.

Modifying the message: 'maybe they brought in something from where they came from'

A third position was the argument that Orkney might be a rural
idyll but that these positive attributes cannot be associated with
the accused parents because they were incomers. This perspective
could be seen to accord with Hall's idea of a negotiated reading.
This was espoused by a minority of the groups in my research but
is still worth mentioning as a clearly distinguishable point of view.
These participants accept the positive representation of Orkney and
Orcadians but challenge the media image of an island united in
support of the parents. Some adopt that position because they know
people from the islands, either directly or as friends of friends, and,
in Scotland, the case was subject to extensive discussion and gossip.
Thus one woman speaks about the opinions of two native Oracadians,
relayed to her via her mother-in-law. 'They say something must have
happened up there. [...] he says there is satanical whatever, there's
definitely *something*' (Group 11). Another recounts the point of view
of a friend from Orkney: 'According to my friend the local people were
nothing to do with it, not at all implicated in it. [My friend thought]
it was just typical incomers causing trouble again, giving the island a
bad name, causing trouble for the island people' (Group 7, f). A third
person describes how he became more suspicious about the accused

parents after sounding out several Orcadian acquaintances: '... that was through speaking to Orcadians, one in particular coloured my view of it. [He] said, they were all incomers, people bringing in things. Whether it was true or not, I know that coloured my opinion after that.' Turning to me (the English facilitator of this group discussion) he added: 'No disrespect to certain people here though, but [as] some of them are English [...] maybe they brought in something from where they came from' (Group 19, m).

This view was echoed in several other groups of Scottish people: 'The accused people weren't Orcadians themselves, they were all outsiders [...] That they were English made it more suspicious' (Group 18, f); 'A lot of them (the accused) have moved up there [...] I think it is more the criminal element that's being put in there' (Group 21, f).

Indeed, in one of these groups one woman had not realised that the accused parents were incomers, but on hearing this information she was prepared to reconsider her previous assertion that the parents were innocent:

> m: The thing that made me think about it was the fact that they are all incomers. They weren't local people, they were all English incomers.
> f: That sheds a different light on it, that makes you think (Group 4).

It is worth noting that all the respondents quoted above live in Scotland and many claim some kind of direct or indirect access to opinion on Orkney. They came to their conclusion in spite of, rather than because of, the media coverage of the case. They had either picked up information from the media and reinterpreted this to reach different conclusions than those implied in media reports or they had accessed gossip and friends-of-friends to gain their own impressions of community reactions.

Different conceptual sentences, but a common grammar: similarities between these three accounts

On the face of it, the three positions outlined above may appear very different. In traditional media terms those taking the first position are following a dominant reading, while those adopting the second or third position might be described as reading the Orkney coverage against the grain or, in Hall's terms as adopting oppositional and negotiated readings respectively. A great deal of investigation has focused on the diverse ways in which people interpret or respond to specific programmes (usually shown to research participants on video) (e.g. Morley 1980). The concern in such work is to examine how people resist the intended meaning of the programme producers (or the preferred meaning as identified by the researchers). In this sense the second interpretation outlined above is the most clearly resistant or oppositional. The research participants who declare that islands were likely to harbour child abusers, consciously oppose the predominant presentation of the Orkney story. They resist what they see as the manipulative self-presentation of the Orkney parents and refuse to accept what they understand to be the preferred meaning of most of the press and television reporting. Sometimes they quite self-consciously read against the grain.

However, the limits of the terminology 'opposition' and 'resistance' must be recognised. First, as I have already pointed out, it is important to draw a distinction between how people understand the message, and how they respond to it (a distinction often blurred by the concept of reading). More important still, the fact that people can resist such meanings does not mean that the media have no influence. It simply means that a particular message (the Orkney parents must be innocent because Orkney is such a nice place) can be disputed. This resistance is itself supported by other media messages. Positive reporting about Orkney may be challenged by drawing on books or films or other television or press representations of island life as strange or backward, however this cannot be used as grounds for generalising about audience resistance to media power in any broader way.

Rather than highlighting the differences between these three types of response it is more important to identify their shared framing. These first three groups have more in common than divide them. They may differ about whether or not Orkney is a nice place or whether or not the accused parents were therefore nice people, but they all retain the underlying construction that abuse does not happen in nice places/communities. They also often share the assumption that neighbours would be aware if abuse was taking place. Whether or not they accept the specifics of the coverage of the Orkney case, they are accepting a similar framework of thinking. They may construct different types of conceptual sentence, but they are working within the same rules of grammar. They share a fundamental acceptance of sites of danger which are (differently) entangled with ideas about class and normality, and concepts about urban versus rural, England versus Scotland, modern versus old-fashioned, and Christian versus pagan.

Outright rejection: refusing the relevance of story placing

It would be wrong to imply that people had fixed commitments to each of the three positions outlined above or were unreflective about their assumptions. Explicit rejections of this sort of logic are evident in many of the focus groups from at least one individual at least some of the time. People make statements such as 'It's going on in normal families and normal communities' (Group 46, m) or 'I think sexual abuse could happen anywhere. It doesn't surprise me that it is Orkney, doesn't surprise me that it wouldn't be Orkney' (Group 11, f). Indeed, several participants are quite conscious, and critical, of the way in which the media mobilised a sense of place for ideological ends. One condemns the way Orkney was repeatedly portrayed as 'a nice place to be, sort of middle-class, cucumber sandwiches stuff' (Group 23, f). Another comments on the manipulative devices employed in a particular documentary about the case:

> They had a documentary on BBC Scotland and the kind of closing shot in the documentary was this beautiful sunset over the west of Orkney, the sun going down on the island. [...] The sort of message that came from that sort of closing still was: how could anything like that happen in a place like this? (Group 32, m).

Even so, although many people are aware of such devices and expressly state that abuse can happen anywhere very few are able to maintain this position throughout the discussion. Many admit to 'gut instincts' or 'intuitive responses' that contradict their expressed intellectual position. Some of those who explicitly reject the relevance of ideas about geography and community in assessing the Orkney case, go on to implicitly use such notions as they talk about it in more depth. Sometimes they become self-conscious about this as they talk and reflect on the way certain cultural assumptions had been 'hammered' into them. For example, one man observes:

> I seem to be saying that it doesn't surprise me that something nasty happens there because I don't like [the place]. I try not to make sweeping generalisations [...] but I would have thought 'yeah, it happened'. I can't really escape that because it's been hammered into me (Group 14, m).

The few people who are able to position themselves consistently outside such discourses are worthy of closer attention. These people are clear that place and community have nothing to do with their judgements about Orkney. This position is often combined with the assertion that neighbours would, in any case, not necessarily be aware if abuse was taking place.

Those who consistently articulate a rejection of media promoted assumptions about dangerous/safe places/communities often describe events in their own lives which convinced them that abuse could be carried out 'right under your nose' but in complete secrecy. For example when one research participant asserts that the community would have known if anything had been going on because 'It sounded like a right close-knit community, you know, everybody knows each other's business.' Another responds: 'Well, I live in a small [housing] scheme and there was a scout leader charged with abusing boys over 20 odd years, and nobody knew about it and he was supposed to be a respected member of the community' (Group 34, f).

The three groups who collectively and vehemently reject the idea that abuse is linked with certain types of place have compelling personal and political experiences which have led them to this position. One group, whose members retain a complete and absolute rejection of such discourse, are a group of charity activists working on projects in the less economically developed world.[5] These participants make it clear that they completely reject the idea that it would ever be possible to judge the likelihood of abuse on the basis of the type of place or community in which it was supposed to have occurred. They talk at length about stereotypes of Africa and India and about how these influence public attitudes and political policies in different parts of the world.

The second group who consistently rejects media discourse about Orkney as a place is a support group for incest survivors. Several women in this group are highly critical of the way in which Orkney was pictured 'like a wee postcard' which implied 'like nothing ever happens here' (Group 6, f). They speak about the way in which pictures can deceive. One woman who was hosting the group meeting in her home fetched her own family photo album to show me how pictures could lie. Another talks at length about her anger at such superficial judgements and her own experience of being abused in a 'nice' middle-class family and the difficulty of drawing attention to her plight. Her parents presented a normal, respectable front to the world; the abuse she suffered was well-hidden, including from close friends and neighbours.

A similar proactive rejection of the notion that abuse only happens in certain types of place/community also comes from a third group, a group of neighbours active in their local community centre. This centre is in a notoriously deprived and 'rough' area of Glasgow, the type of place, they say, which job-seekers should avoid giving as an address for fear of discrimination. This group is very conscious of how an area's reputation can influence judgements about its inhabitants. They explicitly deconstruct media representations of Orkney, resenting the way in which those on the side of the parents had tried to exploit a wholesome and middle-class image of the locale. They contrast this privileged image with the stigma attached to their own inner-city area. As one women declares:

> A lot of people questioned if it did or didn't happen because it was Orkney. [...] If the same sort of thing had happened [in this area] in Campbell Street everybody would have just thought 'Och, that must have happened there.' [...] Because people tend to look at an area and just say 'Oh that's a ghetto [...] and yes, it probably did happen there' (Group 8, f).

In each of the last three groups cited above, participants are at the receiving end of stereotypes about places of safety and danger. They are also actively involved in working with other people in similar situations (i.e. the incest survivors self-help group and community centre). These factors seem to help them to step outside the grammar that associates sexual abuse with certain types of places and not others. At the very least it ensures they are careful not to suggest they ascribe to any such sentiments in the group context. Perhaps it is only these few groups who can be truly said to be oppositional in Hall's terms and to challenge the broader hegemonic framing of the issue.

CONCLUSION

This chapter has highlighted how one particular factor, story placing, can operate. It has highlighted how journalists mobilise and reinforce culturally embedded notions about the type of place where violence occurs. Such analysis of media coverage can usefully be applied to a range of topics. In focus groups I conducted about AIDS, for example, story placing proved important in how the media reported, and how people responded to, information about AIDS in Africa. Some people found the idea that HIV originated in Africa easy to accept because of pre-existing images of the 'dark continent' (Kitzinger and Miller 1992).

Comparison across different case studies could also be illuminating. It would be interesting, for example, to examine how journalists describe the home of paedophiles who have abducted and imprisoned children. The house of the Belgian rapist and murderer Dutroux, complete with dungeon, would be a case in point, as would the house of Frank and Rosemary West who buried bodies in the basement. Often in such cases attention drawn to the normality of the scene exploits the contrast rather than challenges it. This was comprehensively illustrated in descriptions of the house dubbed by the media 'The House of Horrors' where the Wests hid the bodies of their murder victims (Wykes 1998). Captions read 'So Normal, So Chilling' and descriptions underlined the contrast between scenes of apparent 'normality' and acts of extreme 'depravity': 'On the wall the infamous address is written in wrought iron. A lucky horse shoe above the door completes the suburban scene' ('The Last Rites', *Mirror*, 9 March 1994). We were treated to computer simulations of the interior of the house; encouraged to imagine that we are walking through the rooms. We were shown photographs of the bedroom: 'On the bed is a small cuddly toy – and a model of Paddington Bear is on a shelf behind ...' (*Mirror*, 7 March 1994). We were led into the 'beige-tiled' bathroom (beige being the ultimate non-entity colour) and told how this was filled with everyday items: 'a crushed tube of toothpaste, an arrangement of plastic flowers'. We were invited into the lounge, where 'a cushion perches on the knitted settee cover. It's embroidered with the word "Dad"' (*Mirror*, 8 March 1994). The irony is that very similar descriptions are used by journalists visiting the homes of parents protesting their innocence.

This chapter has also offered additional reflections on media influence and audience reception processes. It has shown how some people, at least some of the time, were influenced against the social workers and in favour of the parents through the emotive descriptions of Orkney combined with their pre-existing ideas about the type of place in which child sexual abuse would or would not occur. The social and geographical placing of a story in any particular case is thus a crucial analytical tool. However, it would be wrong to create a simplistic model of how such story placing operates on audiences. The group discussions indicate how complex this process can be. Media influence does not always result in a neat absorption of the predominant media message; not everyone accepts Orkney as a peaceful rural idyll or agrees that this made the incomers unlikely abusers. Nor are judgements solely based on the media representations of the Orkney case; other cultural images are important and personal contact and 'gossip' is a factor. However, the underlying logic of the association between certain types of place and abuse is accepted by many research participants (even if sometimes against their better judgement). The media (both in their reporting of the Orkney case and in other reports about crime and sexual violence) play a part in helping to maintain this assumption.

Of course, the media have also been a conduit for public statements that sexual abuse happens across all classes and strata of society, in villages as well as cities, in rural as well as urban locations. Although the notion that sexual abuse might happen in normal homes is acknowledged as a fact, it is rarely developed at the level of symbolism (for further discussion of this last point see Chapter 7). It is perhaps not surprising then that although people often know intellectually that sexual abuse can happen anywhere, this fact is rarely fundamentally absorbed into people's ways of thinking.

This chapter suggests the need for a nuanced and socially embedded understanding of how cultural representations intersect with our sense of sites of danger. It challenges those who exaggerate textual polysemy by pointing to the common understanding of the dominant media message across a wide range of groups. As other studies have found, there is often a clear and common sense of the preferred meanings in media texts across a wide range of groups (Morley 1980:140). It also challenges those who would use evidence of negotiated or superficially oppositional readings as evidence for optimism. Such readings are not necessarily radical, nor are they necessarily resourced from some media-free zone. Truly alternative frameworks of understanding, such as that necessary to refuse any attempt to link sexual abuse with only certain types of places, can be identified. However, such frameworks (so alien to most media representations) are not commonly accessible. They are forged through alternative networks in spite of media coverage and are the exception rather than the rule.

7
Social Currency, Stranger-Danger and Images of Abusers

How do journalists portray perpetrators of sexual violence? How might such profiles impact on who we think about as dangerous and relate to our everyday ways of knowing? This chapter steps back from the specific case studies of how people think about particular scandals to consider public perceptions of sex offenders in general.

This chapter shows how journalists often promote stock images of child abusers, perpetuating unhelpful stereotypes which highlight the threat from 'psychotic' strangers and obscure the more common form of abuse; by known, trusted and 'well-adjusted' adults. I also show how the media fail to confront the fact that child sexual abuse is overwhelmingly committed by men, and thus evade the questions about masculinity and male power that feminist analysis of sexual violence suggests we should address. This chapter also broadens out the terms of the enquiry. My research highlights the ways in which stories about threatening outsiders are integrated into day-to-day experience circulating in parental encounters and community discussions. Certain stories and rumours, I argue, have a great deal of 'social currency' or exchange value. The social structuring of such exchange is a key to examining public responses to mass media representations and developing an understanding of how media messages operate within, parallel to and through social interaction.

BEASTS, DEVILS, QUEERS AND SISSIES: IMAGES OF SEX OFFENDERS

'It is impossible to identify a paedophile on sight, the abuser could be anyone, including a respectable member of the community.' This is an important message from organisations campaigning to protect children. The media sometimes explicitly acknowledge this. However, a different impression is conveyed by the way in which abusers are often represented. The media, especially the tabloid press, tend to present sex offenders as very different from other men, and often imply that they are easily identifiable misfits (for critiques see Brownmiller 1975/1977; Benedict 1992; Kitzinger and Skidmore 1995a; Meyers 1997; Soothill and Walby 1991). A chilling piece of footage featured in the coverage of the Soham murders in 2003 in the UK; it showed a school caretaker speaking to journalists, expressing his concern for the missing children and his horror that men with such proclivities might be living in the community. It was this man who was eventually charged with the murders. It is only with the benefit of hindsight that the irony of such an interview becomes apparent.

At the crudest level sex offenders are often personified as either devilish, bestial or sub-human. For every one headline using a straightforward term such as 'man' for someone who has sexually abused a child (e.g. 'Man sought over sex assault') there are three headlines describing them in terms such as 'fiend', 'pervert', 'monster' or 'animal' (Kitzinger 1999). Such reporting is often accompanied by disturbing mug shots of these 'beasts' with captions or headlines drawing attention to their distinctive appearance, e.g. 'Evil Mr Staring Eyes' (*Sun*, 2 May 1991). If the photograph makes the abuser look too normal, then some parts of the media will resort to the Jekyll and Hyde metaphor identifying the picture with captions such as 'Smile that hid the violent depravity of sex fiend headmaster' (*Star*, 12 April 1991).

Feminist theorists point out that, in fact, one of the few things that distinguish people who commit sexual violence from people who do not, is that the former are usually male. Although women do sometimes commit sex crimes they are much less likely to do so. Feminists argue that this should have implications for how we theorise about sexual violence and how we analyse masculinity, sexuality and power (Brownmiller 1975). The media, however, mainly fail to engage in this debate.[1] Instead, they represent men who assault children as the 'personification of evil'. They use language of supernatural extra-social forces and condense the problem into the individual criminal in ways which displace consideration of social context and social process which shape crime. (For a discussion of this issue in the reporting of crime in general see Cohen 1972; Hall *et al.* 1978; Cohen and Young 1973; Golding and Middleton 1982.) Journalists also usually evade remarking on the gender of sexual assailants and then subtly (or not so subtly) present abusers as 'unmanly'.

One strategy to distance child sex abusers from 'ordinary men' or traditional ideas about masculinity is to associate attacks on children with homosexuality. There is a striking asymmetry here in labelling of male-on-female and male-on-male attacks. When a man attacks a girl this is never identified as a heterosexual assault, but when a man attacks a boy this is often identified as homosexual. Analysing all national British press reporting for one year, for example, showed that the abuser or act of abuse was explicitly identified as 'homosexual' in 50 newspaper articles and headlined as such seven times, e.g. 'Man tells of homosexual abuse by care staff' (*Independent*, 10 October 1991). By contrast no assailant or assault was ever explicitly identified as heterosexual. This was in spite of the fact that most of the reported incidents involved attacks by men on girls.

Unlike the use of terms such as 'monster' and 'beast' which is much more likely to occur in the tabloids, identifying abuse as gay in a discriminatory way is evident in both tabloid and 'quality' press. A case in point is the coverage of the Frank Beck case, a man who over many years assaulted boys in the care home in which he worked and also raped a young woman in his care. This coverage often included implicitly homophobic statements. The most liberal UK newspaper, the *Guardian*, for example, uncritically reported dismay at the fact that a care worker was allowed to foster two boys 'even though there were complaints that he was homosexual' (*Guardian*, October 1991).[2] It is hard to imagine the parallel sentence 'he was allowed to foster two girls even though there were complaints that he was heterosexual'. Such blurring of homosexuality and paedophilia was evident in the reporting of other cases too. In one ill-advised phrase a journalist for the *Sunday Times* stated that police investigating a sex murder had interviewed 92 men: 'Not all of them were paedophiles; sometimes they were straight men' (*Sunday Times*, 23 June 1991). Here being 'straight' and being a paedophile are used as mutually exclusive categories.

The figures presented above do not take into account all the references that may imply homosexuality when abusers are introduced as 'bachelors', for example, or described as effeminate. Take the example of the social worker, Frank Beck, again. The young woman he attacked was a lesbian. When he raped her he stated that he was going to show her what 'a real man' was like. This reported statement could have been used by journalists to explore the definition of what it meant to be 'a real man' and, indeed, to reflect on compulsory heterosexuality. However, instead, the bulk of reporting simply reiterated gender and sexual stereotypes. Frank Beck was 'a sissy':

Frank Beck had a lonely and disturbed childhood – and grew up to be a sex monster. Before he was 13 he was sexually assaulted by a man on a train. And he was teased about being like a girl. Students at agricultural college dubbed him Mrs Beck. Beck stood out from other boys because he did not drink, swear or know about girls (*Star*, 30 November 1991).

THE DANGER THAT PROWLS OUR STREETS

'Sexual violence against children is most often perpetrated by someone they know.' This fact is sometimes included in media reporting of abuse. However, the actual balance of coverage gives a very different picture. 96 per cent of newspaper articles about how to protect children focus on threats from strangers, only 4 per cent even partially address the most common category of abuse, abuse by fathers, uncles, stepfathers, brothers and other family members (Kitzinger and Skidmore 1995a). Most news reports also focus on stranger-attacks (apart from cases where the allegations are contested) (see Collings 2000). The abduction and murder of children by strangers is cause for national shock and alarm. But headlines such as 'WEEP, 3 children murdered in 100 hrs as Britain sinks to a new low' (*Sun*, 14 August 1991) ignore the fact that 150 to 200 children meet their death every year at the hands of their own mother or father; one child is killed in this way every two or three days, year in, year out. Where are the headlines about these startling figures? Like murder, sexual abuse is often a 'domestic' crime. A large proportion of such abuse is by relatives or friends of the family (NSPCC 1992). Front-page treatment of these cases, however, is rare.

Stranger-danger stories have great appeal to journalists. The random and public nature of such attacks makes every reader or viewer potentially at risk from the 'pervert on the loose'. Such cases often combine sex and murder. They also have ongoing narrative momentum (the appeal by parents for the missing child, the eventual tragic discovery) and they come with their own available images (the little girl in her school uniform, the security video footage of her last journey, the police searching wasteland). By contrast, incest cases are far less easy to report. This is sometimes because of ethical and legal restrictions. The Press Complaints Commission's guidelines, for example, quite rightly advise journalists that: 'Care must be taken that nothing in the report implies the relationship between the accused and the child' and 'the word incest must not be used where a child victim might be identified' (www.pcc.org.uk/cop/cop. asp). Incest cases are thus often not reported at all, or described as if they involved a perpetrator unrelated to the victim.

Over and above this, journalists may, in any case, see such abuse as less relevant, and less palatable to their listeners, readers or viewers. Some newspaper editors do not see a 'family newspaper' as an appropriate place to mention incest. There is a deep-seated resistance to publicising this aspect of sexual abuse, both within media organisations and among potential sponsors of the charities that promote awareness about child abuse. This is widely remarked upon by children's charities. As one representative from Kidscape (an organisation promoting child safety) explains, 'Advertisers, people who want to sponsor us, [think that stranger-danger] is a subject they're happy to talk about. [But] people don't want to be associated with child abuse as incest.'

The same is true, in her experience, of journalists:

It's a message we try to get across to the press [that most children are abused by people they know] but they're very wary, [...] it's not a fun subject, it's likely to put readers off, may upset readers, and it's easier and safer to concentrate on strangers and bullying (See Kitzinger and Skidmore 1995b).

PUBLIC PERCEPTIONS OF ABUSERS

The message that abusers 'could be anyone' has reached people to some extent. Most research participants state that that 'intellectually' they know 'it's not just men in dirty macs'. 'It could be anybody', 'Most normalest person', 'They don't wear a badge' (Group 43). However, many also admit they would find it very hard to believe allegations made against anyone who was part of their own social circle. Here it is worth having a closer look at how people talk about 'paedophiles' both in the concrete and in the abstract.

Research participants routinely distance themselves from anyone who could possibly commit such an act. Indeed, expressions of disgust and incomprehension, particularly by and between men, seem to be an important ritual as some groups settle down into the discussion.

A geezer's [...] got to be sick to be able to do it to his own daughter ... just physically, I personally physically couldn't do it (Group 40, m).

It's just beyond me, because I've got a daughter as well. I think that the people that do these things must have something seriously wrong with them mentally ... to actually comprehend doing it. I couldn't personally feel sexual toward [...] a harmless child (Group 4, m).
m: Anyone who's normal just doesn't understand it, it's incomprehensible.
m: It's a no-no, isn't it. It's just like a brick wall (Group 43).

The obscenity of abuse is beyond comprehension, people shrug their shoulders and make statements such as '*Obviously*, I don't know any child abusers, but I can't imagine what sort of person could do that' (Group 14, m).

This assumption that they cannot possibly know any child abusers is often accompanied by a sense that, if they did meet an abuser, they would instinctively know.

Sometimes, even in spite of their own better judgement, people have a very clear mental image of a child abuser. One trainee journalist, for example, describes her reactions to attending court and acknowledges her own prejudices:

I've been to a child abuse case and I just remember this man [...] just looked like a hollow with the cheekbones and *just* how you imagine a child abuser to look like. [...] even though you're innocent until proven guilty, because he fitted the image I could imagine him doing it (Group 23, f).

Others say they think of men who abuse children as 'Mr Ultra Creepy! People that you just look at, [and] you see a dodgy guy' (Group 20, m). The look of the eyes is often mentioned; responding to a TV image, one person commented: 'He had these wild eyes [...] if you were going to draw up a picture of someone who was abusing children, it would have been a picture of him really' (Group 19, f). One woman recalled 'a case in the East End a couple of years ago – there was a bloke who looked particularly odd, he had staring eyeballs' (Group 23, f). Others mentioned the police mug shot of the Moors murderer, Myra Hindley, which is endlessly reproduced in the British press. One man imagines abusers to have 'staring eyes'; he says: 'Staring eyes [...] like Myra Hindley [...] when you see a photo you think "oh yeah, I can tell"' (Group 14, m).

People also often assume that child abusers are mentally disabled or obviously mad. A child abuser is likely to be '... inadequate in some sort of way aren't they, and aren't quite the full ticket' (Group 43, m). The person most likely to pose a danger is 'a fruitcake' (Group 43, m); 'a nutter' (Group 4, m); 'a maniac wandering the streets' (Group 18, f).

Child abusers are also often described as 'weedy' and 'not very butch'. One research participant says she would expect an abuser to be 'thin, weasly like [...] in a scrawny suit' (Group 23, f). Another talks of 'a little guy, sort of thin, anorak type' (Group 20, m). Abusers are 'effeminate' and may be what one research participant describes as 'the lives with his mother type'.

> m: The sort of unmarried bachelor type, never married, never had children.
> f: Someone that couldn't conduct normal sexual relationships.
> [...]
> f: Didn't relate to women.
> f: Not butch at all, I never imagine a butch abuser (Group 23).

Sometimes paedophiles are explicitly assumed to be gay. Some people are self-conscious and ambivalent about this stereotype, but still feel that it influences them. One man for example, says that he reluctantly gives himself licence to discriminate against gay men, for the sake of his boys:

> If a man's homosexual why does that mean he naturally preys on young boys? It's daft really. Your prejudice is clicking in, I like to think I'm an extremely liberal person but it all goes out the window as soon as my own family becomes involved (Group 37, m).

Other groups, however, are less ambivalent. A few move seamlessly between discussing paedophilia and homosexuality. The following exchange, for example, occurs in the middle of a discussion about 'it' (child sexual abuse) and I have to clarify what they are talking about:

> m: Once it was illegal, wasn't it. Then it was optional. Now they've made it legal and I'm thinking of emigrating before they make it compulsory! [laughter]
> JK: What's 'it'? What's 'it' in this case?
> m: Poofters! [laughter]

m: I actually think they made it legal for men because half the MPs are bent (Group 40).

Indeed liberalising laws against homosexuality and allowing gay men or lesbians to work with, or adopt, children is, in some groups, identified as a failure to protect children from potential abuse. (Such embedded knowledge is not, of course, only evident among ordinary lay people, it informs the anti lesbian and gay legislation in various countries and is used to defend discriminatory ages of consent for gay men.)

Class and education also come into people's assessment of who is likely to abuse children. Well educated men are sometimes seen as less liable to abuse. One trainee journalist, for example, who was self-critical of her assumptions about the appearance of abusers, is less reflective about her class assumptions. She is confident that the alleged abusers she has seen in court represent the majority and therefore concludes that intelligence and education must militate against abuse. The defendants, she says, always seemed to be poorly educated or unintelligent. Most 'educated people', she concludes, would intercept their own sexual responses to a child and stop themselves actually doing anything whereas 'Most people you see in court tend not to look overly bright. [...] they are not always very with it' (Group 23, f). A similar idea was echoed in another group which focused on the 'chaotic' (and working-class) nature of the typical 'sex abuse family':

m: I think a lot of the time as well, it's the sort of background people are from. [...] It's normally people, when you see them on the television, with pretty grubby houses and [...] it's always run down.
m: One-parent families, grubby houses.
m: Basement tenement block or something, waste ground or something, its not sort of ...
m: [...] [not] a normal type of person (Group 43).

Intertwined with these ideas is an assumption that abusers would not be the sort of person they might like or admire. This applies to people in the public eye, as well as their immediate neighbourhood. Thus, for example, when discussing whether singer Michael Jackson or filmmaker Woody Allen might be guilty of sexual abuse (both allegations made in the media at various times), responses sometimes seem to be influenced by whether they were fans of, or could identify with, either celebrity.

> f: No, not Michael Jackson, not him [he's not a child abuser].
> JK: Why not?
> f: My son's going to be the next Michael Jackson – he can do all the dance routines [laughter] (Group 8, f).

On the other hand, other participants think both Michael Jackson and Woody Allen are perfectly capable of abusing children because both are 'weird'. Comments about Jackson refer to his 'confused' identity and pet chimpanzee: 'his odd lifestyle ... perhaps that influences our decisions ... he's going white and he's black ... you wouldn't put anything past him. You know, ... how many people have a close relationship with a chimp?' (Group 37, m).

Comments about Woody Allen include references to his shuffling gait and his 'peculiar' or 'alien' ways of thinking: 'He's weird. I think he is quite easily capable of abuse. He's got a warped sense of humour so how does his brain work?' (Group 9).

It is not surprising that people were often confident that no one among their family and friends could possibly be an abuser. They could not imagine any such thing going on within their own social circle or communities. Asked if she could accept it might be happening in her neighbourhood one woman comments: 'I can't imagine it happening to anyone I know, [...] it's very hard to take on board. You couldn't imagine anyone doing something like that' (Group 4).

In another group a woman comments:

> You can't imagine that. Oh my goodness, if a man that lived next door to us, was out doing so and so and such and such and you just ... I can't believe that these kind of things go on. I know that they do, but it is like the ostrich thing. Because if you really ... you just wouldn't go out, you wouldn't do anything (Group 9).[3]

Her neighbour confirms that she feels the same: 'If it is happening in [our area/community] you would tend to say that it can't be happening here. You know the people so well. If it was happening on your doorstep you wouldn't believe it' (Group 9).

But she adds (in a statement that still positioned the threat literally 'beyond the threshold'): 'But it can happen on your doorstep. That is usually where you find these sorts of people. They tend to lurk around playgrounds' (Group 9).

This attitude is shared by several other groups, and in a few cases people flatly deny that sexual abusers could live in their neighbourhood:

f: They wouldn't be living up here if that's the case.
f: [...] No, I don't know of any.
f: Because you all know one another, we all know their businesses and everything. Everybody knows – see, like if [anyone did anything] ... *everybody* would know (Group 10).

On a few occasions however, people do describe particular individuals of whom they feel suspicious, even if they think this is irrational. Invariably suspicions focus on 'loners', those on the very margins of their social circle, often people who are 'too quiet':

I've got a couple live opposite me, must be in their sort of late 60s I suppose ...They really are a pair of recluses, they don't ever come out their front garden. And he goes off about 10 o'clock every night and he's back there in the morning. Strange behaviour, whether he's got a night job or something I don't know but [...] I'm suspicious, what the bloody hell's he up to? [...] [Because] they don't fit the norm, [...] they never say anything (Group 43, m).
They're quiet, they don't get involved with other people, they keep their own personal life to theirself, they don't tell you anything about theirself. [...] Like most blokes sit and talk a lot of old crap when we're having a drink, you know, [but] [not them] ... Too frightened aren't they? (Group 40, m).
He never speaks to anybody and he's totally [into] fishing [...] I'm sure he is going to want to, one day perhaps, he's going to want to sort of become involved in a sexual way and whether he's going to force [it] [...] because saying 'hello' I'm sure is something that bothers him (Group 14, m).

A few people had to confront actual allegations (or convictions) against people they knew. This was often startling because it challenged their stereotypes.[4] One man recalls how a young colleague was convicted for flashing at little girls: 'You would never have known that he was like that. You'd never think anybody his age would do it, he was just one of the boys' (Group 18, m). Another stumbled on child pornography at his boss's house, the last person you would think might be 'like that', he comments, because he was 'built like a brick shit house'. A third was shocked at the conviction of an acquaintance for sexually abusing his daughter. This was totally unexpected because 'He was a real nice chap, and see if anything suggestive came on the television, the likes of women or a bedroom scene he'd say "I've got no time for that, you know"' (Group 26, m).

Sometimes such incidents made people reassess their assumptions. One research participant describes how a local case, 30 years earlier, had made an indelible impression, not least because the man had 'shiny shoes'. Here she is commenting on her mother-in-law's assumptions, as much as her own:

> The chap used to come past my mother-in-law's window every Sunday and he had shiny shoes [...] and she used to draw comparisons to my husband at the time because he wore suede shoes and you should always wear shiny polished shoes ... And two or three months after that [it was revealed in the papers that] he had been [found guilty of sexual abuse] and yet that chap was going up the road with his shiny shoes every Sunday and held up as a respectable member of society. That was about 30 years ago, that always stuck in my head (Group 30, f).

Another recalls his surprise at the conviction of a workmate, even when, in retrospect, his behaviour with his daughter had been obviously inappropriate:

> It had been going on for a good while, she was 14 or 15 when she started but she used to come up the firm and sit on his lap and everything you know [...] [but] you just never ever think, never, that it might be happening with someone you know (Group 40, m).

Another young woman learned the hard way that stereotypes did not always apply. She expresses intense anger at having been so ill-equipped to respond to her younger sister's needs:

> I think they should do something about it because my little sister was sexually abused by our next door neighbour, and [when] she told me, I didn't want to believe her. I knew this man and as far as I was concerned anyone I knew ... he couldn't do it. I didn't want to believe it had happened. [...] She said 'Marie, somebody was touching me and I don't

like it.' I said 'Who was it?' and she said 'Stephen' and I said 'No, no, no, Stephen couldn't do anything like that' (Group 25, f).

However, some people continue to reject the possibility that people they know and like could abuse children. One research participant finds it difficult to consider the possibility that a friend of hers might have abused his nieces as they allege. Her reluctance is, she said, informed by the fact that he is married and 'You couldn't meet a nicer couple and they've got six children, a family of their own, [...] he's such a good person in his daily life, he does charity work for prisoners and things like that' (Group 34, f).

Another research participant vehemently defends a man she knows, even though he was found guilty in court: 'I don't believe it. I don't believe he could do it', she says, 'I've seen him with children and I don't think it's possible. He's *brilliant* with kids' (Group 25, f).

Where most people had difficulty believing that apparently 'nice' men might abuse, this was not usually difficult for those with professional or personal experience. Comments from people with such experience were in stark contrast to the attitude expressed by most. Some Women's Aid workers, for example, commented:

f: [We know that] perverts are just normal men, most of them.
f: I mean some of the men, the abusive men, [that we meet] make you think if you'd met them in any other situation, it'd be, 'what a nice bloke', or it'd be 'very charming' (Group 12).

People who have themselves been abused are often very angry about the stereotypes that protect abusers. For example, one woman countered her friend's difficulty believing that a man she knew could be guilty because he's 'such a good person in his daily life' by describing her own father's abuse of her. She commented: 'Anybody met my father, great man, a hard worker, he was top staff in the office and everything. Anybody to meet my Dad thought "oh perfect, Billy's lovely", nobody would think of him touching his kids' (Group 34, f).

A REFLECTION ON REPRESENTATIONS
OF ACCUSED ADULTS IN CONTESTED CASES

Before continuing, it is worth returning briefly to the Orkney scandal. The above discussion adds another layer to understanding how the media reported and people responded to that case. It highlights some of the underlying ideas about abusers that were mobilised in reporting about, and reactions to, the accused parents.

A clear pattern is obvious in people's general discussions above. People are not surprised when 'social inadequates' are accused of abuse but they are sometimes astounded by accusations against 'respectable', 'moral' or 'normal', masculine men with 'shiny shoes', pillars of the community or those who are 'brilliant with kids'. They also often assume that communities would know if abusers were in their midst and that they personally could judge whether someone was guilty or innocent because of their impressions of that individual's character (until they have to confront evidence to the contrary, and sometimes not even then).

All these assumptions were explicitly used by those supporting the parents in Orkney, by journalists reporting the case, and often by people responding to the coverage. From the very start of the scandal the parents and their supporters appealed to the idea that normal, nice, well-educated parents could not commit abuse (especially involving bizarre rituals). As one of the Orkney mothers commented: 'We're middle-class boring people with boring lives. It's inconceivable that we would even have thought of carrying on like this' (BBC2, *Newsnight*, 15 March 1991). Such assertions were not lost on the audience. This was most clearly and concisely illustrated in the following exchange among a group of schoolgirls:

> f: I just couldn't, I couldn't believe it. I didn't look at them and think: 'Oh they could have done that.'
> f: They weren't, you know ... you have this typical image of a dirty old man that would do it. You know. They didn't look like that.
> f: They were just normal people.
> f: A married couple (Group 22).[5]

The media also emphasised the support of the local population and frequently asked neighbours for their views of the accused parents. Some coverage seemed to suggest that canvassing local opinion was at the very least an important part of this news story and, in some cases, by implication a reasonable way of deciding whether or not the children had been abused. As one report concluded: 'We couldn't find one person who thinks there's anything in the ritual abuse charges' (ITV, *News at Ten*, 12 March 1991).

The irony is that an Orkney man had been convicted of sexual abuse earlier. (It was this case which apparently led to allegations against some of the other parents.) Nobody seemed now to believe that the allegations in this original case were inaccurate. Yet few reports drew attention to the fact that he had been able to sexually abuse his children undisturbed. I could find only two reports that used this prior conviction to challenge the idea that neighbours will always know if abuse is going on. One of these examples appeared in the highly critical *Evening News* article (the one which inverted all conventional descriptions of the Orkney landscape as quoted in the previous chapter). The other, very brief, example appeared in the *Independent*. This raised a question ignored by most journalists in their vox pops with the local population:

> Last November eight children from a family of 15 were taken into care. Their father was already serving a seven-year prison sentence in Aberdeen for abuse of his children. Local people used the word 'horrific' more than once to describe details of this case. Mr Rosie [the local bus driver] said: 'We'd never have thought. He must have been a Jekyll and Hyde character. Nobody could believe it when he was taken away'. As Mr Rosie said this, he recognised the inconsistency of his previous words (*Independent*, 1 April 1991).

'PUBLIC' AND 'PRIVATE' KNOWLEDGE: EXTRA-MEDIA INFLUENCES AND THE SIGNIFICANCE OF SOCIAL CURRENCY

In previous chapters I have been able to establish some direct connections between media presentations of a particular case and people's memories. Such links are harder to examine when exploring something as diffuse as stereotypes of abusers. If there is a connection, in which direction does it operate? Is it simply a question of journalists' and audiences' common cultural repertoire? Analysis of the focus group discussions suggested other factors, over and above media images, may be significant. It became obvious that the nature and type of routine information shared between friends and neighbours might be important in structuring knowledge in this area. Some information is rapidly and widely exchanged, while other information is censored. It is this factor which is addressed in the final section of this chapter.

Stories about attacks by, or threats from, strangers are routinely exchanged in focus group discussion. These accounts are volunteered without awkwardness or hesitation: 'My kids go to school just up the road here. One girl at the school, this was about two weeks ago, she was late for school one morning, some guy tried to get her [...] Police involved, just a weekday morning, half past nine' (Group 43, m).

Indeed, the way in which these stories were introduced assumes that they are already common knowledge: 'There was somebody kerb-crawling up here about a year ago – in Allison Road. Remember? They stopped that wee girl, Clara' (Group 9, f); 'Do you remember a man [...] [in] a white car that was going about [...] and it was down at the school, and he tried to drag in Alex M——?' (Group 10, f).

Such events inevitably become the topic of conversation (e.g. outside the school gate) and parents feel they have a duty to seek out and share such information. These stories also often circulate long after the event.

Structural issues are important here in shaping parents' fears and patterns of communication. Parents talk about the heart-stopping moment when they looked round and realised their young child had disappeared from their side in the supermarket or describe the pattern of worry around a child's first solo journey to school or times when they were late home. 'I've only got Matthew and I keep an eye on him. If he's not home by four thirty, I'm out the window looking, you know what I mean?' (Group 9, f). To be suspicious of family, friends and neighbours was also seen as impractical and untenable. Parents need to be able to trust their nearest and dearest. In addition, while parents often felt they had to, and could, make positive assessments about the people with whom they left their children, the outside world was not under their control: 'When Andrew goes round the corner he could be off the end of the earth' (Group 9, f).

Such fears feed into, and are reinforced by the public profile of stranger-danger. Any incident is often publicised by the school (e.g. letters sent home to parents urging care) or in the local newspapers. Stranger-danger is routinely raised as an issue with pupils (teachers find it harder to discuss the possibility of abuse by friends and family). Classic threats from strangers may also be collectively experienced at the time. Take this example, from a young woman, describing an event at her school some years earlier: 'The rumour went round the school, like, Katy M—— is talking to those weird guys. All the kids took a pure panic attack and like half of them ran down to the car to scare the car away and half of them ran up to the teachers and the police were called' (Group 4, f).

Such incidents, ranging from the man who offers children sweets to the actual abduction of a child also become part of the local folk-memory: 'A wee lassie up from the back of us, she was taken away in a car by a guy when she was young [...] he actually tried to kill her and she played dead basically until he went away' (Group 4, m).

Media stories about stranger-danger are thus complemented, reinforced and reiterated through everyday conversation and the very public, and sometimes collective, nature of some of the experiences.

This is in marked contrast to talk about abuse within one's own community, particularly within families. For a start, such abuse is more private. It often takes place within the four walls of the home, targeting individual children. In addition the victims are less likely to confide in anyone if their abuser is a close and trusted adult, so no one else may ever find out. 'Telling tales' on a family member or close family friend is very difficult because of the power relations and emotional ties between the abuser and the abused and because the victim may feel that he or she is less likely to be believed (precisely because of stereotypes about abusers and the focus on stranger-danger). One teenager, for example, explains how impossible it would ever be to tell his mother about a family friend who offered him money in return for sex:

He's a diamond geezer, you seen him with his kids and [...] I used to be jealous of them because my mum and dad split up and this family was really sort of happy and stuff. And [...] all of a sudden he's in there offering me a tenner to sort of do whatever and it just totally knackered me. You just think, 'oh yeah Sam he's a sound guy' and then all of a sudden he turns out to be this. [...] my mum would never hear anything like that. My mum thinks he's an absolute charmer and he *is* as far as she's concerned and she thinks he's fantastic and I could never sort of turn and just say 'well, look, he tried to do this to me' (Group 14, m).

When abuse takes place inside a family, even where other family members become aware of it, it is unlikely to be discussed outside the home. At a very basic level it is obvious that incestuous abuse is more 'shameful' for the individual victim (talking about being flashed at by a stranger is different from 'admitting' to being flashed at by one's own father). It also is more 'shameful' for the victim's relatives who may be judged for their failure to protect the children.

This gap between the type of accounts of risk and danger which are widely shared, and those which are kept more secret is vividly illustrated in one discussion where a member of the group confronts her friends with her personal experience for the first time. This group of friends and neighbours (meeting in their local community centre) had been making a series of negative judgements about mothers of sexually abused children: 'How could the mother not know?', they asked, 'She *must* know.' (Such opinions were almost ritually exchanged in many of the sessions, certain phrases reoccurring across groups.) This routine exchange is suddenly interrupted by one woman whom I have called 'Alison':

Jan: A lot of women stay with the guy and I can't understand that.
Mike: That's crazy, I don't understand that.
Christine: I mean if I had kids and a guy done anything to my wean [child] ... you'd kill him.
Alison: That's easier said than done. That's crap, Christine, that's crap, that's crap.
Paula: Everybody's different, maybe Christine feels she could do that.
Alison: She must be a big person because I'll tell you something ...
Christine: I'm not big.
Alison: You *must* be, Christine, for the simple reason that my lassie was sexually abused by my father. I'd love to blow his brains off. I'd have loved to have stabbed him. [...] Hey listen, there's not a night goes by but that I wish my Da would drop down dead for the things that he's done. [...]
Christine: Maybe I *say* that right, but maybe I might feel different if I was in the situation, right. But I've never been in the situation so I don't really know.
Alison: Ah well, I've been in the position, I'm in the position. I'm in the position and I've been in the position for years. I've been in the position for eight years now.

The tangible tension as Alison provides this information is in marked contrast to the routine 'gossip' about strange men offering children sweets or, indeed, the very public knowledge associated with the abduction and assault of a child by a 'maniac'. She discovered that her father was abusing her daughter eight years ago and has lived with the consequences ever since, but this is clearly the first time her friend and neighbour (Christine) had heard about it. Here the focus groups – which provided an unusually focused context for debate

– allowed this experience to be discussed publicly for the first time. This highlights the fact that although parents routinely warn each other about any stranger behaving 'suspiciously', even close friends do not usually talk about the assaults committed by fathers, brothers, grandfathers or friends of the family closer to home.[6]

CONCLUSION

This chapter has examined the stereotypes about abusers; their appearance, class, education, age, intelligence, mental illness, physique, social marginality and masculinity (or rather, lack of it). I have argued that the media and broader cultural stereotypes encourage a focus on threats from outsiders rather than a focus on the danger posed by ordinary men close to the child. Media coverage also evades the challenge posed by feminist theorists who point out that patterns of sexual violence should make us question the operation of male power in society.

Public perceptions of abusers largely accord with media coverage. The direction of influence here is not as clear cut as in previous chapters, where a transition in media representation (Chapter 3) or coverage of specific cases (Chapters 4–6) could be shown to inform how people think. Perhaps the most we can say is that media representations and public views mirror each other and that the media can resource stereotypes and amplify some fears rather than others. At the very least they often fail to challenge specific conventional assumptions about abuse. There is much to be criticised in, for example, the iconic display of Myra Hindley's photograph and other images of 'sex beasts', the reinforcement of prejudices against people with mental disability or illness, the failure to analyse the gendered nature of sexual violence, the subtle and not so subtle homophobia which informs much discussion of men abusing boys, and the unreflective canvassing of 'community opinion' about contested allegations without asking probing questions about previous convictions.

This chapter has highlighted that it is not simply a question of media influence. It has also revealed the role played by broader socio-cultural factors and the importance of the 'social currency' of different stories and how these circulate in day-to-day conversation. I have argued that we need to broaden our understandings of reception and meaning-creation processes beyond the media (while always keeping the media within the frame). We need to pay attention to how people interact and not only what they say but how they say it. Analysis of discussions in focus groups should include looking at how people talk, not just what they say; how they express hesitancy, surprise, or mark out a communication as unusual or 'sensitive' (Kitzinger and Farquhar 1999). Such dynamics give insights into everyday exchanges of information and give clues to group responses; the ways in which communities identify threats, react to them, and demand policy solutions. The findings from the focus group discussions about sexual abuse provide insights into community dynamics which predicted the furore about known abusers being relocated in 'the community' and the subsequent push for legislative change. It is this next crisis in the child sexual abuse story that is the focus of the subsequent chapter.

8
Audiences as Activists: The 'Paedophile in the Community' Protests[1]

Under what circumstances do media audiences become social activists? What makes people come out on to the streets, joining together as mourners, or protesters or citizens? How do ordinary people become transformed into collective actors who create news events themselves and organise to demand change? People are always more than simply passive media consumers, and sometimes they respond so actively to media events that they transform themselves into campaigners. Some public responses to media stories are immediate, highly visible and dramatic. Such events would include momentous national disasters or terrorist attacks (the shuttle explosion; 9/11), televised acts of injustice (the Rodney King beating), the assassination of a political leader and the death of celebrities (e.g. Princess Diana). What is going on when particular media events seem to trigger dramatic collective responses? Can such moments of popular (re)action be seen as unequivocal evidence of direct media effects or are they so momentous in their own right that the media processes are barely relevant? In some cases people argue the events 'speak for themselves'; nine-eleven was momentous with or without the cameras (although the same number of deaths in another country would not, of course, generate the same response). At other times the media is blamed for causing an over-reaction. Detractors of public responses to some events dismiss them in terms such as copycat riots or media induced hysteria. Neither representations of the media's role adequately accounts for how journalists and camera crews mediate our sense of ourselves, our communities, our national identity, our world, and our sense of anger, mourning or injustice. This chapter takes a closer look at these processes. It does so by looking at the media campaigns, and the wave of public protest and civil unrest in response to convicted sex offenders being released into the community.

The nation is often said by journalists, to 'hold its breath' during the search for missing children or be 'united in shock' at the discovery of the dead body. Parents cling more tightly to their offspring, newspaper readers write in demanding the death penalty for the offender, the parents of the victims lead calls for policy change, petitions are organised, and, sometimes the public take to the streets in protest. This chapter explores the period, in the second half of the 1990s, when sexual abuse became a focus for unprecedented local action across many different UK cities, especially within particular council estates (public housing projects). These public protests were not confined to letter-writing campaigns or signing petitions set up by newspapers. They included demonstrations, civil disobedience and attacks on suspected paedophiles. For a while the professionals looked as if they were losing control of the policy-making agenda as citizens took the law into their own hands. The police had to be brought in to protect released sex offenders. Monitoring, supervision, treatment and housing of offenders were disrupted and policy-makers had to reconsider legislation, policy and practice. What motivated people to act as they did, and what was the role of the media in this process? What additional perspective can examining these cases give us on the relationship between the media and their audiences?

THE RISE OF THE PAEDOPHILE PROBLEM

The origins of the problem that erupted in the 1990s lay several decades earlier. In the very first chapter I introduced the famous serial child sex murderers who populated the 1960s and 1970s. These included people such as Myra Hindley (who, with Ian Brady, was one of the Moors murderers) and Robert Oliver (who was part of a gang that abducted, raped and murdered Jason Swift).

These high-profile serial offenders were, for many years, the public face of sexual violence. They had all been given prison sentences of 20 plus years. In the 1990s, these individuals, dubbed by the tabloids as 'the most hated' people in Britain, were now due for release. Under the law as it stood they could change their names and live anywhere they wanted and their neighbours would not know. In December 1996 Michael Howard (then Home Secretary) introduced legislation to monitor sex offenders after release generating extensive media interest, e.g. 'Paedophile lists for police' (*The Times*, 19 December 1996); 'Crackdown on sex offenders unveiled' (*Guardian*, 19 December 1996). The reporting initially followed routine media practice whereby media agendas are traditionally set by high-status official sources (such as government bodies) (Tuchman 1978). However, media coverage and public debate rapidly shifted as particular communities, and parts of the media, began to agitate for public access to the register and demand that communities be notified when dangerous individuals moved into their neighbourhood. Journalists (and pressure groups) picked up on community notification legislation in the USA. This legislation, know as Megan's Law, was introduced in 1996, named after seven-year-old New Jersey girl, Megan Kanka, who was raped and murdered by a convicted sex offender who lived across the street. Such legislation should, it was argued, be introduced in the UK.[2] Towards the end of 1996, and into 1997, the big story for the media, and major headache for policy-makers, became not government initiatives, but public fear and anger. Headlines in the national press included:

Parents in dark as paedophiles stalk schools (*Guardian,* 24 November 1996).
Paedophile out of prison 'fearful for life and limb' (*Observer,* 15 December 1996).
Jeering mothers drive paedophile off council estate (*The Times,* 11 January 1997).
Stop hiding perverts say protest mums (*Daily Mail,* 3 February 1997).
Town not told of paedophile's stay (*The Times,* 12 October 1997).

Protest rapidly spread from one area to another. It was not only the national media that were important here, the local press were also crucial. Although often ignored when thinking about the media, the local press can play a key role. (Indeed, the local media influence many national and international policy-making processes from road building to the disposal of nuclear waste.) Many of the national stories about paedophiles started out on the front page of local papers and some neighbourhood protests were sparked by local press reports rather than vice versa. Headlines from local papers included:

Angus mums on alert over local sex offender (*Press and Journal* (Aberdeen), 17 June 1998).
Parents besiege abuser's house (*Press and Journal,* 17 July 1997).
Residents pledge to continue campaign (*Leicester Mercury,* 4 July 1998).
Give us the Right to Know (*Torquay Herald Express,* 2 September 1997).
Parents' paedophile poster campaign (*Evening Gazette* (Teesside), 26 January 1998).

Panic hits town over perverts (*Belfast Telegraph News,* 22 March 1997).
Sex offender's home torched (*Belfast Telegraph News,* 6 October 1997).

Such articles often included quotes from the host of local residents' groups that formed in response to the paedophile threat; organisations such as 'Freedom for Children', 'People's Power', 'Parents Opposed to Paedophiles' and 'The Unofficial Child Protection Unit'. Such reports were also often accompanied by photographs of local people marching with banners declaring 'Perverts out' (*Press and Journal,* 9 June 1997) or children carrying placards reading 'Make Me Safe' (*Torquay Herald Express,* 2 September 1997). *The Manchester Evening News* published a front-page spread about a local sex offender alongside a photograph of him in his car behind a smashed windscreen after 'a vigilante mob had vented their anger' (cited in Thomas 1997: 68). The tone of some of this reporting was overtly provocative and was clearly intended both to reflect, and endorse, public rage.[3]

Many newspapers took a more proactive role than merely reporting local unrest (with whatever degree of approval). Some took on the role of guardians of public safety, especially in relation to particular dangerous individuals. Robert Oliver (involved in the brutal rape and murder of Jason Swift in 1985) was pursued by journalists on his release. The *Sun* asked readers to phone an emergency number if Oliver was spotted (*Guardian,* 18 October 1997) and, when he moved to Brighton the local paper, the *Evening Argus,* published his picture on their front page with the headline 'Beware this evil Pervert' (*Evening Argus,* 14 October 1997).

In other cases, journalists alerted people to the presence of paedophiles, either through knocking on the doors of neighbours and asking how they felt about living near a sex offender or through outing them on the front page. The *Sunday Express* printed photographs and details of offenders with their last known address under the headline 'Could these evil men be living next door to you?' (cited in Thomas 1997). The Scottish *Daily Record* produced a similar campaign, devoting the bulk of one issue to asserting a 'Charter for our Children' and demanding 'The legal right for communities to be told when a pervert moves into the area' (*Daily Record,* 25 February 1997). Alongside articles headed 'End the Suffering', 'Pervert's Playground' and 'Monster freed to kill', they published a double-page 'Gallery of Shame' with 38 photographs and names of convicted offenders and details of their offences.[4] Four of these were described as 'people power' success stories; one was 'hounded out of Drumchapel housing scheme because of his sick background' and another 'forced into hiding' while 'PEOPLE power drove sick child molester, Christie, 50 out of Stirling' (*Daily Record*, 25 February 1997).

'MORAL PANICS AND LYNCH MOBS'?

Such media attention and the public reactions it reflected, triggered and amplified presented a major problem for those involved in monitoring and housing convicted sex offenders. The media were accused of whipping up 'hysteria', creating a moral panic and encouraging a lynch mob mentality. Routine community notification and the automatic right of public access to the sex offenders register is in opposition to the requests of many professionals working in this field, including chief constables, chief probation officers and the NSPCC (*Guardian*, 19 February 1997). The main reason for their opposition is the belief that it will not protect children. Instead it may result in vigilante action and drive offenders underground making it less possible to monitor or treat them. Indeed the Association of Chief Officers of Probation (ACOP) documented ten cases where the press had lent editorial authority to campaigns to identify and expel offenders, leading to disruption of supervision and, sometimes, to acts of violence (ACOP 1998). Convicted abusers were driven from their homes, leaving behind arrangements put in place to monitor them (such as electronic tagging and video surveillance) and often absenting themselves from any treatment programmes. The notorious Robert Oliver ended up moving from London to Swindon to Dublin to Brighton. He refused hostel accommodation, his location being repeatedly exposed by the media, and finally took refuge in a police station. One of the ironies was that police and probation services ended up protecting sex offenders from the public rather than vice versa (Adams 1998).

In addition, other people are often caught up in the violence and harassment aimed at sex offenders. Hostels have been attacked (whether or not convicted sex offenders are in residence). The wife and child of one offender were named and driven from their home after it was set on fire. In an earlier case a young girl died after a house in which she had been staying was burned down (*Guardian*, 10 June 1997). In Birmingham, the 81-year-old mother of a convicted sex offender was forced to move and her home wrecked when the

Birmingham Evening Mail twice publicised the address of her and her son. In Manchester, a man was badly beaten by a gang who mistook him for a paedophile named by the *Manchester Evening News*.

The panic about paedophiles has also been used to victimise individuals with no known official record of sex offences (and with no connection to convicted offenders). Sometimes it would seem a convenient way of harassing unpopular or minority members of the community. Reading between the lines of some reports it appears that gay men and those with mental disabilities are particularly likely to be victimised. The *Sunday Times* documented '30 cases where men wrongly suspected of abusing children have been beaten and humiliated by gangs bent on driving them out of their homes' (*Sunday Times*, 2 November 1997).

Clearly the media contributed to the spiral of unrest across the country and some coverage was at the very least counterproductive if not blatantly irresponsible. However, the media did not create community protests out of thin air and it is fundamentally unhelpful to dismiss media and community reactions as moral panic. This concept implies that the panic is totally unjustified and that it is state-sanctioned, neither of which could be asserted in this case without qualification. More fundamentally the theory fails to pay attention to the processes through which a moral panic is engendered and therefore offers a way of glossing over rather than truly investigating public reactions (Miller *et al*. 1998). To accuse the media of whipping up 'hysteria' and creating 'lynch mob' violence is equally inadequate and also ignores key sites through which community reactions evolve. (The very term 'lynch mob' is used to signal irrationality in ways which, in addition, obscure the history of lynching and its position in relation to institutional racism.)

Instead of dismissing public and media reactions as proof of their failure to match the rationality and objectivity of the policy-makers, it is crucial to give detailed attention to the questions raised by the protesters and their criticisms of public policy. This is essential if we are to understand the many complex levels on which the media can play a role in social policy issues.

THEORISING COMMUNITY AND MEDIA PROTEST

The 'paedophile in the community' coverage was driven by factors operating on three levels. The first level concerns policy and practice initiatives. The second relates to local community responses and the role of local media. The third level involves the underlying construction of the paedophile which underpinned the whole debate. I shall deal with each of these in turn.

Policy and practice: new initiatives and unanswered questions

The initial decision to establish a register placed the issue of paedophiles in the community on the public agenda. But it did so in ways that begged more questions than it answered. How will these offenders be monitored? Who should have access to this information? Policy and practice on this issue were clearly underdeveloped and often inconsistent. Legal rulings and professional disputes received extensive media attention. There were, for example, several cases exposing uncertainty about sex offenders' housing rights ('Town considers banning sex offenders from council houses', *Guardian*, 9 January 1997; 'Eviction of paedophile justified, court rules', *Guardian*, 20 February 1997). Confusion also surrounded probation officers' responsibilities to pass on information about their clients to prospective employers. The Home Office originally advised probation officers not to notify employers of sex crime convictions in case employees were sacked leading to court actions for damages. This advice was quickly withdrawn leading to headlines such as 'Home Office confusion on paedophiles' (*Guardian*, 5 December 1996).

Policy on notification to the general public seemed to develop in a similar ad hoc fashion. Particular high profile cases raised questions such as: If a housing officer takes it upon himself to inform tenants about a released sex offender on their estate should he be disciplined? Should schools be told, but not pass on the information to parents, or did this place head teachers in an untenable position? Should police inform the public, but only under very special circumstances? One couple in North Wales, for example, were granted Legal Aid to sue police for publicising details about their sexual offences (*Manchester Evening News*, 9 June 1997). In some cases public warnings were released: 'Police warn of threat to young males: town on paedophile alert' (*Guardian* 15 October 1997). In other cases communities were not informed, or only provided with information after media exposure. In a clear example of direct interaction between the media and policy decisions, one London Council decided to warn parents about a 'very dangerous' convicted abuser who had moved into their area, but only after learning that a television documentary was to name the man (*Guardian*, 27 March 1997). It was not until September 1997 that guidelines came into force clarifying procedures. Police were given the power to warn head teachers, youth group and play group leaders and local child protection agencies that a convicted sex offender had moved into their area, but not to generally broadcast his name unless a professional risk assessment said this was necessary.

In the meantime, public fears and critical media interest were increased not only by the obvious confusion but also by the fact that the Sex Offenders Act left certain loopholes. These loopholes were graphically illustrated by high-profile cases such as that of Graham Seddon, a convicted abuser, detained by officers in June 1997 carrying a bag containing toys. He was, he said, looking for a child. Seddon was (briefly) detained in a Liverpool hospital but could not be kept against his will. The notorious Robert Oliver (convicted in 1985) also slipped through a loophole. Judged to be neither repentant nor rehabilitated this man was released without any compulsion to comply with supervision; legislation compelling such compliance could only be applied to those released after a certain date.

In the second half of the 1990s there was thus a confluence of events (such as the release of particular notorious individuals) and the development of policy and procedures that heightened public attention to this threat. The original highly newsworthy government initiatives set the news agenda, but that agenda was rapidly transformed through the questions it opened up, combined with obvious areas of uncertainty and the subsequent direct action from ordinary citizens.

Neighbourhood reactions: democracy, trust and local networking

The local media clearly fed into neighbourhood responses and helped to identify targets for popular anger. However, concern about children's safety was certainly not a new phenomenon. The paedophile had already been established as public enemy number one and, long before 1996, fear of the predatory paedophile was etched into the bedrock of parents' anxieties. As already discussed in the previous chapter, fears of child abduction are woven into the fabric of parental experience. Parents talk about the heart-stopping moment when they looked round and realised their young child had disappeared from their side or describe the daily pattern of worry every time a son or daughter is late home.

In these focus groups it was also clear that some communities already felt under siege. People spoke about predatory men coming on to the housing estates and, in almost every group, parents described incidents where 'shady' individuals had been seen behaving suspiciously around playgrounds or children had been approached by strangers. Such events inevitably become the topic of conversation (e.g. outside the school gate, see previous chapter).

Some working-class communities also often felt neglected by central government; a lack of public transport or decent shops, poorly resourced schools and an absence of employment opportunities all left them feeling alienated and mistrustful. Housing inequalities further exacerbated the crisis. Released prisoners, including convicted sex offenders, tend to be placed in hostels or offered housing in working-class areas and often on council estates (housing projects). Many protesters expressed anger and frustration at the fact that their fate was to be decided by faceless bureaucrats who rarely lived in such areas themselves. The question often asked in public meetings called to reassure people was 'How would *you* feel if he was living next door to you and your kids?' Council tenants who were expected to put up with living next to an incinerator, playgrounds built on polluted sites, damp housing or a failing local school, now were also expected to tolerate the country's most dangerous predators dumped on their doorsteps. (People living on council estates are also, of course, less likely to have access to private transport, decent public transport, safe play areas and consistent child care, all of which may mute concerns about children's safety.)

Given this background it is hardly surprising that the idea that known sex offenders were to be secretly housed in their neighbourhoods, added insult to injury. The child's placard 'Make Me Safe' perhaps carries more demands than community notification. The very names of some of the protest groups express their anger at the restrictions placed upon their lives (e.g. 'Freedom for Children') and their desire to assert their rights (e.g. 'People's Power'). Some protest groups also chose names that encapsulated their disillusionment with official protection and monitoring procedures (e.g. 'The Unofficial Child Protection Unit'). This disillusionment (and some hope and expectations) was vividly articulated by the founder of the (anti-vigilante) 'Scottish People Against Child Abuse':

> People must be able to sit back and be responsible. If they saw something constructive being done, maybe they would start having trust again in the authorities. The Government is there because we trusted them to look after us and protect our children, but they are not doing that yet (*Scotsman*, 16 October 1997).

Official incompetence was a recurring theme both in local discussion and in national coverage. Internationally high-profile cases of multiple sex abusers (from Dutroux in Belgium to Fred and Rosemary West in the UK) suggested that the professionals could not be trusted to monitor and investigate properly. Dutroux was able to continue his activities even though police were notified that he was building dungeons to imprison abducted children (Kelly 1997). The police were regular visitors to Cromwell Street but Fred and Rosemary West were apparently able to continue to rape and murder their victims undetected. Both these cases served as a backdrop to public concern. In 1997 this concern was underlined with the murder of Scott Simpson in Aberdeen by a known sex offender. The bungling of the Scott Simpson case received extensive coverage. Social services (who were supervising the boy's murderer at the time) were blamed for not following guidelines and failing to convey relevant information to the police. The police were also criticised for 'serious corporate failure' in investigating the nine-year-old's disappearance. The name of Scott Simpson was evoked by those campaigning for community notification in future cases. His murder suggested that the experts and professionals could not provide sufficient protection on their own.

For some protesters it was clear that direct action (ranging from seeking media publicity to vigilante activities) represented the only way of having their voices heard. The local media, for their part, were usually happy to co-operate. Local media have a special remit to address community priorities. Local newspaper editorials demanding (or in effect providing) community notification presented the papers as standing up for their constituents, asserting a strong neighbourhood identity and fulfilling their functions as representatives of 'the people'. While local media have problems representing some local concerns (such as pollution from a factory which is key to providing local jobs), the sex offender presented an apparently clear-cut enemy and outsider. As the *Daily Record* declared: 'the Record believe action must be taken NOW to confront the plague of abuse that wrecks young lives and disgusts all right-minded Scots' (*Daily Record*, 25 February 1997).

In understanding media and public reactions it is important not to be dismissive when the public come into conflict with the experts or when NIMBYism seems to come into conflict with the wider public good. Community concern and the conditions under which people are forced to live should not be underestimated. As a feminist journalist and author Bea Campbell points out, community notification may not be the best way of protecting children, however:

> There is a piety around the notion of 'the mob' which doesn't take responsibility for what some communities endure. A liberal disposition can't cope with what these communities are facing. There are communities, there are children, who live in a permanent panic about when he's going to get out of prison. That's not the tone which infuses the debate (Bea Campbell, conversation with author).

The issue of former neighbours returning from prison to live near their victims is certainly one which has been pushed forward by the peak in media attention. A housing worker faced with press coverage of such a situation expresses some ambivalence about the media's role. On the one hand attention from journalists was unhelpful (resulting in a defensive reaction from parts of the Housing Authority and whipping up unnecessary fear on the estate). However:

> The media were useful in that the tenants had tried telling their housing officer and had not succeeded in persuading her to listen. It is a shame that the council obviously felt inaccessible so that they had to go to the press. There are lessons to be learned from that. But the press made sure that the council reacted (Housing Officer, interview with author).

In this particular case, local and national media attention also led to further enquiries from tenants about other individuals on this estate. This, in turn, led to the exposure of another case in which children might be at risk and there had been a failure in inter-departmental communication. According to the housing officer I spoke with, this led to 'significant policy shifts about the sharing of professional information and adoption of protocols and guidelines to support that'.

The media then cannot be seen as merely interfering in an area best left to the experts. Public debate and involvement in social policy issues is a democratic and practical imperative. Questions from the media and the public (as neighbours, tenants and citizens) can disrupt important policy initiatives, but they can also be vital in pushing issues onto the policy agenda and refining procedures.

However, there were far more fundamental problems with the whole way in which the debate about paedophiles was framed in public discourse (including media coverage and policy-making).

These problems have roots that go much deeper than the immediate concerns raised in the second half of the 1990s. I would like to round off this chapter by problematising the whole way in which the paedophile was constructed as an object of social policy and highlighting some of the problems that were obscured by focusing on convicted offenders.

Framing paedophiles: public, media and policy gaps in addressing risk

Throughout this book the word 'paedophile' has often appeared in inverted commas. I have done this to signal the constructed nature of the term. It is a relatively modern invention. Before the late nineteenth century there was no sense of the sex criminal as a distinct category of person, 'terms like sodomy or carnal abuse were reserved for actual behaviours rather than inner tendencies' (Jenkins 1998:26). Today, however, we think in terms of paedophiles rather than abusive acts. The paedophile has become the dominant way through which sexual threats to children are conceptualised and articulated; however it is laden with ideas and assumptions that confine thinking about this issue to a very narrow focus.

The paedophile as a concept is enmeshed in a series of stereotypes which place the child sexual abuser outside society. Such conceptualisations were amply illustrated in the press reporting about paedophiles in the community. The *Daily Record*'s 'Gallery of Shame', for example, perpetuated all the old stereotypes, highlighting particular words in bold block capitals. Struggling for a variety of negative epithets to describe their gallery of 38 sex offenders the paper ran through the usual list warning readers of 'TWISTED Dickons [who] got eight years for raping two young sisters'; 'WEIRDO Sean Regan who was dubbed "The Beast"'; and 'DEPRAVED paedophile Harley who preyed on terrified children as young as six'. Other convicted offenders were variously described as 'EVIL Herriot'; 'PERVERT teacher'; 'SEXUAL predator'; and 'SEX BEAST'. In among these highlighted adjectives one man was simply described as 'BACHELOR Paritt' (with its gay implications) and three of the descriptions highlighted a disability (e.g. 'DEAF Duff posed as a priest as he prowled the street' and 'DEAF MUTE Eaglesham, 66, carried out a series of sex attacks on a ten-year-old girl') (*Daily Record*, 25 February 1997).

Portraits of paedophiles do more than simply stereotype (and reinforce prejudice against particular minority groups). The term singles out the sexual abuse of children, as if there were no connection between the acts of sexual abuse and exploitation perpetrated against boys and girls and those perpetrated against adult women. Notorious abuser Marc Dutroux in Belgium raped and abused both children and adult women (his oldest known victim was 50) and engaged in trafficking, yet he was continually dubbed a 'paedophile', a term which obscures the fact that this is not just a 'sexual preference' but a way of exercising power and expoiting women and children fror financial gain (Kelly 1998).

Having a special term such as 'paedophile' also supports the view that they are a separate species, subhuman or 'a breed apart' (Hebenton and Thomas 1996). One piece of information released by the Home Office during the height of the paedophile crisis was the fact that, by the time they are 40, one man in 90 has been convicted of a serious sex offence, such as rape, incest or gross indecency with a child (Marshall 1997). This fact, combined with evidence that most perpetrators of sexual assault are never convicted, suggests that every community is likely to have its share of sex offenders. In fact the very term 'offenders register' is misleading. The register will only record that tiny minority of offenders who are reported and caught. It is vital to remember that, according to Home Office research, only around 15–17 per cent of those sexually assaulted by a stranger report the crime. The reporting rate for incest is even lower, estimated to be about 2 per cent (Silverman and Wilson 2002:60). These sorts of facts were not integrated into the narrative of stories about paedophiles in the community. The fact that most paedophiles in the community are undetected and probably well integrated into their neighbourhood was rarely raised. The fact that most people would already know a sex offender was ignored.

To acknowledge that sexual violence is quite so endemic would have undermined the narrative thrust of most paedophile in the community stories. By confining their attention to a minority of convicted serial offenders and defining those who sexually abuse children as a certain type of person, 'a paedophile', the media were able to focus not on society but on a few dangerous individuals within it. The problem of sexual violence was represented by the newspaper image of the man with staring eyes or the evil smirk, the 'beast' and 'fiend' who could be singled out, electronically tagged, exposed and expelled. If paedophiles are literally 'evil personified', then such evil can be exorcised by exclusion of these individuals from society. This individualised approach fits with certain strands in criminological discourse (see Hebenton and Thomas 1996). It also fits with the whole media shift towards 'dumbed down' personalised stories whereby, for example, journalists focus on the noisy and antisocial 'neighbour from hell' rather than examining the problem of sink estates through analysis of employment, recreation facilities and housing conditions (Franklin 1997). Paedophiles are, of course, in this sense the ultimate neighbour from hell.

The concept of the paedophile is flawed. It locates the threat of abuse within the individual (rather than in social, cultural or bureaucratic institutions). In the context of abuse in children's homes, for example, attention can be focused on the cunning infiltrator while ignoring the nature of the care system, funding and resourcing. In the case of other sites of abuse, attention is confined to the outsider and the loner, leaving the role of fathers, and the institution of the family, unquestioned. The paedophile is a creature that embodies stranger-danger. He reflects and sustains a focus on abusers as outcast from society rather than part of it. As feminist activist and academic Liz Kelly argues, the concept of the paedophile helps to shift attention away

> … from the centrality of power and control to notions of sexual deviance, obsession and 'addiction'. Paedophilia returns us to [...] medical and individualised explanations [...] . Rather than sexual abuse demanding that we look critically at the social construction of masculinity, male sexuality and the family, the safer terrain of 'abnormalities' beckons (Kelly 1996:45).

If we adopt the word paedophile and see it as synonymous with child sexual abuse then we narrow the policy agenda. The fact that most children are assaulted by someone that they know virtually disappears from the debate and policies which would be deemed unacceptable if applied to 'ordinary men' become allowable (Kelly 1996:46).

The fundamental critique here is that the notion of the paedophile restricts definitions of the problem and thus limits how we can envisage solutions. The term helps to obscure important aspects of sexual violence and shifts attention 'away from political solutions addressing male power and the construction of masculinity toward a range of "problem-management" solutions' such as long-term incarceration (*The Mail*); risk assessment tribunals for dangerous men (*Guardian* and *The Times*) and individual therapy (*Guardian*) (McCollum 1998:37).

CONCLUSION

This chapter has explored the role of the media, particularly the local media, in engaging with audiences not only as 'receivers' of information but as activists and message creators. I have highlighted the positive as well as problematic impact of coverage during the crisis over paedophiles in the community and identified factors that shaped and maintained the momentum both of media attention and of public anger.

In presenting this chapter I have tried to demonstrate the intertwined levels of analysis that can contribute towards theorising the relationship between the media, social policy and 'the public'. It is not enough solely to focus on the media as a cause of people's beliefs, we need also to consider what motivates those who seek out media publicity and engage in direct action. It is also often unhelpful to dismiss the media as interfering or to blame the press for 'hype'. Instead, it is necessary to recognise the media's role as an avenue for networking between those with common concerns and as a forum for public debate. At the same time, however, it is vital never to accept the terms of that debate as cast in stone and always to question what is left out of the policy agenda as well as what is addressed. There are fundamental gaps in the framing of the 'paedophiles in the community' scandal by the media, not least that it failed to address the problem of most paedophiles in the community. However, this does not make the protests illegitimate. Respecting the concerns people raise, and their responses and engagement with media campaigns in this way means that one can combine detailed analysis of protest and crisis coverage with critical reflection on the underlying assumptions that frame public discourse and shape visions for social policy. Such approaches can, I hope, allow us to develop more grounded theories both about so-called 'moral panics' and about 'audience–text relations'.

9
The Zero Tolerance Campaign: Responses to a Feminist Initiative

This chapter introduces another approach to examining the ways in which people engage with messages about child sexual abuse. Instead of looking at responses to the mass media, it examines a particular public awareness initiative: the Zero Tolerance campaign. In contrast to the mass media's ongoing focus on paedophiles and stranger-danger, this campaign sought to prioritise the issue of abuse by ordinary men, known to, and trusted by, the child. It also attempted to reframe the debate in feminist terms. I use my evaluation of this campaign in order to explore audience reception of particular texts and lead into a subsequent discussion of polysemy, resistance and diversity.

THE ZERO TOLERANCE CAMPAIGN

The Zero Tolerance campaign was launched in December 1992 by the local government in Edinburgh. It was the first major advertising initiative in Britain designed to challenge social attitudes towards assaults against women and girls.[1] The campaign addressed the view expressed by many professionals, activists and researchers in this field that 'sexual abuse of children is an inherent condition of our society' (Miller-Perrin and Wurtele 1988) and that 'the real battle lies in making fundamental changes in a society that allows and even encourages child sexual abuse' (DeYoung 1988:111; see also Finkelhor and Strapko 1988; Murray and Gough 1991; Tharinger *et al.* 1988). It attempted to address the gap that:

> While many prevention professionals recognise that fundamental change in power relationships in families and in society from a sexist to egalitarian distribution will be necessary to prevent sexual victimisation, not enough has been done to link political and cultural life and sexual victimisation (cited in Tharinger *et al.* 1988).

Figure 9.1 The Zero Tolerance advertisement: 'By the time they reach eighteen ...'

Figure 9.2   The Zero Tolerance advertisement: 'From three to ninety-three ...'

The Zero Tolerance (ZT) campaign was explicitly informed by feminist analysis and attempted to reframe the issue in these terms. It highlighted the fact that most perpetrators of sexual assault are male and suggested that there are links between the social construction of male sexuality and the potential for abusive behaviour (Dominelli 1986; Finkelhor 1982; Hearn 1988; Hollway 1981; Kelly 1988; Smart 1989). The campaign drew links between the various abuses perpetrated against women and girls throughout their lives, whatever their age and it linked rape, battering, murder and abuse. Research consistently shows that such abuse is a very common part of growing up (Kelly *et al.* 1989). Rather than present rape as an isolated aberration the campaign designers wanted to draw attention to the continuum of sexual intimidation that children, especially girls, experience. Abuse was defined as everything 'from flashing to rape'.

The ZT campaign was deliberately high-profile and provocative. A central strand of the campaign was the display of huge advertisements on the city's buses and on prominent placards in Edinburgh's prestigious main shopping street. The advertisements showed simple white on black stark statements such as '85 per cent of rapists are men known to the victim', 'Male abuse of Power is a Crime' and 'No Man has the Right'. This attracted intensive media attention. Edinburgh District Council also involved local communities in a series of related events, and distributed leaflets, postcards and little 'Z' badges that people could wear to show their support for the campaign.

The campaign materials were designed to counter some persistent stereotypes in the media about where, and by whom, children are likely to be abused and to challenge the idea that you would automatically know if a child was being victimised. Two of the campaign posters which included a focus on sexual violence against girls are reproduced in Figure 9.1 and Figure 9.2. The posters used words and images to stress that abuse is committed by ordinary men who often appear perfectly pleasant and respectable. The designers deliberately chose to locate their images indoors (focusing on violence in the home rather than on the streets/in parkland/wilderness, etc.). Fathers as well as strangers were clearly identified as potential perpetrators and the posters were designed to challenge class stereotypes. The women and girls in the pictures were shown in 'posh' surroundings, with evocations of the Victorian era (e.g. china dolls). In addition, there are no visible signs of physical or mental damage. This was both because ZT designers did not want to produce more images of women as victims and because they wanted to make the point that abuse was often hidden. It was also a response to research which showed that people might turn away from scary or upsetting images rather than engage with them.

RESEARCHING PEOPLE'S RESPONSES

The mixture of hostile and supportive media coverage, the large postbag received by Edinburgh District Council and the increase in self-referral to support agencies suggested that the campaign was having an impact of some kind. There was also extensive anecdotal evidence about the way in which the posters, combined with the little badges, were encouraging discussion and helping some people to seek help. (For example, a youth leader, wearing the Z badge, told me it had prompted a boy to confide in her about his abuse.) However, Edinburgh District Council also wanted to examine responses among people who might not write letters to the newspapers and get a more detailed sense of how the materials were 'working' (or not).

A two-stranded approach was adopted to evaluating the campaign. Along with a colleague, Kate Hunt, I conducted a street survey in Edinburgh of 228 people. I also organised 30 focus group discussions (17 groups were conducted around the Edinburgh campaign, a further 13 were held to assess responses in neighbouring Strathclyde when the campaign moved there). (For a full report of these evaluations see Kitzinger and Hunt 1993; Hunt and Kitzinger 1996; Kitzinger 1994.)

The survey gives a basic idea of people's awareness of the campaign and their reactions to it. 64 per cent were already aware of the campaign prior to being questioned about it, 76 per cent were positively in favour of it (only 6 per cent had a negative reaction to it). The campaign had also provoked a lot of discussion. Over one in three (39 per cent) of those who were already aware of the campaign had talked about it with someone else. The survey also highlighted some differences in responses between men and women, and younger and older respondents; 12 per cent of men but only 2 per cent of women disliked the campaign and people over 50 were twice as likely to be critical as those under 50.

The focus group research was designed to allow a more in-depth exploration of the reception processes and to unpick some of the reasons why different people might react differently. In addition to the 30 focus group discussions entirely focused on the ZT campaign, I used the ZT advert shown in Figure 9.1 as a focus for discussion at the end of about half of the 49 groups which discussed child sexual abuse in general. Quotes from my general groups have ID numbers 1–49, quotes taken from groups which focused solely on ZT are identified with code numbers 50–79.

In all of the groups which discussed the campaign materials a similar format was followed. I started by asking people what (if anything) they remembered about the campaign and what they thought about it. They were then shown the poster images, without their captions, and invited to reconstruct the strap-lines. Finally, the actual caption was revealed and their comments sought. Such methods are designed to tell us more about reactions than effect *per se*. However, they can give us some insight into the latter, especially where research participants had already been exposed to the ZT campaign in natural settings and could talk about their reactions at the time and memories of the materials. (For a full evaluation and discussion of the campaign 'impact' see the publications cited above.)

General comments and reactions

The discussion in focus groups reflects the overall positive responses evident in the street survey. People make comments such as 'I think it's eye-catching and terrific', 'they got people talking', 'it made me think'. Although a few people thought the campaign might damage Edinburgh's reputation, others express great pride in their city's initiative:

> We are seen as this capital city and quite well respected all over the world and quite cultured, if you like. [...] I think for that to have started in Edinburgh – I'm really proud of the fact. That is brilliant [...] and [they] put it in the most noticeable place in Edinburgh, apart from flying a banner from the top of the castle! (Group 56).

Some men felt the message was very thought provoking and many woman saw the campaign as empowering 'It lets you know you don't have to put up with it' (Group 51); 'It gives women strength [...] It's making you aware of your rights' (Group 12); 'It's like some injection of power, that brings you courage and you just feel great' (Group 59). Some women reflect on the importance of such a campaign from a very personal perspective:

To me that was the most vivid one [No Man Has the Right]. Simple and straight to the point – 'No man has the right' […] Years ago someone said something similar to that to me and that really changed … it didn't change my life overnight but it changed the way I thought […] It was like a realisation. I'm not meaning to be dramatic, but I remember thinking 'that's right'. It suddenly sunk in (Group 65, f).

Some women who had been sexually abused express a strong sense of identification with the campaign:

You know that sort of prickly feeling, like when you see something and think … oooooooh! It was when all the posters were up along the tripods right along Princes Street […] I couldn't believe it. I was going along in the bus and I thought: 'There's one, there! There's another one. They haven't got them all along Princes Street [have they]? … YES! They have!' It was very good. [I felt] 'Yes, this is what I want. I want people to see this […] Next month it will be on the buses. They'll go by and you'll go: 'Yes, I'll get on that one. Look at that!' (Group 16).

In contrast to one police officer who worried that the campaign might be 'scaremongering' or 'upsetting', the survivors were very positive about the campaign. They welcomed the way in which ZT placed the issue in the public domain, relieving them of the main burden of placing it on the agenda:

It let's you know it's there. It is not because somebody is standing there saying 'I was raped as a child' that it's there […] The council definitely deserve a round of applause for that, because they're relieving the burden of bringing it up into everyday life from the people who are affected by it.

They also felt the campaign could be important for children currently growing up in abusive situations: 'It's because of the absence of posters like that when we were little that we had to keep it down – we had to deny it – bury it deeper and deeper.'

Common readings and reported positive impact

The focus group discussions reveal a high degree of consensus about the main meaning of the images and show the level of sophistication people bring to their readings of such representations. The picture of the two children playing with their dolls is identified as 'nostalgic', like 'a Father Christmas card picture' (Group 15, f), and 'old fashioned' (because of the black and white print and the type of clothing and toys). It is also identified as having the sort of aspirational qualities associated with advertisements. The image is described as similar to 'an advert for Habitat' or 'Mothercare' (Group 5, f). People make comments such as: 'It's like the Dulux shade cards' (Group 9, f); 'An insurance advertisement "secure yourself and your child" ... safe little ideal, happy, playing environment' (Group 2, f).

Research participants were usually clear that the image was 'middle class' and (until they saw the caption) thought that it projected the suggestion of happiness and security:

> f: ... nice wooden floor, nice middle-class, very comfortable.
> f: Lots of toys, very expensive dolls house (Group 5).
> A happy home, isn't it? You can imagine mum down the stairs, just about to shout up 'Tea's ready!' (Group 4, f).

People often comment that the campaign imagery is not what they expected, saying they were more used to images of frightened, poor or despairing children (the type of image often used to advertise children's charities): 'It's always this image that the kids are dirty, not clean and well-looked-after' (Group 56, f). When shown the image on its own, those who had not seen the campaign could not imagine the caption. They draw on their knowledge of more conventional advertisements to suggest captions such as 'give money' (Group 13). Some emphasise notions of innocence and vulnerability suggesting captions such as 'The age of innocence' (Group 19, m); 'Don't spoil our innocence' (Group 4, f) or 'It would be nice if all little girls felt this safe' (Group 58, f).

When shown the actual caption 'By the time they reach eighteen one of them will have been subjected to sexual abuse', those who had not already seen the poster on public display express considerable surprise. It sometimes takes a few moments to 'digest' the messages but then, once again, a high consensus is clear in how most people interpret the meaning of the advertisement. The combination of traditional image and disturbing words is identified as particularly powerful:

> Well it seems like little, idyllic, naive, two happy little girls playing and the idea of abuse seems all that more sort of negative and oppressive and bad (Group 20, m).

The picture on its own doesn't tell the story, [but ...] when you then wrap it with all the other phrases on there it completely turns it around (Group 19, m).

Some people comment that it was important that the images themselves were attractive and 'benign' rather than horrifying and 'off-putting'. As one young man remarks: 'It lures you in' (Group 20). Some say that when they had seen the posters up in Edinburgh this had caused them to read a message they would normally have avoided:

These posters with the pictures, talking about the violence and with the non-violent pictures there. In a way they made me think. Even today they made me think more about it. If it had been a sort of violent picture I would just have sort of dismissed it because I don't like violence, you know, I don't like dwelling on it particularly (Group 58, f).

f: These visual images are quite peaceful but the words are frightening. [...] Personally, for me, you need a peaceful, domestic scene but what the writing gives you is the horror.

f: There are so many bad images, I think people are quite inured. You turn on the television and you're just sick of all these horrible images (Group 64).

Another woman describes how this affected her sister who was visiting Edinburgh:

We passed one of these posters and she was looking at it, saying about what a lovely looking room that was and then she sort of realised what it said and it was kind of a shock. So I think it's quite good, because it draws them in and then it shocks them out of their comfortable idea of what life is like [...] I think it's quite a good wee twist (Group 56, f).

Many research participants also read the advertisement as conveying the message you can't tell by looking whether someone is being abused:

[It's] Implying that every child looks safe, but they aren't (Group 19, f).

Things might seem normal (Group 17, f).

You never know what goes on in anybody else's life (Group 58, f).

It's not necessarily obvious. I mean your friend's child could be experiencing it and you wouldn't be able to detect it (Group 12, f).

Obviously there's a lot could be going on there that you don't know about (Group 57, m).

f: It's just like the issue really, it's sort of hidden child abuse, it's hidden and that shows that it's there.

f: Looks like sort of happy family you know, well cared for but are they? (Group 22).

Research participants also recognise that the focus is on including abuse by known men: 'It explodes the myth, that rapists are guys who jump out of a dark alleyway' (Group 50, m). One man talks quite specifically about the concerns the caption generated for him:

That bit at the bottom – 'husband, father, stranger' ... That makes me feel uneasy, and anything that makes me feel uneasy, makes me think. That's what's really good about it. I go to work and put my bairns [children] in the nursery, what's going on in the nursery? What's going on with my bairns? (Group 53, m).

Some research participants draw attention to the contrast between these posters and routine mass media coverage 'The stranger gets publicised, if it's the husband or the father it gets swept under the carpet' (Group 51, f). Some also contrast the information in the poster with the sort of advice they had been given at school or from parents. One 16-year-old, abused by her mother's boyfriend, explains: 'Kids need to know. We did stuff on strangers at school, it made you more scared of strangers [...] but it wasn't strangers that were doing it to me' (Group 48, f).

Another woman, sexually assaulted by her father, comments that the message on this poster was '... the opposite of what I was told. I was told "Don't get in a car with strange men". That was the only time you would ever get harmed, if you did something like that' (Group 6, f).

Most research participants were also clear that the advertisement emphasised that abuse did not only happen in chaotic working-class families. The advert, they say, conveys the message that 'it's not just like deprived kids and deprived families' (Group 22, f); 'even if a girl's brought up nice, [...] she can still be abused' (Group 51, f); 'It makes you think it's not just some kid in the slums with an alcoholic parent'

(Group 21, f); 'It could be someone living in a mansion, it could be someone living in a hovel' (Group 53, m).

The above discussion shows a close correlation between the intended message of the producers and the understanding of that message by audiences. It also shows how a particular strategy (using attractive images to draw viewers in) had been effective in reaching some people. Some research participants report that the campaign had made them change their minds, that it had raised their awareness and made them think and talk more about the issue. One man, for example, says that the advertisements made him think about how he used power over his children: 'Every time I've shouted at my kids I've sat back and thought "how could I have done that better?"' (Group 53 m); another comments: 'There's a message for every male here [...] I don't think men can say "this is nothing to do with me"' (Group 50, m). Others describe ways in which the campaign generated conversations, or encouraged women and children to seek help (for further discussion of the effects see Kitzinger and Hunt 1993).

'Effect' in action

In addition to people reporting that the advertisements had had an impact on them, this was also sometimes evident in the focus group themselves. Some of the transcripts show how the discussion of materials (albeit in the artificially focused setting of a focus group) could shift ideas and lead people to change their minds. For example, research participants often puzzled over the suggestion that one out of every two girls would encounter some form of abuse by the time the time they were 18. Much criticism focused on the statement 'from flashing to rape' in the advert shown in Figure 9.1. Individually people often criticise this caption for either 'hyping up' or 'diluting' abuse statistics ('you think, oh well they're only talking about flashing'). However, in the focus groups this statement frequently generates discussion between people about their own experiences of being flashed at, a process which often leads participants to state that it should not simply be dismissed as a joke. The caption also led to the gradual exchange of information previously excluded from common knowledge. This process was vividly illustrated in one group of friends in their early twenties. They initially dismissed the poster's suggestion that 50 per cent of girls would encounter some form of abuse. They saw this as an exaggeration, until, that is, they tentatively began to reflect on their own experiences when they were between the ages of 13 and 16. This culminated in the following exchange:

f2: ... all these years I'd just thought 'Oh that was the night I lost my virginity'. I hadn't even took the time to think about what actually happened [...] He forced me. Now I'm thinking, for fuck's sake, when I lost my virginity I was raped. I remember actually thumping him to get him off me and he wouldn't get off. [...] He said 'If you don't do it now, you'll never do it'. [...] I was too young, I didn't want to do it [...] I couldn't physically get him off me. I was beating him and I couldn't get him off. It was all over.

f1: The first time I got drunk, I lost my virginity. I didn't want to do it either. I was pretty young as well.

f3: You see, I'm the exact same. I was steaming [drunk] and in retrospect I wish it had never happened [...] So that's every single person in this room.

In fact, at that stage it was not 'every single person' in the room. The only man present had not commented. However, later in the session he remarked:

m4: One thing, which I have never ever told anyone about [...] I was at a party when I was 16 [...] I was staying overnight [...] and I woke up and there was somebody in bed beside me, groping me. [...] It frightened the absolute life out of me (Group 4).

The young women's descriptions of 'losing their virginity' and the young man's account of being groped had not previously been discussed among this group of friends. The research participants' willingness to share these experiences at this point was partly facilitated by the focus group discussion. However, it was actually triggered by the controversial caption 'from flashing to rape ...'. This caption seemed to give permission for a continuum of experiences to be explored and taken seriously. It had this sort of effect on dynamics within several groups, and often came to be positively evaluated by participants during the course of the discussion, precisely because they began to reflect on, and exchange, their own experiences.

The next part of the chapter looks more closely at how people identify (or not) with the posters, how some 'misread' the message, and explores some people's ideological opposition to the campaign.

Identification with the images: class and ethnic identity

All the pictures from the ZT posters were usually identified as being located in a well to do home. If people only identify with images that closely reflect their own lives you might expect the middle-class imagery to alienate working-class people. However, no one says that they do not identify with the home portrayed because of the obvious wealth of the surroundings. If questioned closely some research participants agree that the images show homes far wealthier than their own ('It would take a week's wages to buy a doll's house like that'). However, they seem to identify closely with the scene. One man (a manual worker on the railways) responds to the picture of the old woman and young girl by saying: 'That's my wean [pointing at the child] [...] I've just left my weans in the house with their grandmother [...] That's my house, there's my horrible mother-in-law and there's one of my weans' (Group 53, m).

Later, looking at the advertisement showing the two girls playing together he adds: 'I see an advert like that and I tense up because these wee girls there (pointing at the two girls) that's my son and wee daughter. That's anybody's kids' (Group 53, m).

The middle-class symbolism of the pictures seems to be easily read as 'Everyfamily' and the children as 'Everychild': 'They look just like an ordinary wee couple of girls – like anybody's kids, and you realise something's going to happen to them – it could happen to your kid' (Group 51, f).

Some also felt that the campaign's middle-class imagery effectively redressed stereotypes in the media, making comments such as 'If it could happen to them it could happen to anyone' (Group 18, m); and '[it's] showing it's universal' (Group 58, f).

Thus initial concerns by some commentators on the ZT campaign, that the images were too 'middle class' and would not 'speak to' working-class people, were not borne out by the audience research. Such concerns underestimate the sophistication with which people read the images and ignore the ZT campaign's exaggerated play on advertising conventions.

Different issues arose around the 'whiteness' of the images and some non-white research participants were clear that they could not see the images as universal (I use the term 'non-white' or 'ethnic minorities' to include research participants who identified as British Asians and/or black). Research participants from ethnic minorities were more likely to scrutinise the ZT materials to see whether or not they included 'black imagery' and to comment on this aspect. Whereas some white people did not seem to notice that one of the children in the 'from flashing to rape' poster was non-white, this was often noted by research participants from ethnic minorities. These participants were often concerned about stereotyping non-white men as abusers or further problematising black/Asian families. At the same time some felt that it was vital to explicitly include non-white people in the images. One woman, for example, comments that abuse is such a 'silent issue amongst the black community. They keep it right under the carpet' and is concerned that 'maybe [...] that [the campaign] had just sealed that' (Group 59, f). In this sense, the 'whiteness' of the images appears to be more of a problem than their middle-class emphasis (this 'whiteness' was not just about the nature of the models, but also the surroundings, decor, the white doll etc.). The nostalgic, almost Victorian, look of the posters could also be alienating. As one woman comments: 'I wouldn't associate that with my own home or my mother's [...] they are very whitey, whitey.' She adds that if the images had clearly included black people:

> I would have taken slightly more notice, I would have related to it maybe a little bit more. [...] But the pictures were just average: what you see in a magazine, white people, that's it. You just get so used to it [...] You don't even consciously think about it until later [...] [But] there is like a screen between me and that picture [...] . It was good but [I am] like detached from it (Group 59, f).

The western feminist emphasis on male abuse of power was also not always seen as appropriate by women from different cultures:

> We are Asian or whatever, there is a hierarchy within the house and if you happen to be the top female [...] For white people, yes, it is legitimate maybe just to relegate it to males' abuse of power [...] but for people like us it is not true, it is not reality. I live with my aunts and uncles and whatever and my husband could be the last person meting out the abuse (Group 59, f).

Over and above issues of identification, some people's responses to ZT varied in other ways. Whereas most people quoted above apparently understood the main thrust of the ZT campaign, some of the group discussions revealed some 'misinterpretation', resistance and more outright opposition. There are three aspects I wish to highlight here: 'misreadings' of the image, resistance to the statistics and opposition to the gender-politics of the ZT campaign.

Polysemy and 'misreadings'

The above discussion shows congruence between the producers' intentions and most people's interpretation of the campaign. However, some research participants responded quite differently.

One example of a misreading was evident when three different working-class respondents, at first glance, thought that the bare floorboards shown in the advert in Figure 9.1 indicated that the family were too poor to afford a carpet. It was only when they looked at the rest of the picture that they corrected themselves. This is an interesting example of how the same symbol – stripped floorboards – may be read differently by people from different socio-economic backgrounds. Their ability to then re-read the advert in ways more congruent with the intentions of the producers, however, shows a level of cultural bilingualism.

A second and more sustained example, which suggests the polysemy of an image was evident in some people's insistence on looking for symptoms of abuse in the pictures of the two girls. When they were shown the picture without the caption some people thought the girls in Figure 9.1 looked happy. Once they had seen the caption, however, they sometimes revised their opinion, saying the children looked sad or lonely. Several even decide which of the two children is the obvious victim. This is partly a function of what people expect to see. For example, some people expect a child who has been sexually abused to be withdrawn and limp, sitting in the corner with her head down (rather like the images used on the television news and in some children's charity advertisements). Indeed some people try very hard to read the ZT photographs in this way, looking for signs of abuse:

> The little girl doesn't look secure to me – sucking her thumb and the way she's sitting (Group 2, m).
> *That's* the one who's been abused – She's very withdrawn (Group 51, f).
> I think it's *that* one, she's got her legs crossed (Group 17, f).

One woman even says that she had always misread the picture caption when she'd seen it up around Edinburgh. It was only in the research context that she read the caption correctly:

f: I've seen that one. I thought that [caption] said 'One of them *has* been [abused]'. I would say that one. [...] Because she is sitting dead dour! [laughter] [...]
f: Like if she was, like, kind of 'away' you would know that she would be the one (Group 10, f).

Invariably the 'dark-skinned' child was selected as the victim, although no one who selected her made reference to this fact. Indeed few of the white groups explicitly identify her as black or Asian and several even assumed the children were twins.

Renegotiating the statistics

In addition to circumnavigating the photographer's efforts to show children without visible signs of abuse, some people re-negotiate the statistics through reinterpreting the images. They cannot believe the implication that one in every two girls would encounter some form of abuse and try to interpret the poster accordingly. A few people recall the picture from memory as having shown three or four (or even ten) children rather than two. When shown the actual picture they try to find more children than are actually there. One man, for example, peers closely at the image and asks 'Is there a baby in the chair or is it a doll?' (Group 19, m).

People also resist the message by complaining that 'flashing' should not be included as a form of abuse. Such a broad definition of abuse is, they say, ridiculous and misleading: 'Maybe a father will take a wee lassie in the bath with him and wash her. Is that going to be classed as sexual abuse, because she's seen you naked? You know, from the ridiculous to the sublime!' (Group 53, f).

Others feel that the poster is obviously biased and that 'statistics can be used to prove almost anything' (Group 57, m). Research participants make observations such as 'The only thing that leads me to doubt them is that they are such round numbers [...] I'd be interested to know what percentage error there are on these' (Group 50, m) or 'Some of the statistics which have been quoted have been carefully selected to further the point of view which the organisers of the campaign want to get across' (Group 57, m).[2]

Even if they accept the statistics some people object to them being publicised. As one man asks: 'What are you going to tell women? Simply don't know any men? Just forget about them? [...] Just keep away from men? Don't have anything to do with them?' (Group 53, m).

Others acknowledge that the figures might be true but are quite clear that, in one woman's words, 'the men I know aren't going to behave like that' (Group 50, f). Research participants also sometimes interpret the statistics presented in the campaign in ways which distance the information from their own lives. For example, one retired woman, reacting to a campaign statement that almost 50 per cent of female murder victims are killed 'by their partner or ex-partner', suggests that these are mainly prostitutes murdered by their clients. The figures are therefore, she explains, not applicable to 'ordinary people'. In addition there are some suggestions that the statistics displayed by the ZT campaign are not as bad as they might seem because the figures included 'bogus' cases such as 'date rapes' which should not really count. People relate this back to stories they recall from the mass media:

> f1: They'll go so far and then say 'no'. They don't say no at the very beginning and that's bound to be included in that statistic. Women who have reported it because they have agreed at the beginning and then turned round and say 'no' [...]
> f2: Well there was a case in the paper just about a fortnight ago [...] about a young lady lawyer and a male lawyer and she allowed him to stay the night in her apartment [...] she undressed in front of him and so he assumed that was an invitation and so he tried it on and she sued him for rape. [...] I'm sorry for the woman that is genuinely raped [...] but by the same token, if [...] the situation grows and grows and grows and he's getting the come on, I think that girl's got everything she deserves (Group 54).

In this way many people manage to keep rape and assault as the preserve of 'stranger danger' or misfortunes that only happen to women who 'ask for it'.

Ideological questioning and opposition

The above discussion addresses forms of negotiation with the campaign material. Some of this is informed by ideological opposition but is not always explicitly presented in this way. There are also examples of outright opposition and rejection. The strongest and most focused area of opposition concerned the gender-politics of the presentation. Indeed, this was the subject of extensive press attention. The *Sunday Times*, for example, lambasted the campaign for being 'anti-male', a 'poisonous' 'grotesque libel' and a 'Goebbelsstyle exercise in hate propaganda' (*Sunday Times*, 9 October 1994). Within the focus groups some were concerned about the focus on girls 'at the expense' of boys. This was a complaint not simply from men and was a perspective which came from a variety of different positions. One woman who had herself been abused says she knew how important public recognition was and therefore 'I felt sorry for the boys who were left out of that' (Group 6). Another survivor of abuse stresses the importance of recognising that some perpetrators are female (Group 16, f). A third woman says she felt excluded as the mother of a son: 'The reason I think about boys being abused is because I've got a son. I think, [...] "Oh God you know, hope it doesn't happen to Duncan"' (Group 5, f).

Some people think the issue of sexual abuse of children should be kept quite separate from male violence against adult women. Focusing on child sexual abuse as a problem for girl-children is also seen by some as undermining the 'dignity' of the problem: 'It's kind of making abuse a little girlies' thing. You know, there is something in that that is kind of denying it the dignity it deserves. It is something that happens to people and is perpetrated by people' (Group 6, f).

For some this is a question of strategy:

> f: We're not disagreeing at all that there are problems, or saying that it's not the true state of affairs but you don't solve it by this antagonistic ...
> f: You don't help these men to sort themselves out by alienating them further.
> f: Or help the women help themselves either. [...]
> f: This is just anti-male, it's nothing more (Group 58).

There was a worry about how men might react:

> I think men are beginning to feel threatened in all walks of like because they're looking around and they're seeing women doing everything. [...] I sometimes feel that we women aren't as tactful to them as we could be. We're actually laying ourselves open for future maybe verbal abuse, if you like, and here we are ganging up against them. Whereas if this was widened to include any violence ... (Group 64, f).

A few men did indeed say they felt excluded, attacked and insulted by the posters. One man angrily asserts:

It could be *my* little girl, it could be *my* mother, it could be *my* sister that's raped or attacked or whatever. [But] I'm rejected on the same side as the rapist [...] . But let me tell you that my aggression toward that male is probably greater because it's *my* little girl, *my* wife, *my* mother, *my* sister and I've seen what can happen to them and how they might then be nervous of me. So I want to get back to sorting out the males, that not only would attack my mother, my little girl, etc., but they would attack *me* as well. What I'm saying is that I'm also a victim of this male abuse of power (Group 53, m).

The explicit feminist emphasis of the campaign is clearly rejected by some people. Presenting sexual violence and abuse in this way was seen as 'sexist' and 'old-fashioned':

I don't think you nowadays say 'Men do this and women do that'. It's persons, people, how they are, their personalities, [...] it's abuse of people (Group 55, f).
It's the 'male abuse of power' that is offensive [...] It's too limited, it's restrictive and it's way too sexist. [...] It pisses me off right now just looking at it, it really does. And it pisses me off in that sort of really aggressive feminist butch 'I hate men' way, you know, and I just think that's a non-starter as a position these days (Group 58, f).

The pendulum, according to some respondents, has swung too far against men and their side of the story is no longer heard:

f1: The man's position [is] being rubbished, I think we women have done a lot of harm.
f2: We've done ourselves more harm than good (Group 54, f).

CONCLUSION

The method I have adopted here and the type of alternative material I am researching means it is much harder (although not impossible) to detect media influence in this context than in the contexts addressed in previous chapters. Some influence is clear; however, it is most interesting to address the data discussed in this chapter in ways which focus more closely on how people 'read' a message and use this to reflect on both the concept of 'code' and of 'polysemy'.

The focus group data discussed here shows a high degree of consensus about the central message of the ZT campaign. With a few striking exceptions, people show considerable skill and a shared cultural understanding in interpreting some highly complex messages conveyed by the style of image, and the juxtaposition of text and photographs.

Within this common consensus about the intended meaning there are some variations in people's reactions. People differ in how they feel positioned by the ZT campaign and how they feel about it. Although most respondents supported the campaign, some people resist the message because they disagree with its feminist perspective. Others agree with the message but feel it is not relevant to them. Some research participants from ethnic minorities relate to the posters differently from white participants (attending to distinct elements in the images, and thus seeing it in a different way). They feel the messages do not address their communities, but are also wary of stereotypes that might be reinforced by more 'black' images. Younger people and women are more receptive to the campaign, older people and men are more critical (this observation from the focus groups is backed up by the statistical differences evident in the survey results).

This research also reveals that the advertisements could, on occasion, be interpreted in quite a different way than that intended by the campaign designers. In particular it shows how dominant ideas (about 'the look' of a victim or the likely frequency of abuse) may lead a minority of people to 'see' more children in the image than there actually are or to believe they could detect symptoms of abuse in one of the children. This finding echoes results from my own previous work on AIDS. I found that people sometimes 'misread' a Health Education advertisement aimed at convincing them that people with HIV looked just like anyone else. The advert showed a page in which the words 'eyes', 'nose', 'mouth' were positioned on the page as if on a face. The caption read 'how to recognise someone with HIV'. The message was that they look just like anyone else. However, some people superimposed familiar media images of people with AIDS onto this abstract advertisement. Thus people made comments to the effect that the advert was trying to say that if you have HIV you show certain symptoms: 'their eyes are all black underneath', 'his face is all skinny', 'their hair drops out' (Kitzinger 1995). In this sense materials which attempt to challenge mainstream imagery can clearly be read in a polysemic way, so that they are interpeted in ways which more closely correspond to more familiar representations.

This chapter has looked at how people relate to a campaign trying to counter many of the stereotypes in the mainstream media and attempting to introduce a feminist perspective on the issue. The campaign clearly attracted attention, was thought-provoking and generated conversations. In some groups it was evident that the campaign changed people's thinking, even shifting their assessment of their own experiences. Some women felt supported in resisting abuse in their own lives, some men felt challenged positively to reflect on their own behaviour and attitudes towards women and children. However, it is also evident that the campaign met misunderstanding, criticism, resistance and outright opposition. Clearly the potential for one campaign to influence people is limited in the face not only of its own qualities or flaws but also the context in which it is operating. The ZT campaign was trying to introduce a frame of understanding sexual violence which was alien to many people. It also had to compete with pervasive mainstream imagery. The degree of positive support for the campaign and the extent to which it engaged people is testimony to its success. A well-designed campaign can provide important alternatives, offering symbolic support and provoking some people to rethink some of their assumptions. However, the impact of a single campaign can never compare to the power of the mass media. Any individual message will be read in its broader social and cultural context and may be overwhelmed by more pervasive representations. This research showed that sometimes it is hard for individual alternative messages to be understood or even 'seen'.[3]

10
Conclusion

This book has explored the ways in which people engage with diverse media, ranging from headline news reports to individual documentaries, from soap opera story lines to specific advertising campaigns. Each chapter has offered different ways of exploring 'audience–text relations' and theorising about media power. Each offers a distinct insight into how messages influence us and how we might resist them.

The cumulative evidence confirms previous research highlighting the fact that people are not dry sponges uncritically absorbing all that they hear and see. We bring our experiences, our identities, our politics and other sources of information to bear on our engagement with any individual text. Audiences are far more diverse and far more creative than they are often given credit for. These are all fundamental premises of active audience theory and have been amply illustrated in the data presented in this book so far.

Nevertheless, my research reveals that in spite of, and sometimes *because* of this, the media are a crucial resource in constructing our sense of the world around us. The mass media can help to define what counts as a public issue, impact upon our understandings of individual cases, shape suspicions and beliefs, and resource memories and conversations. The media also influence how we think about ourselves and each other, impacting on how we relate to family, friends and 'outsiders'. They can even help us to interpret the most intensely private experience and influence our hopes and our fears for the future.

The most important conclusion from my research is that we should not see ideas about audience activity as contradicting theories about media power. Instead, we should see them as integral to any efforts to understand how that power operates. Acknowledging that audiences are 'active' does not mean that the media are ineffectual. Recognising the role of interpretations does not invalidate the concept of influence. Elihu Katz, whose eminent career spans so many different approaches to audience research, makes this point very cogently. It is not that 'the multiplicity of factors which mediate between television and viewers undermine media effects', he points out 'but rather that it is only through such complex mediations that any effects could occur at all' (Katz, cited in Livingstone 1997:321). Gaining a better understanding of this interplay is one of the challenges for media studies research.

In this final chapter I revisit my key findings about these 'complex mediations', summarise the role played by the media in shaping the public perception of child sexual abuse and consider what my findings can tell us about how both texts and audiences 'work'. This allows for a critical reassessment of some key terms from media studies theory. I conclude by suggesting ways forward for both textual analysis and audience reception research.

THE MEDIA'S ROLE IN REPRESENTING SOCIAL ISSUES

The mass media are a key arena through which contemporary social issues are defined. The research presented in this volume shows that when the media start to publicise an issue they can:

- help to expose new problems. Their status as definers of social reality and agenda-setters makes their involvement in such processes crucial to social transformation
- redefine the very nature of the issue (e.g. with the shift from an exclusive focus on stranger-danger to recognising incest)
- publicise accounts that support conversations about previously taboo topics, shifting interpersonal interaction and contributing toward a spiral of recognition
- popularise new types of discursive construction
- provide a forum for the formation of new types of identity and identity performance ('the victim', 'the survivor').

The way in which the mass media cover an issue is also crucial. The media can:

- help to confront or evade certain aspects of the problem (e.g. that most sexual abuse is committed by men known to the child)
- play a role in constructing or maintaining ideas about certain 'types of people' (e.g. the paedophile)
- promote iconic images of perpetrators (e.g. Myra Hindley's police mugshot)
- perpetuate false associations (e.g. the confusion between gay men and child molesters)

- support or challenge our assumptions (e.g. that we would know if anyone in our community was likely to abuse children)
- popularise new forms of understanding, including disseminating novel, professional or lay diagnostic terms (e.g. false memory syndrome)
- set up high-profile crisis cases that act as common landmarks in public thinking and shift (or divert) attention onto new aspects of the problem (e.g. controversies about disputed allegations).

The way in which journalists question their sources and present their accounts can:

- clarify, or skate over, contradictions in the ways we/they think (e.g. drawing attention, or not, to the fact that neighbours may express shock at one man's conviction for sexual abuse, but still be emphatic that they would know if it were happening in another family)
- evoke empathy with, or alienation from, different sources of a story in ways that may encourage audience identification with one side rather than another (e.g. parents versus social workers)
- present, or fail to present, information that supports different ways of understanding events (e.g. that some families in the 'Cleveland crisis' included men with previous convictions for sexual abuse, Chapter 4)
- challenge or reinforce stereotypes (e.g. contrasting the 'ordinariness' of the accused parents in Orkney with conventional notions about the appearance and behaviour of 'paedophiles').

The media help to frame the problem, defining what is relevant to the debate and how it should be approached. They can:

- help us to think about the solutions to social problems in particular ways (e.g. public notification when convicted sex offenders are released into the community)
- act as a forum through which pressure is brought to bear on policy-makers
- help people to understand social problems and become activists within their communities.

HOW TEXTS 'WORK'

The success of the media in achieving such outcomes will, in part, relate to the nature of the coverage. Key factors include the extent and consistency of coverage across different media outlets and the presentation (or withholding) of particular facts and explanations. Media influence also relates to the reiteration of key phrases, the use of evocative images and dramatic tension, the way in which narrative trajectories are played out and the timing of when different elements in a story emerge. Other key factors are the plausibility and reputation of different sources quoted in the reporting, the use of emotive personal accounts and the ways in which journalists employ techniques such as textual and visual to appeal to audience identification. In this book I have identified three particularly significant media devices (which often combine some of the features outlined above). These are:

- 'media templates': This term highlights the ways in which journalists encourage analogies with prior events. These analogies can become templates that pattern our understanding of the main issues involved and influence our assessments of the likely rights and wrongs of a case. These templates shape our memories of the past, and, crucially, influence how we interpret new stories as they unfold
- 'story branding': This term refers to the labelling of news events in ways that summarise the essence of the story in particular ways. The 'branding' focuses our attention on some aspects of events rather than others (e.g. branding Orkney 'the dawn raids case')
- 'story placing': This term refers to the way in which journalists create an ambience for a story, using references to geography, landscape, culture and community to invite a particular attitude towards a news event. However, my research shows that people may also draw on more diverse cultural imagery of place than that presented in news reporting alone.

HOW AUDIENCES 'WORK'

The impact of coverage cannot be assessed independently from how audiences engage with the media, and what they bring to their 'readings' of newspaper reports or TV programmes. When media coverage influences us it is usually through, not in spite of, our interpretive engagement with it. When a message is particularly powerful it is often because we respond to it by mobilising aspects of our own experience. In Chapter 3, reviewing the dramatic impact of the media's (re)discovery of sexual abuse in the 1980s, I showed how this tapped into a vast reservoir of previously ignored or suppressed personal experiences. It encouraged people to reassess life events and talk about them in new ways. In Chapter 6 I explored the importance of empathy with accused parents and how this connected with people's own fears of state surveillance. Chapter 7 illustrated the ways in which media reports could tap into personal hopes and fears. This chapter also highlighted the importance of the 'social currency' of different media and personal accounts. I demonstrated how anecdotes about stranger-danger become integrated into everyday talk, while knowledge about threats closer to home is less often shared with friends and neighbours. Chapter 8 explored how responses to 'paedophiles in the community' linked into the focus on stranger-danger and reflected people's concerns for their children and their pre-existing sense of community disenfranchisement.

The above examples all demonstrate how the power of particular themes within the coverage was actually strengthened by audience engagement. However, it is important to remember that audience activity can also weaken the potential impact of the media. It is this aspect of audience 'power' which is more usually emphasised in the existing literature. Researchers looking at audience activity point out that we critique, reinterpret, appropriate or resist media messages, potentially undermining their ability to influence us. Evidence of such activity emerged in all my different research projects and is summarised below.

My research confirmed that people sometimes choose to avoid coverage and that they often profess to approach the media with a high degree of cynicism ('The paper'll blow everything out of proportion anyway'; 'You're never going to know what really happened'; 'You just know whenever you are watching the news that you are not actually getting the facts'). It also identified clear examples where people rejected the predominant media message because of what they saw as distorted reporting. Aspects of coverage that could alienate people include:

- a perceived lack of openness or excessive efforts to image-manage by source organisations (see Chapter 5)

- 'over the top' emotive reporting which could make audiences feel manipulated (see Chapter 6)
- a perceived history of bias (e.g. against social workers, see Chapter 4).

In addition, my own observations of how people discussed child sexual abuse identified two further ways in which a dominant message might be resisted or reinterpreted:

- Image-text disjuncture: There were a few occasions when people were more influenced by the visuals shown on television than by the interpretation offered to them by the voice-over (see Chapter 6)
- The boomerang effect:[1] There were a few occasions when media coverage produced the opposite result to that which might be anticipated. This is evident among the minority of research participants who took on board the frequent assertion that the Orkney case was 'just like Cleveland' but responded to this analogy in a very different way from other research participants. Instead of the analogy confirming that this was yet another social work 'cock-up', they thought that the apparent similarities between the two cases suggested that the social workers must have had strong cause for acting as they did. Everyone was well aware of the furore caused by the previous crisis in Cleveland so, these research participants reasoned, social workers would not have risked a similar intervention without carefully considering its necessity (see Chapter 4).

Media coverage thus may have, embedded within it, strands which some people use to reject, subvert or invert the main preferred meanings. Aspects of the coverage which impact on most people in one way may have the opposite effect on others.

In addition, people may resist a message by drawing on a wide range of other texts and discourse including fictional accounts, broader cultural representations, specialist publications or the Internet. Personal and professional networks and people's own life experiences also provide alternative perspectives. The notion of 'the audience' as a single homogeneous mass is a myth. Some of the different perspectives people bring to an issue relate to variables such as age, gender, ethnic identity, socio-economic status or sexual identity.[2] People draw on:

- their own sense of identity and group loyalties
- political frameworks for opposition
- information from trusted professionals
- 'gossip' and community networks
- work experience around the issue
- direct personal experience.

This last category, personal experience, was particularly influential. It allowed some people to reject stereotypes about abusers ('Anybody to meet my Dad thought "oh perfect, Billy's lovely", nobody would think of him touching his kids') and to disown suggestions that abuse only happened in certain types of communities or families. It also gave some a 'gut response' to certain images presented by the media which was quite different from that intended by those who produced the image. A clear example of the latter was the woman who became very distressed when I produced a photographic still from the TV news coverage showing the children reunited with their families in Orkney. This apparently happy image of children holding hands with their parents was profoundly disturbing to her. It brought back painful memories of being sent home to her abusive father (see Chapter 5).

As the above examples make clear, even quite pervasive media messages do not operate successfully on all of the people all of the time and people are quite capable of responding to the same message in a variety of ways. In some ways this challenges any simplistic notion of media influence. However, in other ways it makes the common themes that ran through my focus group discussions all the more striking. Given that people are sceptical of the media, may avoid looking at some coverage, reinterpret it and draw on a whole range of alternative sources of information about a case in the news, it might be surprising to find any common strands in how people think at all. But my research found very strong commonalties (often regardless of age, gender, class or ethnicity, all aspects of identity that are frequently cited as being associated with diverse 'readings' of media texts). While it is important to highlight diversity where it existed, this should not lead us to ignore the common themes. What is striking in my research is the shared perspective of the majority of the research participants, and the recurring nature of the language, images and emotions recalled by such a diversity of groups.[3]

It is therefore also important to acknowledge the limitations to people's independence from the media. My research highlights the following:

- Avoiding coverage, forgetting it or 'not really paying attention' does not necessarily 'protect' people from media influence. Instead it may leave them with the crudest impressions based on headlines or dramatic images alone. Indeed, the inattentive or disengaged audience may actually be more, rather than less, vulnerable to absorbing dominant themes and associations (see Chapters 4 and 5).
- Expressed cynicism is also not a guarantee of independence from media influence. People may not trust how journalists represent a crisis, but they may still rely upon them as their main source of ideas about what happened.
- Alternative sources of information are less accessible or pervasive than the dominant mass media message. Although some people do have access to information from trusted professionals or specialist publications this is less part of most people's everyday environment than the information distributed by the mass media.
- Pervasive themes and media devices (such as templates and branding) can influence people in spite of their preferred political position (see Chapters 4 and 5).
- Even personal experience, which seemed to offer the most profound alternative framework for understanding child sexual abuse, is not completely independent of the mass media.

Given the significance of personal experience of abuse as a platform for criticising the media it is worth expanding on this last point. My research confirms the argument that we do not evaluate our own lives in a media-free zone. When the media ignore a personal experience, however dramatic or widespread, people may find it difficult to define it, talk about it or protest against it. Cultural representations inform how we understand and label events in our lives, and sexual assaults are surrounded by competing notions of what counts as abuse and what counts as consent. This means that a woman repeatedly forced to have sex with her father and uncle may not see it in terms of assault (see Chapter 3). Even if someone does define his or her experience in such terms this may be kept strictly private and so have limited influence beyond the individual. Sometimes people do not bring their own experience to bear on their own understanding of child sexual abuse. They may dismiss it as highly unusual ('I must be the only person this happens to') or simply not consider the implications of what has happened to them for their broader assumptions (see the discussion in Chapter 7).

REFLECTIONS ON KEY TERMS AND THE IMPLICATIONS OF AUDIENCE ACTIVITY FOR MEDIA INFLUENCE

The analysis presented in this book suggests the need for clarity and caution when applying some key terms from audience reception theory. Here I want to revisit concepts such as 'decoding', 'polysemy', 'oppositional reading' and 'resistance'. These are all invaluable tools. However, some accounts (particularly in textbooks for students) seem more concerned to use them to demonstrate and celebrate diverse audience responses rather than consider the origins or consequences of such responses. Little effort has been put into pursuing Hall's original proposition that texts carry 'preferred meanings'. Some accounts of the debate completely ignore Hall's call for audience research to locate 'significant clusters' of meaning and link these to the social and discursive positioning of readers, drawing up a 'cultural map' of the audience and *relating these to social and political processes*' (Hall 1973, my emphasis).[4] Failing to pursue this can mean that descriptions of audience activity, in all its diversity, appear to imply that power is magically transferred from the media text to the audience.

In Chapter 3 I examined debates about 'active consumption' and 'creative appropriation'. I showed how, in my data, audience activity could not be separated from the nature of the texts. I therefore argued for the ongoing importance of 'positive images'. I also argued that people's ability to find positive reflections of their own lives from unexpected sources should not be seen as every individual's birthright. It should be examined alongside a consideration of the conditions that facilitate or inhibit such appropriation activity. Abused children, prior to the mid 1980s, had no place to stand from which to creatively appropriate mainstream texts, precisely because of the cultural and social vacuum surrounding their experience.

Throughout the book I have also drawn attention to any examples of 'oppositional' or 'resistant' readings. However, rather than demonstrating weak media influence these examples are often, I have argued, better understood in terms of intertextuality. For example, some people opted to read representations of the Orkney islands or the accused parents in a way diametrically opposed to the dominant message in the news reporting at the time. Instead of seeing the island as a rural idyll they decided it was a sinister backwater populated by hippies prone to devil-worship and child abuse (Chapter 6). People may resist one message because of the plethora of alternative messages in other, more ubiquitous cultural products. In all these cases we need to think about what counts as an interpretation that truly breaks with the mainstream frame (rather than merely inverting it). People's ability to deconstruct, reconstruct or oppose a particular message should not be seen as inherently progressive. There is a need to go further than simply documenting the various ways in which people 'decode' or 'resist' messages to identify the origins of such diverse readings and reflect on why they matter. Rather than seeing these patterns as evidence of 'consumer sovereignty', we should examine how they are shaped by their socio-political context, including by the conduct of people's social interchange (structured by social conditions and the policing of information exchange by stigma, see Chapter 7). Audience responses are not free-floating. They are themselves products of time and place, embedded in power structures, shaped by patterns of everyday life, conventions, common sense and language.

Finally I want to consider the notion of 'polysemy' and its sister concept of 'decoding'. My study shows that people share highly sophisticated understandings of the meaning of words and images from the dominant culture in which they live. It highlights the skill with which people 'read' the ZT adverts and also highlights the consistency with which news reports about Orkney communicated messages about social work malpractice and the threat to any family. People share very similar 'readings' of the core 'meaning' of the story. It would simply not be true to say, as Hobson suggests about the soap opera *Crossroads*, for example, that there were as many readings of the 'Orkney cases' as there were readers and viewers of news reports about Orkney (see Hobson cited in Chapter 2 this volume).

There were examples of genuinely polysemic readings in my data but these were a very small minority. My research suggests that most readings, most of the time, by most of the intended 'home' audience, will have more in common than divides them. This does not mean that they will respond to the message in identical ways. The distinction is sometimes blurred by terms such as 'decoding' and 'reading' which conflate misunderstanding with a conscious reinterpretation of the message (Corner 1986:56).

This links to a second point; polysemy is sometimes a deliberate part of the text encoded by the producers rather than something which indicates audience independence from the text. Soap operas, as Hobson points out, are structured in ways that interweave diverse perspectives from different characters and their serial nature encourages active engagement from their fans. I would add that even news reports deliberately incorporate a level of polysemy. They do this through the very institutional structure of 'balanced reporting' that invites viewers to see 'two sides' to the debate. Such basic levels of 'polysemy' are recognised by media producers as essential to maximising audiences and maintaining credibility or stimulating pleasure. It does not mean that the text has no ideological effect. On the contrary, the hegemonic power of a programme may actually depend on its ambiguity. Jhally and Lewis's study of *The Cosby Show*, for example, combines an understanding of the programme's different pleasurable appeals to black and white audiences, with a clear argument about how it might impact on people's thinking (Jhally and Lewis 1992). Similarly a 'balanced' news report may still convey a particular frame very powerfully in spite of, or even because of its 'balanced' nature. News reports define not only the importance of the issue but also the axis of debate, the range of relevant experts called upon to comment and the spectrum of reasonable opinion (Williams *et al.* 2003).

I suspect that 'genuine' polysemy (i.e. polysemy that originates in the decoding process of the audience in spite of the intentions of the producers) is much rarer than some writers imply (at least where encoders and decoders live in the same dominant culture).[5] Polysemic moments make for intriguing anecdotes, and have high 'social currency' among scholars. But I suspect this results in a disproportionate emphasis on such incidents. A systematic attempt to track such examples in my own data suggests a rather different way of interpreting such moments. The 'boomerang effect' and the way in which a couple of people privileged their own reading of news film footage over the preferred meaning offered by the news anchor were the clearest examples of polysemy that I could find in my focus group discussions in relation to mainstream news reports. More examples of apparent polysemy (as well as more examples of negotiated and oppositional readings) were evident in my research into responses to the feminist-inspired ZT campaign. Here it seemed that some people could quite literally 'not see' some aspects of the campaign message because these messages did not conform to their expectation (for similar findings see Kitzinger 1995 and Tulloch 2000:118, 195–6). This suggests an intriguing possibility: perhaps genuinely polysemic readings are more likely to occur when a text breaks with the frame offered by mainstream coverage. The more 'alternative' the message, the more likely the audience are to mobilise polysemic interpretations or to resist it.

The concept of polysemy thus should not be evoked as a mantra guarding against media power. Some texts are more polysemic than others, some invite polysemy and some have polysemy thrust upon them. The concept should always be used with attention to context and consequences.

So where does this leave us? What are the implications for future research?

IMPLICATIONS FOR FUTURE RESEARCH

Analysing media coverage

My research demonstrates the on-going importance of critically assessing, and attempting to intervene in, media coverage and cultural representation. We may not always be able to predict audience responses, but it would be quite wrong to dismiss textual analysis as completely out of touch with the real sites of meaning creation. Even if we cannot specify all the possible meanings a text may offer its audiences 'we can still elucidate tendencies and likelihoods, specifying the different registers and discursive strategies at work' (Dahlgren 1995:31). Analysis of media coverage (and the development of campaign strategies) can, however, be refined and developed through a better understanding of how audiences might engage with different texts (news coverage, documentaries, soap opera story-lines or advertisements). Research into how people actually view, discuss, recall and understand such representations confirms some parts of textual analysis, but challenge others. It also produces new insights into what aspects of texts might be most significant. My audience research underlines that such analysis should include considerations of the facts that are offered or withheld as well as examining more subtle representation processes, e.g. narrative trajectories and repetition, images and phrases, invitations to imaginative empathy and the structuring of identification. In particular I hope that the concepts of 'story placing', 'branding' and 'media templates' – concepts directly drawn from the focus group data – may provide useful tools for analysing media accounts in the future.

Studying audiences: 'new influence research'

My research also demonstrates both the importance, and the feasibility, of pursuing questions about media influence through qualitative audience reception work. Such work should never define people only in terms of their interaction with the text, or see them as individuals. It should always include consideration of people's social networks and what they bring to their engagement with any newspaper article, TV programme or campaign message. Ideally it should also explore the links between audience understandings, the nature of media coverage and the media production processes.

I hope the work presented in this volume, whatever its limitations, suggests some methodological and theoretical ways of advancing such research. I think that ongoing work is needed on the complex interaction between the 'personal' and the 'cultural' that explores both audience acceptance and audience resistance as sites of power and includes analysis of common readings alongside acknowledging differences. We also need research that pursues comparisons across different formats and genre (something I have not explored in any great detail here) and work that addresses the potential and limitations of new media forms.

Luckily I do not think we are starting with a blank slate; let me break with convention here and conclude not simply with a call for further research but a suggestion that we make better use of existing work. There is now a substantial body of research which, I believe, offers plenty of scope for refining our understanding of audiences. I have previously, perhaps somewhat mischievously, attempted to identify this as the 'New Effects Research' (Kitzinger 1999). Such efforts have not met with much success. Does this indicate the amount of 'baggage' carried by the word 'effects' or does this indicate audience 'resistance'? Here I will adopt a more acceptable term and describe this body of work, as others have begun to, as the 'New Influence Research' (Corner 2000).

New Influence Research incorporates a hybrid collection of research involving focus groups, interviews, ethnographies and various innovative exercises with audiences to explore the interaction between media representation and how people talk, interact and think. One strand of such research was developed by researchers based at the

Glasgow University Media Group during the late 1980s and 1990s. This includes research on the impact of media reporting of topics as diverse AIDS, industrial disputes, public health issues, terrorism and breast cancer (See Eldridge 1993; Henderson 1996; Kitzinger 1990, 1993; Kitzinger and Henderson 1999; Miller 1994; Miller *et al.* 1999; Philo 1990, 1999; Reilly 1999). Similar research emerged from Liverpool University around the same time including a detailed study of how people responded to different televisual representations of nuclear power (Corner *et al.* 1990) and another on economics (Gavin 1998). Under this rubric I would also include an impressively wide-ranging set of studies from many different countries including Australia, Norway and the USA. This includes work addressing, for example, how people integrate media representations into their discussion of war, gun control, welfare, social policy and how news reporting and TV programmes are used in constructing ideas about racism or ethnicity or interact with accounts of femininity and identity (see, for example, Entman and Rojecki 2000; Gamson 1992; Gripsud 1995; Jhally and Lewis 1992; McKinley 1997; Tulloch and Tulloch 1993).

This work bridges not only many of the national but also the disciplinary divisions that have bedevilled media research in the past. Each author adopts a slightly different approach and has a different way of envisaging 'influence' and attending to what people say. What this work shares, however, is an in-depth method of enquiry which engages in sustained explorations of audience responses while also giving serious attention to the nature of the text(s). All these studies are rooted in a keen understanding of audiences as active participants in the creation of meaning. Their findings offer sharp reminders of how media power might operate.

The debate about audience research is bursting with manifestos for the future of the field. For some commentators our destiny lies in studying the emerging new media, for others in examining how media producers conceptualise their audiences. Some argue for a focus on audience choices and pleasures, others for a broad sociology of how people consume media technologies. All these directions may prove productive. My plea here is simply that we do not abandon investigating questions of media impact. Quite how the media might impact on how we think is one of the most contested questions within media studies. It is also very difficult to study. However, the challenges are not insurmountable. I hope that the methods and theories expounded in this book, and the whole new body of 'New Media Influence Research' that I have highlighted above, may provide a fruitful way of developing the debate. In this way I hope that audience reception research can move towards, developing a nuanced understanding of how media influence operates (when and under what circumstances), at all times maintaining a clear conceptualisation of who is trying to communicate, what, to whom, and why.

Epilogue:
Implications for Journalists
and for Child Protection

This book has focused on the debate about audience reception and media theory, however, my task would be incomplete without at least briefly reflecting on some of the practical implications of my research.

IMPLICATIONS FOR CHILD PROTECTION

For those concerned with child protection the research presented in this book underlines the need to develop and maintain good links with media personnel, especially TV producers. The aspect of television that makes it most feared – its invasion of the private space of the home and its accessibility prior to literacy – also makes it a very powerful tool in the battle against sexual abuse. Some of the 'success stories' evident in my analysis suggests that positive media messages about child sexual abuse provide an important resource and that child protection professionals can work productively with media producers.

The data presented in this volume also highlights the ongoing need to challenge misleading stereotypes about abusers and to improve public understanding of the intervention process when sexual abuse allegations are made. This, of course, is not necessarily just a PR exercise, gaining public trust can also include improved training, better resources and greater transparency and accountability.

Finally, my research highlights some of the attitudes with which child protection practitioners will have to engage in everyday practice and in policy making. Sensitivity to everyday ways of understanding child sexual abuse, and presumptions about the intervention process, are important in working with clients and providing information and support. Direct public awareness campaigns, unmediated by mass media production values, may also provide an (albeit limited) alternative avenue for challenging sexual violence. The ZT campaign discussed in Chapter 9, and its evaluation, suggests ways in which such strategies might be pursued.

IMPLICATIONS FOR MEDIA PROFESSIONALS

This book has some clear messages for all those working within the media, e,g. journalists, editors, programme producers and script-writers. The survivors of abuse who spoke to me argued strongly in favour of 'realistic' and 'hopeful' media representation. They yearned for portrayals of survivors which showed what they had endured without parading them as part of some kind of freak show. Every portrait of an abuse survivor carries a burden of representation which, they felt, would directly impact on how friends and families saw them ('You don't know if they are watching it, or putting you in the film and watching you'). They praised 'emotional realism' in programmes which explored the complex feelings they might have about their abusers, their mothers and themselves. (Similar issues are noted by women who have experienced domestic violence, see Schlesinger *et al.* 1992.) Such representations helped them to think through and talk about their experiences ('We've got some kind of communication with the telly and can talk to each other about the way Beth is'). It also affected their own self image. Media images could be disempowering ('Victims on TV, they're like a big shadow, all blacked out. That makes me feel terrible'). But the media could also support them in feeling more positive ('Watching Beth [in *Brookside*] has really helped me').

There are also clear messages for how journalists represent abusers. As one young woman commented, she wished the media had made her better able to respond supportively when her little sister told her about being abused by a neighbour. The neighbour did not fit the media stereotype of a paedophile and so she had been dismissive of her sister's disclosure. Media personnel also need to think seriously about how they represent the intervention process. It is important to recall the comment by a teenager who felt that media reporting of social workers had 'put a barrier up' and stopped her from seeking help (Chapter 5).

There are many guidelines available on-line to help journalists think about the practice and ethics of reporting about children and/or sexual violence both nationally and internationally. Guides have been produced by, for example, UNICEF (www.unicef.org), Human Rights Watch (www.hrw.org), Press Complaints Council (www.pcc.org.uk), Presswise (www.presswise.org.uk) and the International Federation of Journalists (www.ifj.org) (see Jempson 1997; Jempson and Searle 1999; McCrum and Hughes 2003; McIntyre 2002). I would also recommend publications such as Byerly (1994) for those engaged in journalism training. Here I would also suggests the following cluster of questions to complement those guidelines:

- You might envisage your primary audience as adults, but what about children (especially for TV output)?
- What image of social work intervention are you offering to mothers or fathers who suspect their children are being abused (or to the abused children themselves)? Is it accurate? Is it representative? Does it reflect the range of ways in which social services operate?
- What image of abuse survivors is being presented, and what impact might this have on survivors and on those currently being victimised?
- What levels of complexity are you reflecting in the stories?
- What are the opportunities and the dangers in turning suffering into entertainment?
- How do you select the stories that are news worthy, and what overall image of the problem does this promote to 'the public'?
- How do values such as sensationalism, novelty, human interest or timeliness impact on you or your editor's focus?
- How does a concentration on events, rather than underlying issues, influence what is reported?
- What are the issues behind the headlines, and are there innovative ways through which these might be addressed?
- How does the 'angle' you select organise your account? How might you make this transparent to your audience? What other angles might you have adopted?
- When moving onto a 'new angle' on an issue what dimensions of the problem are being left behind?
- When describing the site of an alleged attack what images are you challenging or reinforcing? How do you employ 'story placing' to destabilise or confirm conventional ways of understanding the sort of places and communities in which children are abused?
- When describing an abuser what stereotypes are you drawing upon or challenging?
- Is it ever appropriate to describe an abuser or act of abuse as 'homosexual'? Do you equally describe other assaults as 'heterosexual'?

- When representing someone who is protesting their innocence how do you present them?
- When seeking, for yourself, to assess someone's guilt or innocence what informs your judgement and how do you present this to your viewers/readers/listeners?
- What shorthand 'branding' do you use to label a controversial case and why? What consequences do you think this might have?
- Which cases do you link together and why? How do you use analogies from history and is this appropriate? What is your knowledge of previous events based upon? (see Chapter 4).
- When an issue or case is the subject of controversy how do you decide what is the continuum of relevant and reasonable opinion? How do you use the concept of 'balance'?
- How can you ensure you represent perspective or voices which are structurally disadvantaged in any particular situation (this may be parents or it may be social services bound by rules of confidentiality)?
- How can you nurture good relations with diverse sources to allow you to research all dimensions of a story?
- How can you represent 'the voice of the child' without direct access? Who speaks 'on the child's behalf'?
- What can, and should, you say about cases before they come to trial?
- When using a vox pop or canvassing local opinion in a report, what is its status? How do you, as a journalist, contextualise such comments or question those who are commenting?
- When representing an 'expert opinion' how do you assess or contextualise this expertise? How do you question the professionals involved?
- How can you challenge common-sense but inaccurate assumptions or draw attention to contradictions?
- How can journalists challenge powerful professional consensus and open up new questions?
- How can you evaluate short-term tactical gains versus long-term strategies for child protection (e.g. concerning community notification for released sex offenders)? How do you reflect local and national/international concerns?
- What are the limits of your own knowledge about a controversy? What can you research? What are you unlikely to ever be able to discover? How do you acknowledge your own limitations?

REFLECTIONS ON THE POLITICAL ECONOMY OF THE MEDIA

Media personnel are not operating in conditions of their own making. Many of the questions I have raised might be considered unrealistic by journalists just trying to do their jobs. Some of the criticisms of the media that I have highlighted should also be seen in the context of current changes in the media. If we are to have a healthy media, we also need to consider the political economy of media ownership and production.

Historically 'soft' journalism and media (e.g. soap operas, discussion shows and magazines) have been an important avenue through which 'women's problems' gained a public profile. Formats other than hard news still offer potential for addressing key social issues (the character of Beth in *Brookside* was clearly a positive example of this, see Chapter 3). However, the expansion of 'soft' under-resourced journalism (Franklin 1991) can also simply lead to a proliferation of ill-informed stories which rely on emotive accounts rather than engaging with critical debate (whether these are the family tragedy stories from Orkney or dwelling on ever more horrific accounts of sexual violation).

Many of the problems with media coverage highlighted in this book may also be exacerbated by lack of resources, pressures of time, and deteriorating employment conditions for journalists. Reducing the number of full-time specialists employed on newspapers means that there will be even fewer journalists able to write about issues with knowledge of the wider debates or a first-hand understanding of the history. Obsessions with 'up to the minute' reporting in the broadcast media could lead to further deterioration in reporting of past events. There will be little space for thoughtful journalism which might challenge one injustice (such as children being taken into care unnecessarily) without perpetrating another (such as misrepresenting routine social work practice). Time constraints already mean that complex ideas have to be presented in simple sound-bites. Lack of time may also undermine efforts to access the most vulnerable and 'difficult' of interview sources. While happy to exploit off-the-peg voyeuristic presentations of suffering, highly pressurised media production processes are unlikely to create conditions under which survivors might assert more positive and critical representations. At the same time journalistic research may increasingly consist of merely 'going through the cuttings' and recycling media-defined truth, resulting in the proliferation of formulaic journalism. The crass use of media templates and stereotypes is likely to be exacerbated, while opportunities for innovative or investigative journalism are likely to diminish. In this context 'alternative' media and other avenues for communication and education continue to be essential; critical media studies also have a vital role to play and we need to continue to defend quality and diversity in mass media production.

Appendix

FOCUS GROUP DISCUSSIONS ON
GENERAL VIEWS OF CHILD SEXUAL ABUSE

Group no.	Group description	No. of people	Gender	Age
Group 1	University students 1	6	6f	20s
Group 2	University students 2	6	5f, 1m	20s
Group 3	Television editors	5	3f, 2m	20s–30s
Group 4	Neighbours 1	5	4f, 1m	30s
Group 5	Academic colleagues	6	6f	20s–30s
Group 6	Survivors support group 1	5	5f	20s–40s
Group 7	Postnatal support group	5	5f	30s
Group 8	Neighbours 2	3	3f	20s–30s
Group 9	Neighbours 3	5	5f	30s–40s
Group 10	Community centre group	10	10f	20s–50s
Group 11	Community centre group	8	8f	20s–30s
Group 12	Women's Aid workers	4	4f	20s–40s
Group 13	Charity/activist group	7	4f, 3m	20s–40s
Group 14	Friends	5	3f, 2m	20s
Group 15	Social workers	4	3f, 1m	20s–30s
Group 16	Survivors support group 2	5	5f	20s–40s
Group 17	Youth group	9	6f, 3m	16–20
Group 18	Evening class	4	1f, 3m	30s
Group 19	Church attenders	6	2f, 4m	30s
Group 20	Friends	3	3m	16–20
Group 21	School pupils	6	3f, 3m	16
Group 22	School pupils	5	5f	16
Group 23	Post-grad trainee journalists	6	5f, 1m	20s–30s
Group 24	Youth group	9	5f, 4m	16
Group 25	Youth group	6	5f, 1m	16
Group 26	Retirement club	8	3f, 5m	60s–70s
Group 27	Bowling club	6	6m	60s–70s
Group 28	Unemployed workers centre	4	3f, 1m	20s–30s
Group 29	Grandmothers/mothers of playgroup children	4	4f	20s–60s
Group 30	Community education workers	7	4f, 3m	20s–50s
Group 31	Community women's group	10	10f	20s–50s
Group 32	University lecturers	4	1f, 3m	30s–50s
Group 33	Community group	7	5f, 2m	20s–40s
Group 34	Women's centre group	11	11f	30s–50s
Group 35	Knitting circle	6	6f	60s–70s
Group 36	Football fans	5	5m	20s–30s
Group 37	Local government workers	6	6m	20s–40s

Group no.	Group description	No. of people	Gender	Age
Group 38	Neighbours 4	6	3f, 3m	30s–40s
Group 39	Trainee journalists	3	1f, 2m	20s–30s
Group 40	Factory workers	5	5m	30s–50s
Group 41	Neighbours 5	7	4f, 3m	30s–60s
Group 42	Pub group	6	6m	30s–60s
Group 43	British Telecom workers	8	1f, 7m	20s–50s
Group 44	Flatmates	3	3f	20s
Group 45	Friends	3	3f	20s
Group 46	Friends	3	3f	20s
Group 47	Football fans	4	4m	20s
Group 48	Survivors support group	3	3f	14–16
Group 49	Indian academic visitors	3	1f, 2m	30s–50s

Total no. of participants discussing general perceptions of child sexual abuse = 275.

FOCUS GROUP DISCUSSIONS ON THE ZERO TOLERANCE CAMPAIGN ONLY

Group no.	Group description	No. of people	Gender	Age
Group 50	Office workers	5	2f, 3m	20s–40s
Group 51	Neighbours	13	13f	20s–50s
Group 52	Youth group	9	9f	13–15
Group 53	Transport and railway workers	5	2f, 3m	20s–50s
Group 54	Members of the Christian Women's Guild	4	4f	50s–60s
Group 55	Single parents involved in Gingerbread	6	6f	20s–40s
Group 56	Women's aid workers	5	5f	20s–30s
Group 57	Police officers	3	3m	20s–30s
Group 58	Marriage guidance counsellors	4	4f	30s–50s
Group 59	Black women's support agency workers	4	4f	20s–40s
Group 60	Police officers	3	1f, 2m	20s–40s
Group 61	Social workers	4	4f	20s–40s
Group 62	School staff	5	2f, 3m	20s–40s
Group 63	Rape crisis workers	5	5f	20s–40s
Group 64	Health workers	4	4f	20s–40s
Group 65	Women's aid workers	4	4f	20s–40s
Group 66	Meridian workers	3	3f	20s–40s
Group 67	Housing workers	4	3f 1m	20s–40s
Group 68	ZT Implementation group 1	10	10f	20s–50s
Group 69	ZT Implementation group 2	5	3f, 2m	20s–50s
Group 70	School pupils	5	3f, 2m	16
Group 71	School pupils	3	2f, 1m	16

Group no.	Group description	No. of people	Gender	Age
Group 72	School pupils	6	3f, 3m	16–17
Group 73	School pupils	3	3m	16–18
Group 74	Youth club group	4	4f	15–18
Group 75	Youth club group	6	3f, 3m	16–18
Group 76	Youth club group	5	5m	16–19
Group 77	Youth club group	5	3f, 5m	16–17
Group 78	Youth club group	6	4f, 2m	14–17
Group 79	Youth work trainees	6	6m	16–18

Number of focus groups for ZT studies = 30 (no. of participants =154).
Overall total number of focus groups = 79 (total number of participants = 429).

Notes

CHAPTER 1

1. Domestic violence is not the only priority. The International Feminist Movement also addresses global inequalities which feed sex tourism and cross-border trafficking. Distinct priorities have also developed including attention to rape as a war crime. (See Henson 1999; Joseph and Sharma 1994; Kelly and Radford 1998; Omvedt 1990; Stiglmayer 1994; Yoon, undated.) This book, however, is concerned with sexual assaults against children in a domestic context, with a particular focus on incestuous abuse.
2. Some anthologies addressing this issue were just emerging from the USA at this time. These included Louise Armstrong's groundbreaking work: *Kiss Daddy Goodnight* (Armstrong 1978) and the collected volume: *Voices in the Night* (McNaron and Morgan 1982). Invaluable early autobiographies and novels that addressed the subject were Maya Angelou's autobiographical account in *I Know Why the Caged Bird Sings* (published in the USA in 1969, but not in the UK until 1984) and the Pulitzer Prize winning novel *The Color Purple* by Alice Walker (1982).
3. The 40 interviews with abuse survivors and 58 of the focus groups were conducted by myself. Thanks are due to the following people who facilitated the other 21 groups: Lesley Henderson, Rick Holliman, Dawn Rowley, Hannah Bradby and Eddie Donaghy. I would also like to thank Paula Skidmore who conducted some of the interviews with journalists and their sources.

CHAPTER 2

1. My review focuses on work emanating from western European (particularly the UK) and North America (mainly USA) traditions. It is limited in that it pays minimal attention to difference across Europe (e.g. distinct Nordic or French traditions) or to research emanating from regions such as Latin America (see Martin-Barbero 2000). For a discussion of how an Arab-Islamic perspective might challenge western oriented communications theories, see Ayish 2003.
2. All histories are a form of story-telling told from a standpoint in the present and summaries inevitably end up glossing over subtleties in the original texts (Gray 1999). My review is a partial history in the sense that, like any other history, it can be neither comprehensive nor entirely impartial. In my first draft of this chapter my efforts to 'be true' to the original studies and not simply reproduce secondary accounts led me into a maze of complexity and contradictions. In the end I decided to adopt a conventional way of categorising and summarising the key approaches, because it is precisely these conventional categories that help

to underpin contemporary debate in much of Europe and North America. Such accounts therefore have a 'truth' regardless of what happened at the time. I would, however, urge readers who want to develop a thorough understanding of each approach to read the primary materials for themselves.

3. Alternative trajectories can be tracked through looking at the history of film studies. For example, the Payne Fund studies (1929–32) sought to assess the effects on audiences of exposure to the themes and messages of motion pictures. According to some writers it is these studies which 'gave birth to the scientific study of mass communication' (Lowry and DeFleur 1955, cited in Mosco and Kaye 2000:37). This review also does not discuss the dominant research paradigm emerging out of film theory in Britain during the 1970s and 1980s, although this contributed to the dialogue in developing approaches to television audience research. For a discussion of this dialogue see Eldridge *et al.* 1997:127–9.

4. The hypodermic model and the experimental behavioural approach are now both often seen as out-dated. Although such strong notions of media effect continue to thrive within mainstream psychology and to influence policy decisions, some of this work has been severely criticised on methodological grounds. (See Gauntlett 1995, 1998; Barker and Petley 1997/2001.)

5. The two-step model of media influence was pioneered in actual practice much earlier. It was used in 1918 by Parkes who directed British propaganda in the USA. Parkes started his campaigns by first singling out influential and eminent people of every profession as targets in order to encourage American involvement in the First World War (Kubey 1996:197).

6. The 'recipe for adjustment' category is a particularly interesting one and it is fascinating to revisit Herzog's data from a modern perspective. A remark by one of Herzog's interviewees that the radio stories give her 'an idea of how a wife should be to a husband' and warns her of the danger of being a busy-body is interpreted by Herzog as the woman 'using' the media for her own ends. It could equally be used to illustrate the ideological power of media representations (Herzog 1941:90).

7. Within a single country, different cultural interpretations may also produce quite distinct readings of a single film or programme. A study of women's reactions to representations of violence against women reports that a group of British Asian women 'learned' from *The Accused* (a film about a gang rape and the subsequent trial) that drinking and flirting was dangerous. 'They seemed to view the film almost anthropologically as a report upon the wider society', comment Schlesinger *et al.*, '... their reading of the film validated their differences, showing how their culture could operate to protect them from danger' (Schlesinger *et al.* 1992:64). This is in spite of the fact that the film was framed by the western feminist ideals about women's rights and designed to challenge the idea that women who drank and flirted were 'asking for it'.

8. Alice Walker's book was not a straightforward mainstream text. It was at the forefront of addressing sexual violence against girls and was extremely important for incest survivors when it first came out (see Chapter 3). However, the film (produced by the white male director, Steven Spielberg)

was the focus of a major controversy about the image of black people in the media, 'the likes of which had not been seen since the films *The Birth of a Nation* (1915) and *Gone with the Wind* (1939)' (Bobo 2003:307).

9. In Latin America the telenovellas are phenomenally popular with both men and women. Leading theorist Martin-Barbero theorises that their appeal in Latin America is due to the fact that melodrama 'speaks to many people who search for their identity in the primordial sociability of family relations and in the social solidarity of the neighbourhood, region, and friend networks' (Martin-Barbero 2000:152). This work highlights the telenovella as providing a language for popular forms of hope (Tufte 2000; Martin-Barbero 1999).

10. This study was designed on the premise that people do not view individual media messages in isolation, but as part of a patchwork of messages over time. I was also interested in how people might draw on different genre (news, soaps, documentaries, discussion shows) in constructing views on a topic or negotiating with different media messages. The research was also essentially retrospective. Where other researchers have used in-depth observation to explore the immediate interaction between audiences and their television sets, I wanted to tap into people's memories and their uses and understandings of media messages long after the naturally occurring media-watching event, and in a broader social context. Rather than assuming that 'consumption' and the relationship between text and audience is confined to the moment of viewing/reading (and the conversations which take place in the family sitting room or on the bus the next day) my research examined what people were left with long after the images had faded from the TV screen.

CHAPTER 3

1. Part of this chapter originally appeared in J. Kitzinger (2001) 'Transformations of public and private knowledge: audience reception, feminism and the experience of childhood sexual abuse', *Feminist Media Studies* 1(1):91–104.

2. I conducted most of these interviews before I became interested in media studies. I rarely asked women directly about the media. But talk about the media was threaded through women's accounts of their experiences and identities. Women also often talked about the mass media in response to questions such as: did you seek help as a child? What did you think would happen if you told? Have you ever talked to your mother about being abused? If you've only recently started thinking about the abuse, what prompted you to start thinking about it? How have friends and family reacted?

3. All names are pseudonyms. Names indicate that the quotes come from interviews conducted during the 1980s, Group ID numbers indicate that quotes come from the focus groups conducted during the 1990s.

4. Taking some element of 'control' over the timing or process of submitting to the inevitable might also be seen as a survival strategy. For a discussion

of experiences of abuse that are trivialised or discounted see also Gavey 1999; Kelly and Radford 1996.

5. Louise Armstrong, who wrote one of the very first books on this subject (*Kiss Daddy Goodnight*) describes a similar experience of going to the library to research incest. There was, she writes, 'virtually nothing that did not lead to a door marked "taboo", with all the attendant baggage of myth and divine retribution. I listened at those doors to sombre dialogues about tribal exogamy, the pragmatics of marrying outside the family or clan in order to solidify relations and support with outside peoples. None of which had anything to do with my New York father's political and personal interest or motives' (Armstrong 1994:13).

6. There were other factors which acted as a trigger such as the death of the abuser, or becoming a mother herself. However, the media were most likely to be mentioned as significant. For a discussion of how medical or life events – especially childbirth – influenced women's recall of abuse see Kitzinger 1990b.

7. Media studies is often divided into 'film and television' versus 'journalism studies'. This division allows for close attention to the characteristics of the different media. However, if you start from how people think about a problem (e.g. child sexual abuse) then attempting to write only about TV, or only about the press, becomes nonsensical. Audiences are omnivores. We think about an issue using information, images and ideas from multiple media sources and cannot usually distinguish from which source we obtained each fragment of the mosaic which makes up our point of view. Different media do, however, have different production contexts and ways of addressing audiences. Genre diversity may also be significant. My research cannot explore this in any depth although in comparing reactions to documentaries (Chapter 4) and advertising campaigns (Chapter 9) I can make some general observations about the context of consumption.

8. To reflect on another, more disturbing example, the man who showed pornography to his eight-year-old stepdaughter was also, of course, making use of these representations for his own purposes. However, using porn to groom children to accept sexual assault would hardly be celebrated as a progressive act.

CHAPTER 4

1. This chapter is based on an article which first appeared in *Media, Culture and Society*, 2000, 22(1):64–84.

2. This fact should not pass without comment. Alleged, or even proven, examples of injustice are not routinely used to exemplify issues around other crimes (e.g. mugging, murder or terrorism). Why is there this difference? This is not a simple mirror of 'reality', it reflects complex issues about the politics of categorisation, identification, source strategies and media representation. It is also inextricably intertwined with the operation of social power, class politics and the metaphorical and social status of both social workers and children in society (Aldridge 1994; Franklin and Parton 1991).

3. The case in which the father committed suicide involved a two-year-old being taken to casualty with convulsions and bleeding from the anus. It does not fit into the context in which these research participants raised it (e.g. testing 'for any reason') or with their earlier assumption that fathers and mothers were united against the social workers. Indeed, this child's mother tried to challenge media representation of her family's situation and commented: 'I don't agree with people trying to get rid of Dr Higgs, because other people won't speak out, and the same thing will happen to other people as happened to my daughter' (Campbell 1997:183).

4. The image of the examination as itself abusive was promoted by police surgeons who opposed Higgs and Wyatt. In her evidence to the inquiry one police surgeon made a widely reported statement that the Cleveland paediatricians were guilty of 'outrageous sexual abuse' and that screaming infants had been held down to be examined. After being challenged by the judge in charge of the inquiry and by the Official Solicitor representing the children she withdrew the allegation. Her original accusation had been headlined by the press but 'her reluctant retraction was reported in only one paragraph at the bottom of one report in the *Guardian*' (Campbell 1997:58).

5. Some theorists interpret audience confusion as evidence of weak media influence, e.g. Nordenstreng (1972). However, this ignores the effect of confusion and its origins. Sometimes source organisations deliberately seek to encourage certain 'confusions' or associations. For example, the fact that people conflate the Cleveland and Orkney scandals (and transpose details from one into the other) was encouraged by the repeated use of the Cleveland–Orkney analogy in reporting. Similarly, in campaigns against equalising the age of consent in the UK some lobby groups deliberately sought to conflate homosexuality and paedophilia (a confusion also maintained in some group discussions, see Chapter 7). What counts as confusion or clarity is often key to any discursive struggle. In the fierce debate about stem cell research ethics, for example, those pro the research seek to distinguish 'reproductive' and 'therapeutic cloning', those against it insist that they are both 'human cloning' and deliberately 'confuse' the two in their statements to the media (Williams *et al.* 2003).

6. Such framing by association is by no means unique. For an analysis of the meaning of 'Watergate' and how this is reiterated, see Schudson 1992; for discussion of how, in the Ghana coup, Busia was represented as 'another Nkrumah', see Elliot and Golding (1974:243).

7. Of course some research participants with personal experience in this area may have chosen not to discuss it. Not surprisingly no one talked about being an abuser and only one research participant volunteered in a group a personal experience of having been accused of such a crime.

8. The role of specific events has been noted in many case studies of media coverage. Chibnall's work highlights the importance of the 1966 Shepherds Bush killing of three policemen in developing the media's 'Violent Society' theme (Chibnall 1977). Hall and colleagues note the importance of particular crimes in importing the concept of 'mugging' (Hall *et al.* 1978). Golding and Middleton's research on representations

of the welfare state highlights the role of a particular 'benefit cheat' story which acted as a 'precipitating event' in the framing of 'scroungers' (Golding and Middleton 1982). More recently, research focused on audience reception also notes the role of particular reference points. Corner *et al.*, for example, write about the way in which the Chernobyl accident is used as a 'datum event' in discussions of nuclear power (Corner *et al.* 1990).

CHAPTER 5

1. This is partly influenced by the fact that most of the focus groups were conducted in Scotland. Scottish respondents were more than twice as likely to spontaneously mention the Orkney case when invited to write a newspaper headline about child sexual abuse. English respondents were more likely to mention Cleveland. This is partly a result of access to local/regional media coverage but is also connected to perceived significance. People tended to pay more attention to cases in their area.

2. Some people thought that the return of the children proved that the social workers had no evidence at all. They believed (incorrectly) that all the evidence had been heard in a court of law and the case dismissed. People remark that the children had been returned as a result of the Orkney inquiry (e.g. Group 37), or a 'lengthy court case' (e.g. Group 24). 'There was no evidence' (Group 8, f); 'The accusations were found to be unfounded' (Group 23, f); 'It was all a pack of lies' (Group 7, f); 'All claims of sex abuse were dismissed' (Group 21); 'Proved [to be] a load of nonsense, social workers were idiots' (Group 31, f); 'The parents were found not guilty' (Group 17, m).

3. Only a handful of research participants knew that social services had won an appeal against the ruling which returned the children to their parents. This successful appeal ruled that the actions in sending the children home had been unlawful and that social services were entitled to pursue the case to a proof hearing (although they decided not to proceed). Most of the research participants had no knowledge of this, even though it was widely covered in both lunchtime and evening news the following day. The lack of recall of such events is partly due to the fact that this does not 'fit' with the main logic and narrative of the Orkney story and that this news event occurred outside the time frame of peak audience interest.

4. Information, or the lack of it, is crucial. Sometimes the sharing of such information within the group had an observable effect on the expressed attitude of other research participants. In the following exchange, for example, one man, who had originally asserted that no abuse could possibly have occurred in Orkney, began to waver in the light of assertions from two of the other group members. Unusually, these two women knew that social workers had won an appeal against the children's return, and that Sheriff Kelbie's decision to send the children home had been made without hearing all the evidence. The man had not previously been privy

to this information. By the end of the group session he was beginning to shift more towards their point of view:

> m: Something might have happened ... but not on that scale.
> f: He's coming over to our side!
> JK: What makes you think that it might have happened?
> m: Just hearing all the new evidence.
> JK: What evidence?
> m: Well, basically the judge not actually listening to everything beforehand and the social work department actually appealing (Group 4).

5. There has been a great deal of debate about 'embedded journalists' in the Iraq war. Less attention has been paid to 'embedded journalists' in abuse scandals. Some newspaper and television reporters became very close to parents in Orkney. A certain amount of empathy and identification became important to some in obtaining and maintaining good access (Kitzinger and Skidmore 1995a). In addition, because of the need to protect the identity of the children, parents were interviewed with their backs to the camera. This showed that TV reporters were themselves clearly moved during the interviews with parents, their emotional response underlined by the fact that cameras focused on their faces rather than the parents.

6. The nature of the language used to describe a case is crucial here. Other researchers have noted the importance of particular key phrases in promoting certain associations. Labels such as 'smart bombs' or phrases such as 'a war on drugs', 'the drift back to work' or 'winter of discontent' help to set up ways of thinking about and remembering events in the news (see Chibnall 1977:12, 21; Philo 1990; McLeod *et al.* 1991:246; Reese *et al.* 2001:41).

7. As with the Cleveland case before it, the reporting also clearly reinforced the idea that social workers were completely insensitive and made parents worried about turning to social services for help (see Chapter 3). In this case I also found evidence that the coverage influenced abused children too. One girl, who was abused during the Orkney crisis, waited for several years before confiding in anyone. This was because 'I thought I'd get sent away if I told.' Now in a support group for young incest survivors (run by social services) she feels she was misled. Journalists, she says, 'make social workers out to be big and bad [...] . They sort of put a barrier up' (Group 48).

8. The image of social workers in the news media is generally negative (see Aldridge 1994). Fictional representations echo this. Since Orkney the case has fed directly into further portrayals. See, for example, the portrayal of social workers' behaviour in a case of 'suspected Satanic abuse in a small Highland community' (*Flowers of the Forest*, BBC2, 21.30, 26 October 1996). See also the depiction of a condescending naive social worker using leading questions and jumping to conclusions to take a child into care. In this programme an eight-year-old girl is snatched from her distraught parents and forced to leave her doll behind (*Rumpole of*

the Bailey: Children of the Devil, ITV, 29 October 1992). It is worth noting that although there are dramas that invite empathy with police officers (*The Bill*), fire-fighters (*London's Burning*), lawyers (*LA Law*), and doctors and nurses (*ER, Casualty*). There is no equivalent for social workers. (For analysis of the overwhelmingly negative image of social workers in film see Freeman and Valentine, 2004.)

9. The family tragedy scenario can stop people assimilating other information and debate even when it is clearly included in a text. In their study of a programme about leukaemia near a nuclear power plant, for example, Corner *et al.* conclude 'the sheer power of the depiction it offered of one family's tragedy, backed up by the programme's own "dark" framing of the industry ... tended to crystallise meanings at the lower level for our respondents, leaving the wider reach of speculation relatively unassimilated' (Corner *et al.* 1990:100).

CHAPTER 6

1. When we were seeking financial support from the council in Cambridgeshire to work against child sexual abuse in the early 1980s we confronted an irony. Stereotypes of place counted in our favour. 'The Fens', a deprived, rural area around Cambridgeshire was historically seen as just the sort of place where incest and 'in-breeding' would occur. This was explicitly mentioned by one local government officer as a reason why we should be funded.

2. On one level, people's ability to reconstruct particular elements of a story may tell us more about their familiarity with a certain genre of reporting than their actual memories of that story. Certainly research participants' attempts to reconstruct the Orkney story demonstrate people's familiarity with journalistic conventions as well as sophisticated understandings of the format and structuring of news bulletins. Audience groups routinely recognised the establishing shot in the script-writing exercise as a scene-setter, and their scripts included inventing live satellite links with Orkney, on-site interviews as well as studio-based reports (see also Kitzinger 1993). Indeed, research participants sometimes joked about the process of script-writing, making reference to programmes such as *Whose Line is it Anyway?*, *Have I Got News For You* and *Drop the Dead Donkey* as they did so (these are radio and television shows that satirise news and media production processes). People combined their knowledge of TV news conventions with language taken from the (tabloid) press and informed by radio programmes. While acknowledging the role of both choice of images and genre familiarity, it is not possible to dismiss the news script reconstructions produced by research participants as merely a product of these two factors. Research participants' talk and script-writing about Orkney were also explicitly informed by actual memories of events at the time.

3. This film had been scheduled for a repeat showing on TV during the height of the Orkney crisis but was cancelled because it was considered inappropriate. However, some people remembered it anyway.

4. Richardson and Corner (1992) report a similar finding about perceived text-image disjuncture in how people responded to television representations of 'fiddling' state benefit. In their study some viewers perceived a mismatch between a 'benefit cheat's claims to poverty and the evidence displayed on camera of his ability to buy cigarettes, own a video and have a well-furnished house. Sometimes, of course, programme producers use this as a deliberate device.

5. This group refused to produce a 'typical' news bulletin about Orkney, choosing to produce a deliberately oppositional account instead. Their script consciously inverts everything they remembered and the bulletin opened with the promise that they were going to reveal 'The facts that lurk behind the stone walls of this Orcadian backwater' (Group 13, m).

CHAPTER 7

1. The links which feminists assert exist between masculinity and sexual violence are disowned by rhetoric around the alleged effeminacy or immaturity of abusers. The media often evade examining the gender issues. Among all the articles about causes and prevention of sexual abuse during 1991, I could only find two which included statements about the gender imbalance in patterns of abuse. One of these was in parody form and attributed to a social worker with 'a largish body', 'jeans' and a 'determinedly unmade up face' (*The Times*, 19 October 1991). More attention was paid to other features of abusers, e.g. in one case the abuser's orthodox Judaism was the subject of extensive comment in the press. The fact remains that, as David Finkelhor has pointed out, and feminists have been asserting for many years. 'The most obvious characteristic of sexual abusers has been one of the least analysed: they are almost all men' (Finkelhor 1979:75).

2. The *Sun* explicitly stated that gay men were 17 times more likely to be paedophiles than heterosexuals. The statement which was in an article by Anne Atkins, *Sun* columnist and 'vicar's wife', resulted in a Press Complaints Commission ruling stating that the article 'failed to distinguish between comment, conjecture and fact' (*The Pink Paper*, 6 February 1998).

3. It is instructive to look at people's use of the term 'imagine' and compare the difficulty people said they had imagining that a neighbour was a paedophile, with the ease with which they 'imagined' how the parents in Orkney must have felt (see Chapter 5).

4. Another reaction, usually referring to older incidents, was to state that they had always known something was odd about the behaviour of this individual, but no one had ever named it as abusive. Several participants described cases where everyone had known this particular man had a reputation for exposing himself to little girls, or all the boys at school had known this teacher was a 'slimeball', but it was only years later that he was taken to court. It was thus only in retrospect that people recognised the signs. This seemed partly a historically rooted phenomenon, some

of those free to abuse with impunity during the 1960s and 1970s being 'brought to book' as the social climate changed.

5. Although in a few cases the parents' 'scruffy' or 'hippy' appearance in TV news footage was used against them (see previous chapter).

6. In my work on AIDS, for example, there was similar evidence of stigma and silencing of some accounts, such as personal experiences of homosexuality, whereas other stories, such as the 'vengeful AIDS carrier tale' had great social currency and had become 'urban myths'. This helped to shape public understandings of AIDS (Kitzinger 1993).

CHAPTER 8

1. This chapter is based on an earlier version published in Franklin, B. (ed.) (1999) *Social Policy, the Media and Misrepresentation*, London: Routledge.

2. This call was given added impetus in the UK when eight-year-old Sarah Payne was abducted and murdered in the summer of 2000. Several tabloid newspapers took up the campaign for a 'Sarah's Law' modelled after Megan's Law and, most notably, the *News of the World* pledged to name and shame every one of the 110,000 convicted child sex offenders in the UK.

3. Other reports urged caution and restraint. The *Aberdeen Press and Journal*, for example, reported efforts to reassure the public and condemn vigilante action: 'Crowd (self) control' (*Press and Journal*, 6 August 1997); 'Police and community condemn vigilantes' (*Press and Journal*, 10 June 1997). Similar reports and editorials appeared in other papers, e.g. 'Sex crime vigilantes not answer' (*Yorkshire Evening Post,* 6 February 1997); 'Have faith in the police to shield our children' (*Express on Sunday,* 10 August 1997).

4. The *Bournemouth Evening Echo*'s 'Protect Our Children' campaign involved setting up a register of convicted sex offenders, compiled from newspaper reports. This was, however, available only to workers with children. Other papers, such as the *Guardian*, adopted a policy of only 'outing' offenders if there was evidence that supervision had broken down and children were at risk.

CHAPTER 9

1. For information about the campaign as it is now, see www.zerotolerance. org.uk/index.htm. Since I conducted my original study the campaign has been taken up and adapted for use across the UK. However, it is the initial Edinburgh campaign and its subsequent implementation in Strathclyde which will be addressed here. The initial ZT materials were developed by Edinburgh District Council Women's Committee in consultation with groups working with victims/survivors of domestic violence and sexual assault. The campaign drew on research into initiatives undertaken in other countries, especially Canada (see Westmount Research Consultants Inc. 1992). For evaluations of other campaigns see, for example, Weaver and Michelle 1999.

2. A belief in the statistics was reinforced by the status of the source of the posters (the District Council). This was seen as a respectable organisation rather than a marginal pressure group. In one group the first response to being shown the strap line was to pick up the poster to see who had produced it: m1: 'Aye I think its quite a high figure'; m2: 'Just trying to see if there's a stamp, some kind of respectable stamp on it who done it, whether that's an actual realistic figure. It must be though cause it's eh ...' [interrupted] (Group 20).

3. This underlines the value of using different types of study to assess 'media power'. If I had only used this data to attempt to generalise about how 'messages' influence us I might have concluded that any such impact was rather dispersed.

CHAPTER 10

1. I borrow this term from other authors who have noted similar effects (Corner *et al.* 1990:87; Curran 1987).

2. The following broad patterns were evident in my sample. Older participants in my research were more likely than younger people to express overtly homophobic attitudes confusing paedophilia and homosexuality. They were also more likely to see increases in media attention to sexual abuse as merely 'a fad'. Being working class, black or gay was explicitly identified by research participants themselves as making them more critical of 'the authorities' and feeling more vulnerable to oppressive state intervention (Chapter 5). Men often feel more implicated as potential abusers and they were more likely than women to spell out their lack of understanding of, and intense disgust at, men who abuse children. They were also more likely to be alienated by messages which drew attention to gender asymmetries in sexual violence (i.e. that most perpetrators are male) (Chapter 5). However, as Morley pointed out in his original *Nationwide* study, this is not a one-on-one mapping and there are other sources of difference depending on how people mobilise. (In the Nationwide study, for example, there were differences between working-class people active within the trade union movement and those who were not.) Demographic variables thus act as proxy measures for how these may structure politics and experience. The significance of such variable will very depending on the topic. For example, gender was particularly pertinent in reactions to the ZT campaign because of the specifically gendered message of the initiative. All the same only 12 per cent of men disliked the campaign.

3. A similar finding is observed by Corner and colleagues. Noting both the differences, but also the commonalities in people's responses to a programme about nuclear power, they conclude that the 'divergence between the groups should not be allowed to obscure the more important convergence – the power of the affective dimension, even on groups who reject its legitimacy, comes through in many ways. This may be of considerable significance in the shaping of public opinion about the issue' (Corner *et al.* 1990:105).

4. In any case, as Hall himself observes, 'the encoding/decoding model' was not intended to be 'a model which would last for the next 25 years for research. I don't think it has the theoretical rigor, the internal logical and conceptual consistency for that. If it's of any purchase, now and later, it's a model because of what it suggests. It suggests an approach; it opens up new questions. It maps the terrain' (Hall 1994:255).

5. My work was based within a single country, all groups, with one exception, were based in the UK. However, this conclusion is supported by cross-cultural work. As Kerby comments, reflecting on Katz's famous work on cross-cultural readings of *Dallas*, 'One can view the glass as half-full or half-empty. Katz chose to see differences across nationalities as evidence of viewer activity. Looked at another way one can marvel at the similarity in response within a given culture and ask why so many responses are so uniform' (Kerby 1996:192–3).

References

Adams, D. 1998. The 'At Risk' Business. *Police Review*. 30 January. pp. 16–17.

Adorno, T. and Horkheimer, M. 1983. The Culture Industry: Enlightenment as Mass Deception. In: Curran, J. *et al*. eds. *Mass Communications and Society*. London: Arnold. pp. 349–384.

Alcoff, L. M. and Gray-Rosendale, L. A. 1993. Survivor Discourse: Transgression or Recuperation? *Signs: Journal of Women in Culture and Society* 18(2), pp. 260–290.

Aldridge, M. 1994. *Making Social Work News*. London: Routledge.

Ang, I. 1985. *Watching 'Dallas': Soap Opera and the Melodramatic Imagination*. London: Methuen.

—— 1989. Wanted: Audiences. On the Politics of Empirical Audience Studies. In: Seiter, E. *et al*. eds. *Remote Control: Television, Audiences and Cultural Power*. London: Routledge, pp. 96–115.

Angelou, M. 1984. *I Know Why the Caged Bird Sings*. London: Virago Books. (Originally printed in USA in 1969 by NY. Random House.)

Armstrong, L. 1978. *Kiss Daddy Goodnight*. New York: Profile Books.

—— 1994. *Rocking the Cradle of Sexual Politics: What Happened When Women Said Incest*. Reading, Massachusetts: Addison-Wesley.

Ashendon, S. 1994. 'Governing Child Sexual Abuse'. PhD thesis, Birkbeck College.

ACOP [Association of Chief Officers of Probation] 1998. *Recent Cases of Public Disorder around Sex Offenders which have Impeded Surveillance and Supervision*. London: ACOP.

Atmore, C. 1994. Witch Hunts, Icebergs and the Light of Reason: Constructions of Child Sexual Abuse. In: Borland, H. ed. *Communications and Identity: Local, Regional and Global*. Canberra ACT: ANZCA.

—— 1996. Cross-cultural Media-tions: Media Coverage of Two Sexual Abuse Controversies in New Zealand/Aotearoa. *Child Abuse Review* 5(5), pp. 334–345.

—— 1998. Towards 2000: Child Sexual Abuse and the Media. In: Howe, A. ed. *Sexed Crime in the News*. Melbourne: Melbourne Federation Press, pp. 124–144.

—— 1999. Towards Rethinking Moral Panic: Child Sexual Abuse Conflicts and Social Constructionist Response. In: Bagley, C. and Mallick, K. eds. *Child Sexual Abuse and Adult Offenders: New Theory and Research*. Aldershot: Ashgate, pp. 11–26.

Ayish, M. 2003. Beyond Western-Oriented Communication Theories. A Normative Arab-Islamic Perspective. *Javnost* X(2), pp. 79–92.

Barker, M. and Brooks, K. 1998. *Knowing Audiences: Judge Dredd, its Friends, Fans and Foes*. Luton: University of Luton Press.

—— and Petley, J. eds. 2001. *Ill Effects: the Media/Violence*. 2nd edn. London: Routledge.

Bailey, V. and Blackburn, S. 1979. The Punishment of Incest Act 1908: A Case Study of Law Creation. *The Criminal Law Review*, pp. 708–718.

Barbour, R. and Kitzinger, J. eds. 1999. *Developing Focus Group Research.* London: Sage.

Barry, A. 1993. Television, Truth and Democracy. *Media, Culture and Society* 15(3), pp. 487–496.

Barry, K. 1979. *Female Sexual Slavery.* New York: Avon Books.

Barthes, R. 1966/1977. The Death of the Author. In: Barthes, R. ed. *Image, Music, Text.* London: Fontana.

Bass, E. and Thornton, L. eds. 1983. *I Never Told Anyone: Writings by Women Survivors of Child Sexual Abuse.* New York: Harper and Row.

Bell, D. 1995. Picturing the Landscape. *European Journal of Communication* 10(1), pp. 41–62.

Bell, S. 1988. *When Salem Came to the Boro: The True Story of the Cleveland Child Abuse Crisis.* London: Pan Macmillan.

Bell, V. 1993. *Interrogating Incest: Feminism, Foucault and the Law.* London: Routledge.

Benedict, H. 1992. *Virgin or Vamp: How the Press Cover Sex Crimes.* Oxford and New York: Oxford University Press.

Bennett, W. and Lawrence, R. 1995. News Icons and the Mainstreaming of Social Change. *Journal of Communication* 45(3), pp. 20–39.

Best, J. 1990. *Threatened Children: Rhetoric and Concern about Child-Victims.* Chicago: University of Chicago Press.

Blumler, J. 1978. Purposes of Mass Communication Research: a Transatlantic Perspective. *Journalism Quarterly* 55, pp. 219–230.

—— 1980. Mass Communications Research in Europe: Some Origins and Prospects. *Media, Culture and Society* 2, pp. 59–82.

Bobo, J. 2003. The Color Purple: Black Women as Cultural Readers. In: Brooker, W. and Jermyn, D. eds. *The Audience Studies Reader.* London: Routledge, pp. 305–314.

—— and Seiter, E. 1996. Black Feminism and Media Criticism. In Baehr, H. and Gray, A. eds. *Turning It On: A Reader in Women and Media.* London: Arnold pp. 177–182.

Hamer, D. and B Budge, B. eds. 1994. *The Good, The Bad and The Gorgeous: Popular Culture's Romance with Lesbianism.* London: Pandora.

Brown, L. and Burman, E. 1997. Feminist Response to the 'False Memory' Debate. *Feminism and Psychology* 7(1), pp. 7–21.

Brownmiller, S. 1975/1977 (reprint). *Against Our Will: Men, Women and Rape.* New York: Bantam Books.

Brunsdon, C. 1981. 'Crossroads': Notes on Soap Opera. *Screen* 22(4), pp. 32–37.

Burgess, J. and Gold, R. eds. 1985. *Geography, the Media and Popular Culture.* London: Croom Helm.

Burke, P. 1997. *Varieties of Cultural History.* Cambridge: Polity Press.

Burton, S. et al. 1998. *Young People's Attitudes Toward Violence, Sex and Relationships: A Survey and Focus Group Study.* Edinburgh: Zero Tolerance Charitable Trust.

Butler, J. 1978. *Conspiracy of Silence: The Trauma of Incest.* San Francisco: Volcano Press.

Byerly, C. M. 1994. An Agenda for Teaching News Coverage of Rape. *Journalism Education* Spring. pp. 59–69.

Campbell, B. 1988. *Unofficial Secrets: The Cleveland Case.* London: Virago.

—— 1997. *Unofficial Secrets: The Cleveland Case.* Revised edition London: Virago.

Carey, J. 1977/83. Mass Communication Research and Cultural Studies: an American View. In: Curran, J. *et al.* eds. *Mass Communication and Society.* London: Arnold, pp. 408–425.

Carter, C. 1998. When the 'Extraordinary' Becomes 'Ordinary': Everyday News of Sexual Violence. In: Carter, C. *et al.* eds. *News, Gender and Power.* London: Routledge, pp. 219–232.

—— and Weaver, K. 2003. *Violence and the Media.* Buckingham: Open University Press.

Chibnall, S. 1977. *Law-and-Order News: an Analysis of Crime Reporting in the British Press.* London: Tavistock Press.

Chritcher, C. 2003. *Moral Panics and the Media.* Buckingham: Open University Press.

Clyde, J. 1992. *The Report of the Inquiry into the Removal of Children from Orkney in February 1991.* Edinburgh: HMSO.

Cohen, S. 1972. *Folk Devils and Moral Panics: The Creation of the Mods and Rockers.* London: MacGibbon and Kee.

—— and Young, J. eds. 1973. *The Manufacture of News: Social Problems, Deviance and the Mass Media.* London: Constable.

Collings, S. 2002. The Impact of Contextual Ambiguity on the Interpretation and Recall of Child Sexual Abuse Media Reports. *Journal of Interpersonal Violence* 17(10), pp. 1063–1074.

Corner, J. 1986. Codes and Cultural Analysis. In: Collins, R. et al. eds. *Media, Culture and Society: A Critical Reader.* London: Sage, pp. 49–62.

—— 1991. Meaning, Genre and Context: the Problematics of 'Public Knowledge' in the New Audience Studies. In: Curran, J. and Gurevitch, M. eds. *Mass Media and Society.* London: Edward Arnold.

—— 2000. 'Influence': the Contested Core of Media Research. In: Curran, J. and Gurevitch, M. eds. *Mass Media and Society.* 3rd edn. London: Arnold Publishers, pp. 376–397.

—— *et al.* 1990. *Nuclear Reactions: Format and Response in Public Issue Television.* London: J. Libbey.

—— *et al.* 1997. Introduction. In: Corner, J. *et al.* eds. *International Media Research: A Critical Survey.* London: Routledge.

Cottle, S. 1993. *TV News, Urban Conflict and the Inner City.* New York: St Martins Press.

—— 1994. Stigmatizing Handsworth: Notes on Reporting Spoiled Space. *Critical Studies in Mass Communication* 11(3), pp. 231–256.

Cream, J. 1993. Child Sexual Abuse and the Symbolic Geographies of Cleveland. *Environment and Planning D: Society and Space* 11, pp. 231–246.

Cuklanz, L. 1996. *Rape on Trial.* Philadelphia: University of Pennsylvania Press.

—— 2000. *Rape on Prime-Time: Television, Masculinity and Sexual Violence.* Philadelphia: University of Pennsylvania Press.

Cumberbatch, G. 1998. Effects: Media Effects: The Continuing Controversy. In: Briggs, A. and Cobley, P. eds. *The Media: An Introduction.* London: Longman.

Curran, J. 1987. The Boomerang Effect: The Press and the Battle for London 1981–6. In: Curran, J. *et al.* eds. *Impacts and Influences*. London: Methuen.

—— 1990. The New Revisionism in Mass Communication Research: A Reappraisal. *European Journal of Communication* 5, pp. 135–164.

—— 1996. Media Dialogue: a Reply. In: Curran, J. *et al.* eds. *Cultural Studies and Communications*. London: Edward Arnold, pp. 294–299.

Curthoys, A. and Docker, J. 1989. In Praise of 'Prisoner'. In: Tulloch, J. and Turner, G. eds. *Australian Television: Programmes, Pleasures and Politics*. Sydney: Allen and Unwin.

Dahlgren, P. 1995. *Television and the Public Sphere: Citizenship, Democracy and the Media*. London: Sage.

De Young, M. 1997. The Devil Goes to Day Care: McMartin and the Making of a Moral Panic. *Journal of American Culture* 20(1), pp. 19–26.

—— 1988. The Good Touch/Bad Touch Dilemma. *Child Welfare* LXVII(1), pp. 61–68.

—— 2002. *The Ritual Abuse Controversy: An Annotated Bibliography*. Jefferson, NC: McFarland.

—— 2004. *The Day Care Ritual Abuse Moral Panic*. Jefferson, NC: McFarland.

Dickerson, D. 2001. Framing 'Political Correctness': The New York Times' Tale of Two Professors. In Reese, S. *et al.* eds. *Framing Public Life*. Mahwah, New Jersey: Lawrence Erlbaum Associates. pp.163–174.

Dominelli, L. 1986. Father-Daughter Incest: Patriarchy's Shameful Secret. *Critical Social Policy* 16, pp. 8–22.

Donaldson, L. and O'Brien, S. 1995. Press Coverage of the Cleveland Child Sexual Abuse Inquiry. *Journal of Public Health Medicine* 17(1), pp. 70–76.

Doty, A. 1993. *Making Things Perfectly Queer: Interpreting Mass Culture*. Minnesota: University of Minnesota Press.

Droisen, A. and Driver, E. 1989. *Child Sexual Abuse: Feminist Perspectives*. Basingstoke: Macmillan.

Dyer, R. 1986. *Heavenly Bodies*. London: Macmillan.

Eco, U. 1974. Semiological Guerrilla Warfare. In: Eco, U. ed. *Faith in Fakes: Travels in Hyper-reality*. London: Picador.

—— 1986. *Faith in Fakes: Travels in Hyper-Reality*. London: Picador.

—— 1990. *The Limits of Interpretation*. Indianapolis: Indiana University Press.

Eldridge, J. ed. 1993. *Getting the Message*. London: Routledge.

—— *et al.* 1997. *The Mass Media and Power in Modern Britain*. Oxford: Oxford University Press.

Elliot, P. and Golding, P. 1974. Mass Communication and Social Change: the Imagery of Development and the Development of Imagery. In: Dekadt, E. ed. *Sociology of Development*. London: Macmillan.

Entman, R. and Rojecki, A. 2000. *The Black Image in the White Mind*. Chicago: University of Chicago Press.

Ericson, R. *et al.* 1987. *Visualizing Deviance: a Study of News Organization*. Milton Keynes: Open University.

—— *et al.* 1991. *Representing Order: Crime, Law and Justice in the News Media*. Milton Keynes: Open University.

Feminism and Psychology 1997. Special Issue on Retrieved Memories. *Feminism and Psychology* 7(1).

Finkelhor, D. 1979. *Sexually Victimised Children*. New York: Free Press.

—— 1982. Sexual Abuse: A Sociological Perspective. *Child Abuse and Neglect* 6(1), pp. 95–110.

—— 1984. *Child Sexual Abuse: New Theory and Research*. New York: Free Press.

—— 1986. *A Source Book on Child Sexual Abuse*. Sage: London.

—— and Strapko, N. 1988. Sexual Abuse Prevention: A Review of Evaluation Studies. In: Willis, D. et al. eds. *Child Abuse Prevention*. New York: Wiley.

Fisher, K. 1997. Locating Frames in the Discursive Universe. *Sociological Research Online* 2(3).

Foucault, M. 1990. *The History of Sexuality*. Middlesex: Penguin.

Franklin, B. 1990. Wimps and Bullies: Press Reporting on Child Sexual Abuse. *Social Work and Social Welfare Yearbook 1*, pp. 1–14.

—— 1991. *Newszak and News Media*. London: Edward Arnold.

—— and Parton, N. 1991. Media Reporting of Social Work. In: Franklin, B. and Parton, N. eds. *Social Work, the Media and Public Relations*. London: Routledge.

Freeman, M.L. and Valentine, D.P. 2004. Through the Eyes of Hollywood: Images of Social Workers in Film. *Social Work*, 49(2), pp. 151–161.

Gammon, J. 1999. A Denial of Innocence: Female Juvenile Victims of Rape and the English Legal System in the Eighteenth Century. In: Hussey, S. and Fletcher, A. eds. *Childhood in Question: Children, Parents and the State*. Manchester: Manchester University Press.

Gamson, W. 1992. *Talking Politics*. Cambridge: Cambridge University Press.

Gauntlett, D. 1995. *Moving Experiences: Understanding Television's Influences and Effects*. London: John Libbey.

—— 1998. Ten Things Wrong with the 'Effects' Model. In: Dickinson, R. et al. eds. *Approaches to Audiences: a Reader*. London: Arnold.

Gavey, N. 1999. I Wasn't Raped But...' Revisiting Definitional Problems in Sexual Victimisation. In: Lamb, S. ed. *New Versions of Victims: Feminists Struggle with the Concept*. New York: New York University Press, pp. 57–81.

Gavin, N. 1998. *The Economy, Media and Public Knowledge*. London: Leicester University Press.

Gibbons, J; Conroy, Sue and Bell, Caroline 1995. Operating the Child Protection system: a study of child protection practices in English Local authorities. In: *Child Protection: Messages from Research*. London: HMSO. pp. 68–70.

Gillespie, M. 1995. *Television, Ethnicity and Cultural Change*. London: Routledge.

Gitlin, T. 1980. *The Whole World is Watching: Mass Media in the Making and Unmaking of the New Left*. Berkeley, USA: University of California.

—— 1991. The Politics of Communication and the Communication of Politics. In: Curran, J. and Gurevitch, M. eds. *Mass Media and Society*. London: Edward Arnold.

Glasgow University Media Group 1976. *Bad News*. London: Routledge and Kegan Paul.

—— 1980. *More Bad News*. London: Routledge and Kegan Paul.

Goffman, E. 1974. *Frame Analysis: An Essay on the Organization of Experience*. New York: Harper and Row.

—— 1990 [1959]. *The Presentation of Self in Everyday Life*. Harmondsworth: Penguin.

Golding, P. and Middleton, S. 1982. *Images of Welfare: Press and Public Attitudes to Poverty*. Oxford: Martin Robertson.

Gordon, L. 1988a. *Heroes of Their Own Lives: The Politics and History of Family Violence Boston 1880–1960*. New York: Viking.

—— 1988b. The Politics of Child Sexual Abuse: Notes from American History. *Feminist Review* 28, pp. 56–64.

Gray, A. 1987. Behind Closed Doors: Video Recorders in the Home. In: Baehr, H. and Dyer, G. eds. *Boxed In: Women and Television*. London: Pandora.

—— 1999. Audience and Reception Research in Retrospect: the Trouble with Audiences. In: Alasuutari, P. ed. *Rethinking the Media Audience*. London: Sage, pp. 22–37.

Griffen, G. ed. 1993. *Outwrite: Lesbianism and Popular Culture*. London: Pluto Press.

Gripsrud, J. 1995. *The Dynasty Years: Hollywood Television and Critical Media Studies*. London: Routledge.

Grodin, D. and Lindloff, T. R. eds. 1996. *Constructing the Self in a Mediated World*. London: Sage.

Gross, L. 1998. Minorities, Majorities and the Media. In: Liebes, T. and Curran, J. eds. *Media, Ritual and Identity*. London and New York: Routledge.

Guy, C. 1996. Feminism and Sexual Abuse: Troubled Thoughts on Some New Zealand Issues. *Feminist Review* 52, pp. 154–168.

Haaken, J. 1998. *Pillar of Salt: Gender, Memory and the Perils of Looking Back*. London: Free Association Press.

—— 1999. Heretical Texts: The Courage to Heal and the Incest Survivor Movement. In: Lamb, S. ed. *New Versions of Victims: Feminists Struggle with the Concept*. New York: New York University Press, pp. 13–41.

Hacking, I. 1995. *Rewriting the Soul: Multiple Personality and the Sciences of Memory*. Princeton: Princeton University Press.

—— 1998 The sociology of knowledge about child abuse. *Nous* 22(1), pp. 53–63.

Hagen, I. and Wasko, J. eds. 2000. *Consuming Audiences? Production and Reception in Media Research*. Cress Hill, N.J.: Hampton Press.

Hall, S. 1981/1973. Encoding and Decoding in the Television Discourse. In: Hall, S. *et al.* eds. *Culture, Media, Language: Working Papers in Cultural Studies 1972–79*. London: Hutchinson.

—— 1994. Reflections Upon the Encoding/Decoding Model: An Interview with Stuart Hall. In: Cruz, J. and Lewis, J. eds. *Viewing, Reading, Listening: Audiences and Cultural Reception*. San Francisco: Westview Press, pp. 253–274.

—— *et al.* 1978. *Policing the Crisis: Mugging, the State and Law and Order*. London: Macmillan.

Hearn, J. 1988. Commentary. Child abuse: Violences and Sexualities Towards Young People. *Sociology* 22(4), pp. 531–544.

Hebenton, B. and Thomas, T. 1996. Sexual Offenders in the Community: Reflections on Problems of Law, Community and Risk Management in the USA, England and Wales. *International Journal of the Sociology of Law* 24, pp. 427–443.

Hechler, D. 1988. *The Battle and the Backlash: The Child Sexual Abuse War.* Massachusetts: Lexington Books.

Helfer, R. 1982. A Review of the Literature on the Prevention of Child Abuse and Neglect. *Child Abuse and Neglect* 6, pp. 251–261.

Henderson, L. 1996. *The Issue of Child Sexual Abuse in TV Fiction: Audience Reception of Channel 4's 'Brookside'.* London: Channel 4.

—— and Kitzinger, J. 1999. The Human Drama of Genetics: 'Hard' and 'Soft' Media Representations of Inherited Breast Cancer. *Sociology of Health and Illness* 21(5), pp. 560–578.

Henley, J. 2001. Calls for Legal Child Sex Rebound on Luminaries of May 68. *Guardian.* Saturday 24 February, p. 17.

Henson, M. R. 1999. *Comfort Woman: a Filipina's story of Prostitution and Slavery under the Japanese Military.* Oxford: Rowman and Littlefield Publishers.

Hertog, J and McLeod, D. 2001. A Multiperspectival Approach to Framing Analysis: A Field Guide. In Reese, S. *et al.* eds. *Framing Public Life.* Mahwah, New Jersey: Lawrence Erlbaum Associates.

Herzog, H. 1941. On Borrowed Experience: an Analysis of Listening to Daytime Sketches. *Studies in Philosophy and Social Science* 9(1), pp. 65–95.

Hirsch, S. 1994. Interpreting Media Representations of a 'Night of Madness': Law and Culture in the Construction of Rape Identities. *Law and Social Review* 19(4), pp. 1023–1056.

Hobson, D. 1981(1980). Housewives and the Mass Media. In: Hall, S. *et al.* eds. *Culture, Media, Language: Working Papers in Cultural Studies 1972–79.* London: Hutchinson.

—— 1982. *'Crossroads': The Drama of a Soap Opera.* London: Methuen.

Hodge, R. and Tripp, D. 1986. *Children and Television.* Cambridge: Polity Press.

Hollway, W. 1981. 'I Just Wanted to Kill a Woman' Why? The Ripper and Male Sexuality. *Feminist Review* 9, pp. 33–41.

Hunt, K. and Kitzinger, J. 1996. Public Place, Private Issue: The Public's Reaction to the Zero Tolerance Campaign against Violence against Women. In: Bradby, H. ed. *Defining Violence.* Aldershot: Avebury Press, pp. 45–59.

Husband, C. ed. 1975. *White Media and Black Britain.* London: Arrow Books.

Iyengar, S. 1991. *Is Anyone Responsible? How Television Frames Political Issues.* Chicago: University of Chicago Press.

—— and Kinder, D. 1987. *News that Matters; Television and American Opinion.* Chicago: University of Chicago Press.

Jackson, L. 2000a. *Child Sexual Abuse in Victorian England.* London: Routledge.

—— 2000b. 'Singing Birds as well as Soap Suds': The Salvation Army's Work with Sexually Abused Girls in Edwardian England. *Gender and History* 12(1), pp. 107–126.

Jakubowicz, A. *et al.* 1994. *Racism, Ethnicity and the Media.* St Leonards, Australia: Allen and Unwin.

James, A. and Prout, A. eds. *Constructing and Reconstructing Childhood*. London: Falmer Press. pp. 157–183.

Jay, C. and Glasgow, J. eds. 1992. *Lesbian Texts and Contexts: Radical Revisions*. London: Onlywomen.

Jeffreys, S. 1985. *The Spinsters and her Enemies: Feminism and Sexuality 1880–1930*. London: Pandora.

—— 1990. *Anticlimax: A Feminist Perspective on the Sexual Revolution*. London: Women's Press.

Jempson, M. 1997. *Child Exploitation and the Media: Report and Recommendations*. London: PressWise/ACHE.

Jempson, M. and Searle, D. 1999. *The Media and Children's Rights: A Handbook for Media Professionals*. London: UNICEF/PressWise.

Jenkins, P. 1992. *Intimate Enemies: Moral Panics in Contemporary Great Britain*. New York: Alpine de Gruyere.

—— 1996. *Pedophiles and Priests: Anatomy of a Contemporary Crisis*. Oxford: Oxford University Press.

—— 1998. *Moral Panics: Changing Concepts of the Child Molester in Modern America*. New Haven, CT: Yale University Press.

Jhally, S. and Lewis, J. 1992. *Enlightened Racism: 'The Cosby Show', Audiences and the Myth of the American Dream*. Oxford: Westview Press.

Joseph, A. and Sharma, K. eds. 1994. *Whose News? The Media and Women's Issues*. London: Sage.

Katz, E. and Lazarsfeld, P. 1955. *Personal Influence: the Part Played by People in the Flow of Mass Communication*. New York: Free Press.

—— and Liebes, T. 1988 (1985). Mutual Aid in Decoding Dallas: Preliminary Notes for a Cross-culture Study. In: Drummond, P. and Paterson, R. eds. *Television and its Audience: International Research Perspectives*. London: B.F.I.

Kelly, L. 1988. *Surviving Sexual Violence*. London: Polity.

—— 1996. Weasel Words: Paedophiles and the Cycle of Abuse. *Trouble and Strife* 33, pp. 44–49.

—— 1998. Confronting an Atrocity: the Dutroux Case. *Trouble and Strife* 36, pp. 16–22.

—— and Radford, J. 1996. 'Nothing Really Happened': The Invalidation of Women's Experiences of Sexual Violence. In: Hester, M. *et al.* eds. *Women, Violence and Male Power: Feminist Activism, Research and Practice*. Buckingham: Open University Press, pp. 53–76.

—— and Radford, J. 1998. Sexual Violence Against Women and Girls: An Approach to an International Overview. In: Dobash, R.E. and Dobash, R.P. eds. *Rethinking Violence Against Women*. London: Sage, pp. 53–76.

—— *et al.* 1989. *An Exploratory Study of the Prevalence of Sexual Abuse in a Sample of 1244 16–21 Year Olds*. London: ESRC.

Kepplinger, H. and Habermeier, J. 1995. The Impact of Key Events on the Presentation of Reality. *European Journal of Communication* 10(3), pp. 371–390.

Kitzinger, J. 1988. Defending Innocence: Ideologies of Childhood. *Feminist Review* 28(Spring), pp. 77–87.

—— 1990. Audience Understandings of AIDS Media Messages: A Discussion. *Sociology of Health and Illness* 12(3), pp. 319–335.

—— 1990. Who Are You Kidding?: Children, Power and the Struggle Against Sexual Abuse. In: James A. and Prout, A. eds. *Constructing and Reconstructing Childhood*. London: Falmer Press, pp. 157–183.

—— 1992. Sexual Violence and Compulsory Heterosexuality. *Feminism and Psychology* 2(3), pp. 399–418.

—— 1993. Understanding AIDS – Media Messages and What People Know about AIDS. In: Eldridge, J. ed. *Getting the Message*. London: Routledge.

—— 1994. Challenging Sexual Violence Against Girls: A Public Awareness Approach. *Child Abuse Review* 3(4), pp. 246–248.

—— 1995a. *Evaluation of the Strathclyde Regional Council Zero Tolerance Campaign*. Edinburgh: ZT Trust.

—— 1995b. The Face of Aids. In: Marcova, I. and Farr, R. eds. *Representations of Health and Illness*. Switzerland: Harwood Academic Publishers.

—— 1996. Media Representations of Sexual Abuse Risk. *Child Abuse Review* 5(5), pp. 319–333.

—— 1998. The Gender Politics of News Production: Silenced Voices and Fake Memories. In: Carter, C. *et al*. eds. *News, Gender and Power*. London: Routledge.

—— 1999a. A Sociology of Media Power: Key Issues in Audience Reception Research. In: Philo, G. ed. *Message Received*. London: Longman.

—— 1999b. Some Key Issues in Audience Reception Research. In: Philo, G. ed. *Message Received*. Harlow: Longman.

—— 1999c. The Ultimate Neighbour from Hell? Stranger Danger and the Media Representation of 'Paedophilia'. In: Franklin, B. ed. *Social policy, the Media and Misrepresentation*. London: Routledge, pp. 207–221.

—— 2004. 'Media Coverage of Sexual Violence Against Women and Children' in Ross, K. and Byerly, C. eds. *Media and Women*. Oxford: Blackwell, pp. 13–38.

—— and Farquhar, C. 1999. The Analytical Potential of 'Sensitive Moments'. In: Barbour, R. and Kitzinger, J. eds. *Developing Focus Group Research: Politics, Theory and Practice*. London: Sage.

—— and Hunt, K. 1993. Evaluation of Edinburgh District Council's Zero Tolerance Campaign.Edinburgh: Edinburgh District Council Women's Committee.

—— and Kitzinger, C. 1993. 'Doing it' – Representations of Lesbian Sex. In: Griffin, G. ed. *Outwrite: Lesbianism and Popular Culture*. London: Pluto Press.

—— and Miller, D. 1992. African AIDS: The Media and Audience Beliefs. In: Aggleton, P. *et al*. eds. *AIDS: Rights, Risk and Reason*. London: Falmer Press.

—— and Skidmore, P. 1995a. *Child Sexual Abuse and the Media*. Summary Report to the ESRC.

—— and Skidmore, P. 1995b. Playing Safe: Media Coverage of Child Sexual Abuse Prevention Strategies. *Child Abuse Review* 4(1), pp. 47–56.

Klein, N. 2000. *No Logo*. London: HarperCollins/Flamingo.

Kubey, R. 1996. On Not Finding Media Effects: Conceptual Problems in the Notion of an 'Active Audience'. In: Hay, J. *et al*. eds. *The Audience and its Landscapes*. Boulder: Westview Press, pp. 187–205.

LaFontaine, J. 1998. *Speak of the Devil: Tales of Satanic Abuse in Contemporary England*. Cambridge: Cambridge University Press.

Lamb, A. ed. 1999. *New Versions of Victims: Feminists Struggle with the Concept*. New York: New York University Press

Lazarsfeld, P. F. *et al*. 1944. *The People's Choice. How the Voter Makes Up his Mind in a Presidential Campaign*. New York: Duell, Sloan and Pearce.

Lewis, J. 1997. What Counts in Cultural Studies. *Media, Culture and Society* 19, pp. 83–97.

Livingstone, S. 1990. Interpreting a Television Narrative: How Different Viewers See a Story. *Journal of Communication* 40, pp. 72–85.

—— 1996. On the Continuing Problem of Media Effects Research. In: Curran, J. and Gurevitch, M. eds. *Mass Media and Society*. 2nd edn. London: Edward Arnold.

—— 1998. *Making Sense of Television: The Psychology of Audience Interpretation*. 2nd edn. London: Routledge.

—— 1999. Mediated Knowledge: Recognition of the Familiar, Discovery of the New. In: Gripsrud, J. ed. *Television and Common Knowledge*. London: Routledge, pp. 91–107.

—— 2000. Television and the Active Audience. In: Fleming, D. ed. *Formations: A 21st Century Media Studies Textbook*. Manchester: Manchester University Press, pp. 175–193.

Livingstone, S. M. 1991. Audience Reception. In: Curran, J. and Gurevitch, M. eds. *Mass Media and Society*. London: Edward Arnold.

—— 1993. The Rise and Fall of Audience Research: An Old Story with a New Ending. *Journal of Communication* 43(4), pp. 5–12.

Loftus, E. and Ketchum, K. 1994. *The Myth of Repressed Memory*. New York: St Martin's Press.

Marullo, S. *et al*. 1996. Frame Changes and Social Movement Contraction: U.S. Peace Movement Framing after the Cold War. *Sociological Inquiry* 66, pp. 1–28.

Marshall, P. 1997. *The Prevalence of Convictions for Sexual Offending: Research Findings No. 55*. London: Home Office Research and Statistics Directorate.

Martin-Barbero, J. 1999. *An Interview by Adelaida Trujillo, for the Communication Initiative*. www.comminit.com/interviews_archives8.html.

—— 2000. Cultural Mediations of Television Consumption. In: Hagen, I. and Wasko, J. eds. *Consuming Audiences? Production and Reception in Media Research*. Cresshill N.J.: Hampton Press, pp. 145–161.

McCombs, M. and Shaw, D. 1972. The Agenda-Setting Functions of the Mass Media. *Public Opinion Quarterly* 36, pp. 176–187.

—— 1993. The Evolution of Agenda Setting Research: Twenty-five Years in the Market Place. *Journal of Communication* 43(2), pp. 58–67.

McCollum, H. 1998. What the Papers Say. *Trouble and Strife* 37, pp. 31–37.

McCrum, S. and Hughes, L. 2003. *Interviewing Children: A Guide for Journalists and Others*. London: Save the Children.

McFadyean, M. 1985. Sex and the Under-age Girl. *New Society*, June 14.

McGuigan, J. 1992. *Cultural Populism*. London: Routledge.

McIntyre, P. 2002. *Putting Children in the Right: Guidelines for Journalists and Media Professionals*. International Federation of Journalists.

McKinley, E. G. 1997. *Beverly Hills, 90210: Television, Gender and Identity.* Philadelphia: University of Pennsylvania Press.

McLaughlin, L. 1993. Feminism, the Public Sphere, Media and Democracy. *Media, Culture and Society* 15, pp. 599–620.

McLeod, D. and Hertog, J. 1999. Social control, social change and the mass media's role in the regulation of protest groups. In Demers, D and Viswanth, K eds. *Mass Media, Social Control and Social Changes.* Ames, IA: Iowa State University, pp. 305–330.

McLeod, J. *et al.* 1991. On Understanding and Misunderstanding Media Effects. In: Curran, J. and Gurevitch, M. eds. *Mass Media and Society.* London: Edward Arnold.

McQuail, D. 1977/83. The Influence and Effects of Mass Media. In: Curran, J. *et al.* eds. *Mass Communication and Society.* London: Arnold.

—— 1983. *Mass Communication Theory: An Introduction.* London: Sage.

—— 1990. Communication Research Past, Present and Future: American Roots and European Branches. In: Ferguson, M. ed. *Public Communication: The New Imperatives, Future Directions for Media Research.* London: Sage, pp. 135–151.

McNaron, T. and Morgan, Y. 1982. *Voices in the Night: Women Speaking about Incest.* Pittsburgh: Cleis Press.

Merton, R. 1946. *Mass Persuasion: The Social Psychology of a War Bond Drive.* New York: Harper Brothers.

Meyers, M. 1997. *News Coverage of Violence Against Women: Engendering Blame.* London and Newbury Park, CA: Sage.

Miller, D. 1994. *Don't Mention the War.* London: Pluto Press.

—— *et al.* 1998. *The Circuit of Mass Communication: Media Strategies, Representation and Audience Reception in the AIDS Crisis.* London: Sage.

—— and Andsager, J. 1997. Protecting 1st Amendment? Newspaper Coverage of Hate Speech. *Newspaper Research Journal* 18(3–4), pp. 2–15.

Miller-Perrin, C. and Wurtele, S. 1988. The Child Sexual Abuse Prevention Movement: A Critical Analysis of Primary and Secondary Approaches. *Clinical Psychology Review* 8, pp. 313–329.

Modleski, T. 1984. *Loving With a Vengeance – Mass-produced Fantasies for Women.* London: Methuen.

Moores, S. 1993. *Interpreting Audiences: The Ethnography of Media Consumption.* London: Sage.

Moorti, S. 2002. *Color of Rape: Gender and Rape in Television's Public Spheres.* New York: State University of New York Press.

Morgan, D. 1988. *Focus Groups as Qualitative Research.* London: Sage.

Morley, D. 1980. *The 'Nationwide' Audience: Structure and Decoding.* London: B.F.I.

—— 1986. *Family Television: Cultural Power and Domestic Leisure.* London: Comedia.

—— 1992. *Television, Audiences and Cultural Studies.* London: Routledge.

—— 1995. Theories of Consumption in Media Studies. In: Miller, D. ed. *Acknowledging Consumption: A Review of New Studies.* London: Routledge.

—— 1996. Media Dialogue: Reading the Readings of the Readings. In: Curran, J. *et al.* eds. *Cultural Studies and Communications.* London: Edward Arnold.

—— 1998. So-Called Cultural Studies: Dead Ends and Reinvented Wheels. *Cultural Studies* 12(4), pp. 476–497.

—— 1999. Finding Out about the World from Television News: Some Difficulties. In: Gripsrud, J. ed. *Television and Common Knowledge*. London: Routledge, pp. 136–158.

—— and Silverstone, R. 1990. *Domestic Communications: Technologies and Meanings*. London: Sage.

Morris, M. 1988. Banality in Cultural Studies. *Black* 14, pp. 15–25.

Morrison, T. ed. 1992. *Race-ing Justice, En-Gendering Power: Essays on Anita Hill, Clarence Thomas and the Social Construction of Reality*. New York: Pantheon.

Mosco, V. and Kaye, L. 2000. Questioning the Concept of the Audience. In: Hagen, I. and Wasko, J. eds. *Consuming Audiences? Production and Reception in Media Research*. Cresshill N.J.: Hampton Press, pp. 31–46.

Murray, K. and Gough, D. eds. 1991. *Intervening in Child Sexual Abuse*. Edinburgh: Scottish Academic Press.

Myers, J. E. B. ed. 1994a. *The Backlash: Child Protection Under Fire*. London: Sage.

—— 1994b. The Literature of the Backlash. In: Myers, J.E.B. ed. *The Backlash: Child Protection Under Fire*. London: Sage.

Nava, M. 1988. Cleveland and the Press. *Feminist Review* 28, pp. 103–121.

Nelson, B. J. 1984. *Making an Issue of Child Abuse: Political Agenda Setting for Social Problems*. Chicago: University of Chicago Press.

Nelson, S. 1982. *Incest: Fact and Myth*. Edinburgh: Stramullion.

Nelson, S. in press. The Orkney 'Satanic Abuse Case': Who Cared About the Children? In: Noblitt, J. and Perskin, P. eds. *Ritual Abuse in the Twenty-first Century: Clinical, Forensic and Social Implications*.

Nelson, T. and Willey, E. 2001. Issue Frames that Strike a Value Balance: A Political Psychology Perspective. In Reese, S. *et al*. eds. *Framing Public Life*. Mahwah, New Jersey: Lawrence Erlbaum Associates, pp. 245–266.

Neustadt, R. and May, E. 1988. *Thinking In Time: The Uses of History for Decision Makers*. London: Collier Macmillan.

Nightingale, V. 1996. *Studying Audiences: the Shock of the Real*. London: Routledge.

Noelle-Neumann, E. 1993. *The Spiral of Silence: Public Opinion – Our Social Skin*. 2nd edn. Chicago: University of Chicago Press.

Nordenstreng, K. 1972. Policy for News Transmission. In: McQuail, D. ed. *Sociology of Mass Communication*. Harmondsworth: Penguin.

NSPCC 1992. *NSPCC Fact Pack*. London: NSPCC.

Ofshe, R. and Watters, E. 1994. *Making Monsters: False Memories, Psychotherapy and Sexual Hysteria*. New York: Scribners.

Omvedt, G. 1990. *Violence Against Women: New Movements and New Theories in India*. New Delhi: Kali for Women.

Palmer, P. 1986. *The Lively Audience: A Study of Children around the TV Set*. Sydney: Allen and Unwin.

Pan, Z. and Kosicki, G. 1993. Framing Analysis: An Approach to News Discourse. *Political Communication* 10(1), pp. 55–75.

—— 2001. Framing as a Strategic Action in Public Deliberation. In Reese, S. *et al.* eds. *Framing Public Life*. Mahwah, New Jersey: Lawrence Erlbaum Associates, pp. 35–65.

Parkin, F. 1971. *Class Inequality and Political Order*. London: McGibbon and Kee.

Parton, N. 1985. *The Politics of Child Abuse*. London: Macmillan.

Pearsall, R. 1969. *The Worm in the Bud: The World of Victorian Sexuality*. London: Weidenfeld and Nicholson.

Pendergrast, M. 1995. *Victims of Memory*. Vermont: Upper Access.

Philo, G. 1990. *Seeing and Believing*. London: Routledge.

—— ed. 1999. *Message Received*. Harlow: Longman.

Philo, G. and Miller, D. 1997. *Cultural Compliance: Dead Ends of Media/Cultural Studies and Social Science*. Glasgow: Glasgow Media Group.

Pyck, K. 1994. The Backlash in Europe. Real Anxiety or Mass Hysteria in the Netherlands? A Preliminary Study of the Oude Pekela Crisis'. In: Myers, J. E.B. ed. *The Backlash: Child Protection Under Fire*. London: Sage.

Reavey, P. and Warner, S. eds. 2003. *New Feminist Stories of Child Sexual Abuse*. London: Routledge.

Reilly, J. 1999. The Media and Public Perceptions of BSE. In: Philo, G. ed. *Message Received*. Harlow: Longman.

Rhee, J. 1997. Strategy and Issue Frames in Election Campaign Coverage: A Social Cognitive Account of Framing Effects. *Journal of Communication* 47(3), pp. 26–48.

Richardson, J. *et al.* eds. 1991. *The Satanism Scare*. New York: Aldine de Gruyter.

Richardson, K. and J. Corner 1992. Reading Reception – Mediation and Transparency in Viewers' Accounts of a TV Programme. In: Scannell, P., Schlesinger, P. and Sparks, C. eds. *Culture and Power: A Media, Culture and Society Reader*. London: Sage, pp. 158–181.

Rosengren, K. 1996. Combinations, Comparisons and Confrontations: Towards a Comprehensive Theory of Audience Research. In: Hay, J. et al. eds. *The Audience and its Landscapes*. Boulder: Westview Press, pp. 23–51.

—— *et al.* eds. 1985. *Media Gratifications Research*. Beverly Hills, CA: Sage.

Rush, F. 1980. *The Best Kept Secret: Sexual Abuse of Children*. New York: McGraw-Hill.

Said, E. W. 1978. *Orientalism*. London: Routledge and Kegan Paul.

Schlesinger, P. 1978. *Putting 'Reality' Together: BBC News*. London: Methuen.

—— *et al.* 1992. *Women Viewing Violence*. London: B.F.I.

Schudson, M. 1992. *Watergate in American Memory: How We Remember, Forget, and Reconstruct the Past*. New York: Basic Books.

Scott, S. 1998. Here Be Dragons: Researching the Unbelievable, Hearing the Unthinkable. A Feminist Sociologist in Uncharted Territory. *Sociological Research Online* 3(3).

—— 1999. Dancing to Different Tunes: A Reply to Responses to 'Here Be Dragons...' *Sociological Research Online* 4(2).

Seaman, W. 1992. Active Audience Theory: Pointless Populism. *Media, Culture and Society* 14, pp. 301–311.

Seiter, E. et al. eds. 1989. *Remote Control: Television and Cultural Power*. London: Routledge.

Shah, D. *et al.* 2001. The Effects of Value-Framing on Political Judgement and Reasoning. In: Reese, S. *et al.* eds. *Framing Public Life*. Mahwah, New Jersey: Lawrence Erlbaum Associates, pp. 227–243.

Silverman, J. and Wilson, D. 2002. *Innocence Betrayed: Paedophilia, the Media and Society*. Oxford: Polity Press.

Skidmore, P. 1995. Telling Tales: Media Power, Ideology and the Reporting of Child Sexual Abuse in Britain. In: Kidd-Hewitt, D. and Osborne, R. eds. *Crime and the Media*. London: Pluto Press.

—— 1998. Gender and the Agenda: News Reporting of Child Sexual Abuse. In: Carter, C. *et al.* eds. *News, Gender and Power*. London: Routledge.

Smart, C. 1989. *Feminism and the Power of Law*. London: Routledge.

—— 1999. A History of Ambivalence and Conflict in the Discursive Construction of the 'Child Victim' of Sexual Abuse. *Social and Legal Studies* 8(3), pp. 391–409.

—— 2000. Reconsidering the Recent History of Child Sexual Abuse, 1910–1960. *Journal of Social Policy* 29(1), pp. 55–71.

Soothill, K. and Walby, S. 1991. *Sex Crimes in the News*. London: Routledge.

Sreberny, A. 2002. Media, Muslims and the Middle East: A Critical Review Essay. *Political Communication* 19(2), pp. 273–280.

Stainton Rogers, R. 1989. The Social Construction of Childhood. In: Stainton Rogers, W. *et al.*, eds. *Child Abuse and Neglect*. London: Open University Press. pp. 23–29.

Stanko, E. A. 1985. Incest: Some of Us Learn as Children. In: Stanko, E.A. ed. *Intimate Intrusions: Women's Experience of Male Violence*. London and Boston: Routledge and Kegan Paul.

—— 1990. *Everyday Violence*. London: Pandora.

Stiglmayer, A. ed. 1994. *Mass Rape: The War Against Women in Bosnia-Herzegovina*. Lincoln and London: University of Nebraska Press.

Summit, R. C. 1983. The Child Sexual Abuse Accommodation Syndrome. *Child Abuse and Neglect* 7, pp. 177–193.

Tharinger, D. *et al.* 1988. Prevention of Child Sexual Abuse: An Analysis of Issues, Educational Programs and Research Findings. *School Psychology Review* 17(4), pp. 614–634.

Thomas, T. 1997. How Could This Man Go Free: Privacy, the Press and the Paedophile. In: Lawson, E. ed. *Child Exploitation and the Media Forum: Report and Recommendations*. Dover: Smallwood Publishing Group, pp. 67–69.

Tuchman, G. 1978. *Making News: A Study of the Construction of Reality*. New York: Free Press.

Tufte, T. 2000. The Popular Forms of Hope: About the Force of Fiction Among TV Audiences in Brazil. In: Hagen, I. and Wasko, J. eds. *Consuming Audiences? Production and Reception in Media Research*. Cresshill N.J.: Hampton Press, pp. 275–295.

Tulloch J. and Tulloch M. 1993. Understanding TV Violence: A Multifaceted Cultural Analysis. In: Turner, G. ed. *Nation, Culture and Text: Australian Cultural and Media Studies*. London: Routledge.

—— 2000. *Watching Television Audiences: Cultural Theories and Methods*. London: Arnold.

Van der Gaag, N. and Nash, C. 1987. *Images of Africa: The UK Report*. Oxford: Oxfam.

Valentine, G. 1989. The Geography of Women's Fear. *Area* 21(4), pp. 385–390.

Waldby, C. 1987. *Breaking the Silence*. Dymphna House Inc.

Walker, A. 1982/1985. *The Color Purple*. New York: Pocket Books.

Ward, E. 1984. *Father-Daughter Rape*. London: Women's Press.

Weaver, C. K. and Michelle, C. 1999. Public Communication Compromised: the Impact of Corporate Sponsorship on a Pro-Social Media Campaign. *Australian Journal of Communication* 26(3), pp. 83–97.

Weaver, K. 1998. Crimewatch UK: Keeping Women off the Streets. In: Carter, C. *et al.* eds. *News, Gender and Power*. London: Routledge, pp. 248–262.

West, D. 1985. *Sexual Victimisation*. Aldershot: Gower.

Westmont Research Consultants Inc. 1992. *Evaluation of the Wife Assault Prevention Campaign.Ontario*: Ontario Women's Directorate.

Whitiker, C. 1985. Hollywood Transformed: Interviews with Lesbian Viewers. In: Staven, P. ed. *Jump Cut: Hollywood, Politics and Counter Cinema*. New York: Praeger Scientific.

Whitney, D. and Wartella, E. 1992. Media Coverage of the 'Political Correctness' Debate. *Journal of Communication* 42(2), pp. 83–94.

Williams, C. *et al.* 2003. Envisaging the Embryo in Stem Cell Research: Discursive Strategies and Media Reporting of the Ethical Debates. *Sociology of Health and Illness* 25(7), pp. 793–814.

Wilson, M. 1994. *Crossing the Boundary: Black Women Survive Incest*. Seattle: Seal Press.

Winship, J. 1987. *Inside Women's Magazines*. London: Pandora.

Women's Research Centre 1989. *Recollecting our Lives: Women's Experience of Childhood Sexual Abuse*. Vancouver: Press Gang.

Worrell, M. 2003. Working at Being Survivors: Identity, Gender and Participation in Self-Help Groups. In: Reavey, P. and Warner, S. eds. *New Feminist Stories of Child Sexual Abuse*. London: Routledge, pp. 210–226.

Wykes, M. 1998. A Family Affair: The British Press, Sex and the Wests. In: Carter, C. *et al.* eds. *News, Gender and Power*. London: Routledge, pp. 233–247.

Yoon, B. S. undated. *Military Sexual Slavery: Political Agenda for Feminist Scholarship and Activism*. http://witness.peacenet.or.kr/e_comfort/library/god/god21.htm.

Index of Authors

Subject Index